T0246097

"This book is needed *now*. The rapidly chang[ing] pan-Wesleyanism, and more broadly Protestant evangelicalism in North America means the establishment of new boundary lines. Taking a sober, holistic, integrated, and honest look at one of the most important of the North American 'church fathers,' this work makes for a more unified, empathetic, and ultimately more effective church for reaching a post-Christian world. This book, with the spirit in which it is written, is the kind of work that will simply make the church better in the immediate future."

—**Matt Ayars,** *president and professor of biblical studies, Wesley Biblical Seminary*

"*Jonathan Edwards: A Reformed Arminian Engagement* offers the portrayal of Edwards as a link between Calvinism and Arminianism. This insightful perspective on Edwards, marked by an irenic tone, makes a fresh and creative contribution to the ongoing discussions in Edwards studies. There is unanimous consensus that Edwards was America's greatest theologian, even as this book scrutinizes certain aspects of Edwardsean Calvinism. This page-turner offers a captivating exploration that underscores the real divergences between Calvinists and Reformed Arminians. In the process, it dispels some of the caricatures associated with Arminianism. Matthew Pinson and others in this volume maximize the areas of agreement while shedding light on genuine disagreements. Can Arminians find common ground with Edwards? The resounding answer from Reformed Arminians is a definite yes!"

—**Chris Chun,** *director of the Jonathan Edwards Center and professor of church history, Gateway Seminary*

"This collection of essays is a fascinating exploration of the nuanced differences between Classic Reformed theology and Reformed Arminianism. Utilizing Jonathan Edwards as a case study, these essays identify nuanced differences and similarities between Edwards and Reformed Arminianism on topics ranging from depravity and atonement to grace, free will, and perseverance. Along the way, several contributions also contrast Reformed Arminianism with Wesleyan Arminianism. Any discussion of the differences between the Dordt version of Reformed theology and Reformed Arminianism and Wesleyan Arminianism must engage this book."

—**John Mark Hicks,** *emeritus professor of theology, Lipscomb University*

"This book consists of a serious engagement by Free Will Baptists, who identify themselves as brothers in the Reformed stream of historical theology, with the theology and piety of Jonathan Edwards. Its authors' grasp of the secondary literature is profound, and their interaction with primary Edwardsean texts shows an impressive, sympathetic, and instructive depth of understanding. The authors are insightful concerning their points of difference with Edwards and give a cogent defense of their doctrinal viewpoint, while maintaining a provocative appreciation of the wide range of positive doctrinal and spiritual instruction in Edwards. Because every reader will be edified from the breadth and depth of their critical observations concerning Edwardsean theological formulation, I recommend the book heartily."

—*Thomas J. Nettles, senior professor of historical theology, Southern Baptist Theological Seminary*

"*Jonathan Edwards: A Reformed Arminian Engagement* is a unique collection of essays that truly models the art of charitable, appreciative, and balanced theological disagreement. Pinson and his contributors celebrate the piety and influence of one of America's most important Christian thinkers, highlighting common ground as well as offering pointed critiques of aspects of Edwards's theology that they find most troubling. This book is a must read for anyone engaged in Edwards studies or who just wants a better understanding of classical Arminian theology."

—*Rhyne Putman, vice president for academic affairs and professor of Christian ministries, Williams Baptist University*

"A positive Arminian engagement with Jonathan Edwards seems as paradoxical as the nomenclature of Reformed Arminianism itself. In this creative retrieval of tradition, the authors seek to recover a broader Reformed tradition over against the labels and divisions that have marked the heirs of the Reformation. The beauty and sensibilities of Edwards's writings are realized, while sovereignty, depravity, and assurance are refurbished for Arminian thought. As the landscape of evangelical thought shifts, this nuanced approach with its generous attitude can help to rectify overstated theological partitions."

—*W. Brian Shelton, professor of theology and chair of Christian studies and philosophy, Asbury University*

Jonathan Edwards

Jonathan Edwards

a Reformed Arminian Engagement

Edited by J. Matthew Pinson

ACADEMIC
BRENTWOOD, TENNESSEE

ISBN: 978-1-0877-7746-7

Dewey Decimal Classification: B

Subject Heading: EDWARDS, JONATHAN \ CLERGY--BIOGRAPHY \ PROTESTANT CHURCHES--CLERGY

Printed in the United States of America

29 28 27 26 25 24 VP 1 2 3 4 5 6 7 8 9 10

Contents

Foreword

Michael A. G. Haykin

Jonathan Edwards has been rightly described as "America's Augustine." It is a very apt moniker. For just as one can describe Western Christians, both Catholic and Protestant, as Augustinians, given the undoubted influence of the North African pastor-theologian on occidental Christianity, so one can depict Anglophone Protestant believers as Edwardseans. To be sure, this is something of an exaggeration, but it helps to capture the enormous influence that the New England theologian has had upon successive generations of Christians in the English-speaking world.

Now, one of the great concerns that Edwards has bequeathed to us is how to uphold both divine sovereignty and human responsibility. The eighteenth century was deeply shaped by a hunger for freedom that exploded in various revolutions—political, intellectual, even sexual—and Edwards found himself having to relate his inherited Calvinist tradition to this new world that was framed by this passion for liberty. In Edwards's day, one of the theological perspectives that grappled with the nature of human liberty was one that he both feared and rejected, namely, Arminianism. But, as J. I. Packer once argued, there are various types of Arminianisms. And in this book we encounter what one can well call "Edwardsean Arminianism," that is, an Arminianism that sees in much of Edwards's literary corpus a helpful guide to Christian life and thought.

Yet, even as modern-day Calvinistic Evangelicals do not follow Edwards in all that he believed (for example, his contradictory view of slavery and the slave trade—a view that even his close mentee, Samuel Hopkins, rejected), so the authors of the essays in this fine collection are quite prepared to acknowledge Edwards as an important mentor in their lives and yet part company with him on certain issues that relate to freedom and soteriology.

Yes, a collection of Reformed Arminian essays on one regarded as a quintessential Calvinist is a surprising turn of events, but it is a turn that is both a profitable and an enjoyable read.

Michael A.G. Azad Haykin
Professor of Church History
The Southern Baptist Theological Seminary
Dundas, Ontario
12 November 2023

Preface

Jonathan Edwards is the hero of the New Calvinism. Collin Hansen and other writers have discussed the fascination with Edwards by many in the "Young, Restless, and Reformed" movement. Yet Edwards was a complex and nuanced thinker and preacher whose theological sensibilities are worth engaging from quarters of the church catholic outside Calvinism. This volume does that by featuring essays that consider Edwards's theology from the vantage point of a unique stream of Arminian theology known as Reformed Arminianism.

Contemporary Reformed Arminianism follows the original teachings of Jacobus Arminius and some of the early Remonstrants, who saw themselves and their theology as consistent with the broad stream of confessional Reformed theology in Europe in the sixteenth century. Arminius always saw himself teaching and writing in harmony with the historic Reformed confessions. His thought and its modern rearticulation by those identifying with the historic Reformed tradition (as opposed to many contemporary Wesleyan Arminians) provides an enlightening conversation partner to Jonathan Edwards's thought which, for some, is seen as virtually synonymous with Calvinism. The minority report of the Reformed Arminians pushes back against the characterization of Arminius as non-Reformed. This book aims to engage Edwards's theology critically from within the broad Reformed tradition. Its goal is to offer alternative expressions of fidelity to the early Reformed confessions without the troubling deterministic metaphysics associated with Edwards's thought.

A Reformed Arminian engagement with the thought of Jonathan Edwards, therefore, provides a unique opportunity for constructive theological dialogue that will draw in people from a large number of constituencies, from Calvinist to Arminian to other varieties of non-Calvinists. The contributors to this book hope to challenge the complacency that often accompanies the hard lines too often drawn between confessional traditions and traditional theological systems in the Calvinist-Arminian debate.

This volume originated with a series of papers presented a decade ago at the annual Theological Symposium of the Commission for Theological Integrity of the National Association of Free Will Baptists. At the time I was program coordinator for the symposium under the direction of F. Leroy Forlines, who had served on the Commission for five decades, most of that time as Chairman. When I pitched the idea for a symposium theme on a Reformed Arminian engagement with the Calvinist titan Jonathan Edwards, Professor Forlines was elated, and he encouraged me to collect the papers and edit them for publication. The volume you hold in your hands is the plant that eventually grew from those seeds ten years ago.

Leroy Forlines and his colleague at Welch College Robert E. Picirilli were the chief twentieth-century proponents of a unique variety of Arminianism that has come to be known as Reformed Arminianism. Forlines and Picirilli systematized a homiletical tradition in the Free Will Baptist Church that had been handed down from the first Free Will Baptists in America—English General Baptists who had crossed the Atlantic to the American colonies in the late seventeenth century. Those General Baptists stood in the venerable tradition of writers such as Thomas Helwys and Thomas Grantham.

Forlines was the systematic theologian, while Picirilli was the biblical theologian. Picirilli was the first to use the term "Reformed Arminianism," in the preface to the inaugural volume of the Randall House New Testament Commentary on Romans written by Forlines. Picirilli wrote:

> If there were such a phrase, I would say that Free Will Baptists are "Reformed Arminian." I would immediately be accused of contradiction, of course. If I reminded my accuser that Arminius himself was Reformed, he would probably remind me in

turn that Arminius's followers (after his death) were turned
out of the Reformed Church. Even so, I think that many Christians will be at least a little surprised to learn that there are
"Arminians" who believe in total depravity, in the eternal (conditional) election of individuals to salvation, in Christ's death
as penal, substitutionary (universal) atonement that fully satisfied the just demands of a holy God for the infinite punishment of sin, in salvation (including perseverance in salvation)
that is conditioned on faith and not on works or merit.[1]

Though Picirilli subsequently used the descriptor "Reformation Arminianism"
and Forlines the phrase "Classical Arminianism," "Reformed Arminianism"
had already caught on among some of their younger protégés such as Stephen
M. Ashby and myself.

That terminology signified for many of us a way to engage in what Timothy
George has called "retrieval for the sake of renewal." The prospect that Arminian theology could be renewed by retrieving a Reformed theology shorn of
its undesirable—and unbiblical—associations with a deterministic metaphysic
and a historically idiosyncratic emphasis on an irresistible *gratia particularis*
(particular grace) was enlivening. That is because many younger Arminians at
the turn of the twenty-first century had grown weary of caricatures of "Arminianism" from Calvinists and Arminians alike. The primary caricature was of a
semi-Pelagian works-righteousness reminiscent of Charles Finney that relied
on Holiness models of sanctification and spirituality, confident in the ability of
natural reason to discover divine truth without special revelation or reach out
to God without special grace.

The breadth of Reformed confessional theology before the crystallization
and exclusion process of the Synod of Dort in 1618–1619 gave figures such as
Jacobus Arminius freedom to embody just such a broadly Reformed theology.
Arminius and other thinkers, with the rest of the Christian tradition, affirmed
the *gratia universalis* and *gratia resistibilis* but did so without jettisoning the
beauty of sixteenth-century Reformed thought. (I will discuss this further in
Chapter One.)

---

[1] F. Leroy Forlines, *Romans*, The Randall House New Testament Commentary, Robert E.
Picirilli, gen. ed. (Nashville: Randall House, 1987), viii.

A Reformed Arminian engagement with Jonathan Edwards's nuanced Calvinistic brand of Reformed theology provides a wonderful way to show how Arminians and Calvinists can take part in fruitful dialogue. It also points a way forward in probing ways in which commonalities with Calvinism that arise from the Reformed roots of Arminianism can bring renewal to the Arminian theological project. It is with thanks to God that I and the other contributors of these essays commend this book to readers who share these aims.

J. Matthew Pinson
April 23, 2023

Chapter 1

Arminians and Jonathan Edwards? Really?

J. Matthew Pinson

A book about Arminians and Jonathan Edwards? Really?" one might ask, recalling young "New Calvinists" wearing T-shirts with "Jonathan Edwards is My Homeboy" emblazoned on them.[1] Such a quizzical response is not surprising in our current evangelical climate, for two reasons. First, we evangelicals tend, now more than ever, to remain insulated cozily in our tribes, unlike the evangelicals of a bygone era. Second, what is thought of as Arminianism today is often diametrically opposed to Edwards's Reformed mentality.

To be sure, strong disagreements among Protestants from various confessional perspectives are nothing new. Yet there has always been a degree of warmth and fellowship among many Protestants from different traditions. Everybody read the Calvinist Congregationalist Matthew Henry. Presbyterians appreciated the Baptist Charles Spurgeon's preaching. Baptists quoted Anglican Bishop J. C. Ryle. Someone once asked the Calvinist preacher George Whitefield, "Will we see Wesley in heaven?" Whitefield's response was, "I fear

---

[1] Collin Hansen, *Young, Restless, and Reformed: A Journalist's Journey with the New Calvinists* (Wheaton: Crossway, 2008); a picture of such a T-shirt appears on the front cover.

not. He will be so near the throne, and we shall be at such a distance, that we shall hardly get a sight of him."[2]

Not every evangelical today has a contentious spirit regarding theological differences, including Arminianism and Calvinism. Not too long ago, I was standing in front of a 9Marks book stall at Capitol Hill Baptist Church, which is led by my friend (and Calvinist) Mark Dever. As I was scanning the shelves, my eyes landed on a book by the staunch Calvinist Iain Murray published by Banner of Truth. It was a spiritual biography of John Wesley and some early Wesleyans with an endorsement by the Presbyterian Sinclair Ferguson describing it as a "thrilling history and biography, the bringing to light of forgotten men of extraordinary faith and energy for Christ."[3]

Sadly, however, one need not search too far on the internet about "Arminianism" and "Calvinism" before discovering videos from well-known Calvinist personalities asking the question "Can Arminians be saved?" with the individual assuring, "Yes, sure, it is possible for them to be saved." In an environment in which such a video can be posted, with a straight face and that question in the heading, one can understand why the average reader would be surprised to find a group of Arminians writing appreciatively of a figure like Jonathan Edwards.

INACCURATE PERCEPTIONS OF ARMINIANISM

Still, the fact remains that today's "Arminianism" is almost always marked by what distinguishes it from the Reformed tradition, not by its commonalities with Reformed theology and spirituality. Some of this has to do with caricatures Calvinists often make of Arminianism. Yet there is a grain of truth in some of these caricatures.

Much that passes for Arminianism today is really what we might call "Finneyism," a semi-Pelagian brand of Christianity that de-emphasizes divine sovereignty and overemphasizes individuals and their free will to choose, thereby downplaying the effects of the fall.[4] Of course, traditional Arminianism,

---

[2] J. C. Ryle, *Christian Leaders of the Last Century, Or, England a Hundred Years Ago* (London: Thomas Nelson, 1869), 59–60.
[3] Iain Murray, *Wesley and Men Who Followed* (Carlisle, PA: Banner of Truth Trust, 2003); https://banneroftruth.org/us/store/history-biography/wesley-and-men-who-followed/.
[4] "Finneyism" refers to the thought and practice of the Second Great Awakening revivalist Charles Finney, whose theology and practice de-emphasized total depravity and thus the

whether of the Wesleyan variety or the more Reformed approach espoused in this book, eschews semi-Pelagianism and affirms total depravity.[5] Still, many traditional Wesleyans treat the prevenient grace they believe is necessary for the conversion of sinners like a blanket that fell on humanity as a result of Christ's atonement. In this view, prevenient grace universally reverses the effects of the fall and makes everyone automatically able to respond to the gospel.

Calvinists, like Reformed Arminians, believe that this view grants the doctrine of total depravity with one hand while taking it away with the other. Reformed Arminians affirm that God, in his own mysterious way and timing, gives everyone sufficient grace for their eventual conversion, if they do not resist it. Yet they see this prevenient (beforehand) grace as an individually directed wooing and "suasion." In this way, prevenient grace is not at all like what my friend Stephen Ashby has called a "dense fog" that settled on humanity, mitigating its depravity.[6]

Most self-professed Arminians do not subscribe to penal substitutionary atonement and its concomitant justification solely by the righteousness of Christ imputed to believers through faith. This makes Reformed people wary of them.

Furthermore, Arminians are often caricatured—sometimes for legitimate reasons—as having discarded key orthodox formulations traditionally associated with evangelical Protestantism. Leading Arminian thinkers, for example, comfortably deny the infallibility of the phenomena of Scripture, limiting it to matters of doctrine and morals. Others seem giddy about N. T. Wright and his novel reinterpretation of Pauline soteriology.[7] Still others affirm

---

intrinsic drawing power of the Spirit. Finney played up human ability and absolute free will (without the influence of depravity) in salvation, which could be manipulated through innovative worship methods and psychological techniques. His views were also characterized by the affirmation of Christian perfection and a much more mystical view of sanctification and spirituality, rather than the ordinary-means-of-grace spirituality seen in Reformed theology.

[5] "Semi-pelagianism" is a milder form of the teaching of the ancient heterodox monk Pelagius; it teaches that God gives his grace to those who naturally "do what is in them," overemphasizing human ability in conversion and skirting the doctrine of total depravity and inability.

[6] Stephen M. Ashby, "A Reformed Arminian Response to J. Steven Harper," in *Four Views on Eternal Security*, ed. J. Matthew Pinson (Grand Rapids: Zondervan, 2002), 273.

[7] For opposing Arminian perspectives on N. T. Wright and the New Perspective on Paul, see Joseph R. Dongell, "The Pauline 'New Perspective' and Wesleyan Theology," https://www.atalystresources.org/the-pauline-new-perspective-and-wesleyan-theology/ (pro); and Matthew J. McAffee, "The N. T. Wright Effect: A Free Will Baptist Assessment through the Theology of F. Leroy Forlines," *Integrity: A Journal of Christian Thought* 7 (2019): 25–50 (con). Ben

"postconservative" and "postpropositional" theology. Thus it makes sense that confessionally Reformed Christians would have concerns about Arminianism.

ARMINIUS AS A REFORMED THEOLOGIAN

When one goes back to Arminius, however, one sees none of the abovementioned characteristics. The more one reads Arminius, the more his Reformed convictions become evident. That is true whether one means Reformed in a broad, modern sense or in the more narrowly defined terms of the Synod of Dort that condemned Arminianism as heresy in 1619. Arminius was more broadly Reformed in the modern sense of that term than most Arminians are today. Yet he was fully Reformed in his day, fitting comfortably within the confines of the Reformed confessions and catechisms before the Synod of Dort that condemned Arminianism as heresy in 1619.

Arminius not only affirmed traditional Protestant confessional orthodoxy but he also agreed wholeheartedly with the confessional standards of the sixteenth-century Dutch Reformed churches, the Belgic Confession of Faith and Heidelberg Catechism. When one reads these confessional documents, one sees that the details of "the five points of Calvinism" are not spelled out in them. The same is true of all sixteenth-century Reformed confessional standards. So someone like Arminius, or the authors of the chapters in this book, could subscribe to both documents with no difficulty (of course, no Baptist could subscribe to certain ecclesiological elements in them).[8]

Some Calvinist scholars, following Richard Muller, try to drive a wedge between Arminius and the Reformed tradition.[9] I will grant that increasingly in the late sixteenth century, the teachings of Arminius—like that of precursors

---

Witherington has lodged serious criticisms against Wright and the New Perspective, even having an article on it carried on the Calvinistic Ligonier Ministries website. However, regarding Wright's doctrine of imputation (which denies it), Witherington remarks, "I think Tom is 100% correct in this assessment." http://benwitherington.blogspot.com/2009/02/nt-wright-response-to-john-piper-on.html.

[8] For more on Arminius as a Reformed theologian, see J. Matthew Pinson, *40 Questions About Arminianism* (Grand Rapids: Kregel Academic, 2022), chapters 6–8.

[9] See, e.g., Muller, "Arminius and the Reformed Tradition," *Westminster Theological Journal* 70 (2008): 19–48. See also J. V. Fesko, *Arminius and the Reformed Tradition* (Grand Rapids: Reformation Heritage, 2022). Cf. Thomas McCall's excellent review of Fesko from an Arminian perspective, https://www.thelondonlyceum.com/book-review-arminius-and-the-reformed-tradition/.

of his such as Albert Hardenberg, Anastasius Veluanus, Johannes Holman-nus Secundus, and Gellius Snecanus—began to clash with the mainstream of scholastic Reformed dogmatics.[10] However, the assertion of some scholars that Arminius contradicted *confessional* Reformed theology before Dort simply cannot be sustained, since total depravity is the only point of the five points of Calvinism that was clearly affirmed in the sixteenth-century Reformed confessions and catechisms. What we see, therefore, in Arminius and his early followers in the Netherlands, as well as the English General Baptists, whose major writers came closest to his soteriology, is a warm affirmation of the Reformed faith.

This type of Reformed theology strongly affirmed divine sovereignty but wisely steered clear of the divine determinism into which much Reformed teaching morphed. This was a sovereignty in the biblical sense that God is sovereign and will punish or banish those who do not comply with the terms of his covenant with them. It was a sovereignty in the sense that God providentially rules and guides his creation and that nothing is outside his purview, even when he permits sin and evil that arises from human freedom. It was a sovereignty in the sense of Abraham Kuyper's famous comment, "There is not a square inch in the whole domain of our human existence over which Christ, who is Sovereign over all, does not cry, Mine!"[11]

However, Arminius's view of divine sovereignty was resolutely not a divine determinism in which every thought, intent, and moral choice made by sinful human beings is determined by God and is just as he wants it to play out. It was not a divine decision to give the grace necessary for conversion only to a

---

[10] Wim Janse, *Albert Hardenberg als Theologe: Profil Eines Bucer-Schülers* (Leiden: Brill, 1994); Erik A. de Boer, "Who are the 'Predestinatores'? The Doctrine of Predestination in the Early Dutch Reformation (Joannes Anastasius) and Its Sources (Philip Melanchthon)," in *The Doctrine of Election in Reformed Perspective: Historical and Theological Investigations of the Synod of Dort 1618–1619*, ed. Frank van der Pol (Gottingen: Vandenhoeck and Ruprecht, 2019); Johannes Trapman, "Grotius and Erasmus," in *Hugo Grotius, Theologian: Essays in Honor of G. H. M. Posthumus Meyjes*, ed. Henk J. M. Nellen and Edwin Rabbie (Leiden: Brill, 1994); "Holmannus (Johannes) Secundus," in *Biographisch Woordenboek der Nederlanden*, ed. Abraham Jacob van der Aa (Haarlem: J. J. van Brederode, 1862), 309; Jasper van der Steen, "A Contested Past: Memory Wars during the Twelve Years Truce (1609–21)," in *Memory before Modernity: Practices of Memory in Early Modern Europe*, ed. Erika Kuijpers et al. (Leiden: Brill, 2013), 53; Benjamin J. Kaplan, *Calvinists and Libertines: Confession and Community in Utrecht 1578–1620* (Oxford: Clarendon, 1995).

[11] James D. Bratt, ed., *Abraham Kuyper: A Centennial Reader* (Grand Rapids: Eerdmans, 1998), 488.

select few and purposefully deprive the mass of humanity of that grace, while
still holding them responsible for resisting it and enlarging their punishment
the more they do so. This approach to divine sovereignty was well within the
confines of the Reformed confessions and catechisms of the sixteenth century.

Divine sovereignty and total depravity are the doctrines that made
Reformed theology what it was. God through Christ is Lord over all. He created us for himself and made a covenant with us, and we broke that covenant
and fell and came under his curse. The only way to be redeemed from this
curse is for God in Christ to fulfill the law on our behalf through his sinless life
and his death on the cross and impute that righteousness to us through faith.
Yet the details of the free will-determinism debate and how it impinges on the
doctrines of the universality or particularity, or the resistibility or irresistibility,
of divine grace were left open questions in pre-Dort Reformed confessional
theology.

THE BEAUTY OF REFORMED THEOLOGY

The question then becomes, Can one take advantage of the beauty of Reformed
theology and still be an Arminian on the *gratia universalis* and *gratia resistibilis*
(universal, resistible grace)? Reformed Arminians answer this question with a
resounding yes.

F. Leroy Forlines, the systematic theologian who mentored so many
Reformed Arminians either personally or through his writings, showed what
this looked like. He drank deeply from the well of Reformed scholastic theology as mediated through the two American writers he most frequently quoted:
William G. T. Shedd and Charles Hodge. He joyfully concurred with these and
other Reformed thinkers on total depravity and its far-reaching effects on what
he often referred to as the "total personality"—our intellect, will, and affections.
He agreed that God is sovereign over all and that we can come into our own
as human beings created in God's image only when we bow to the lordship of
Christ in the whole of life. He affirmed the classic Reformed understandings
of penal satisfaction in atonement and the imputation of the active and passive
obedience of Christ to the believer in justification. He rejoiced in the five *solae*
as interpreted by the consensus of sixteenth-century Reformed theology: *sola*

gratia (grace alone), *sola fide* (faith alone), *solus Christus* (Christ alone), *sola Scriptura* (Scripture alone), and *soli Deo gloria* (the glory of God alone).[12]

This Reformed Arminian approach to understanding Christian theology and the Christian life differs from Calvinism on *how one comes to be in a state of grace.* Yet it agrees with Calvinism on *what it means to be in a state of grace.* This agreement with Calvinism on what it means to be in a state of grace touches on the total depravity and inability of humanity to reach out to God without divine prevenient grace. Those who do not resist God's grace will be converted and justified by the imputed righteousness of Christ rendered by the penal satisfaction Christ performed in his obedience to the law and by his sacrifice on our behalf.

Yet the similarities with Reformed theology do not end with depravity, the nature of atonement, and justification. Reformed Arminians also share with Calvinists the Reformed view of sanctification as a progressive growth in holiness and the likeness of Christ. Thus they demur from the entire sanctification and Christian perfection teachings of many Arminians. How this Reformed understanding of sanctification plays itself out in perseverance and spirituality also distinguishes Reformed Arminians from other Arminians. Most Arminians are more moralistic with regard to indwelling sin. They believe that sin in believers' lives (sometimes one sin, sometimes several) severs their relationship with God, bringing about an apostasy from which the apostate must repent and be restored to that relationship. For Reformed Arminians, the doctrine of justification by the imputed righteousness of Christ drives them to a different conclusion. They argue that the believer's union with Christ and the imputation of his active and passive obedience in that union mean that unconfessed sin does not sever that union. Yet, unlike Calvinists, Reformed Arminians still take the scriptural warning passages seriously, affirming that it is possible for a believer to apostatize through unbelief and no longer be in union with Christ and thus participate in his saving benefits. Like Arminius, they agree with the Belgic Confession's understanding of postconversion sin:

---

[12] F. Leroy Forlines, *The Quest for Truth: Theology for Postmodern Times* (Nashville: Randall House, 2001); Forlines, *Classical Arminianism: A Theology of Salvation* (Nashville: Randall House, 2011).

Though we do good works, we do not found our salvation
upon them; for we can do no work but what is polluted by
our flesh, and also punishable; and although we could perform such works, still the remembrance of one sin is sufficient
to make God reject them. Thus, then, we should always be in
doubt, tossed to and fro without any certainty, and our poor
consciences would be continually vexed if they relied not on
the merits of the suffering and death of our Saviour.[13]

Thus, for Reformed Arminians, apostasy occurs only when union with
Christ is broken by unbelief and the once-for-all satisfaction of Christ is
no longer imputed to the individual. This apostasy is irremediable because,
as Hebrews 10 says, the sacrifice of Christ, the great high priest, unlike the
repeated sacrifices of the Levitical priesthood, is unrepeatable. For the apostate,
"there no longer remains a sacrifice for sins," but only a "terrifying expectation
of judgment and the fury of a fire about to consume the adversaries" (10:26–
27). This differs from many Arminians who affirm that a believer can fall away
because of unconfessed sin and can be reconverted repeatedly.

Reformed Arminians also resonate with Forlines's concerns about the "crisis experience" orientation at the heart of much Wesleyan and Holiness spirituality.[14] A consistently Reformed view of progressive sanctification entails a
Reformed view of spirituality centered on what the Westminster Shorter Catechism calls the "ordinary means of grace." God's ordinary means of redeem-
ing people, through both justification and sanctification, are those ordinary
practices—ordinances—the Spirit has ordained in his Word. As the Catechism
says, "The outward and ordinary means whereby Christ communicateth to us
the benefits of redemption, are his ordinances, especially the word, sacraments,
and prayer; all which are made effectual to the elect for salvation."[15] Such an
approach avoids an emphasis on crisis experiences, including a second (or
subsequent) work of grace, as well as an overemphasis on subjectivism and

---

[13] Art. 24, in Arthur C. Cochrane, ed., *Reformed Confessions of the Sixteenth Century* (Louis-
ville: Westminster John Knox, 2003), 206.

[14] Harrold Harrison and Leroy Forlines, *The Charismatic Movement: A Survey of Its Development and Doctrine* (Nashville: Commission for Theological Integrity, National Association of
Free Will Baptists, 1989), 16–18, 36–39.

[15] The Westminster Shorter Catechism, Question 88 (Presbyterian Church in America
Administrative Committee), 396, https://www.pcaac.org/bco/westminster-confession/.

experientialism. It stresses balance between the three facets of the total personality: our reason, our affections and desires, and the choices we make.

Thoroughgoing Reformed Arminians, however, move beyond questions of
what it means to be in a state of grace in their appreciation of Reformed faith
and practice. They follow Forlines into Reformed themes such as epistemology
and apologetics, covenantalism and inaugurated eschatology, an Augustinian-
Kuyperian orientation with respect to cultural engagement, and the sufficiency
of Scripture for ecclesial practice.[16]

THE PROMISE OF A REFORMED ARMINIAN
INTERACTION WITH EDWARDS

A Reformed Arminian interaction with Jonathan Edwards is an ideal way to
get at this nuanced approach to Arminianism. Such an interaction holds out
the promise of enlivening the interconfessional conversation among evangelical Protestants. That is because Edwards asks difficult questions and probes
possible answers in ways neither Calvinists nor Arminians are accustomed to
do. Often, in thinking aloud as he moves toward the solution of a problem over
the course of his work, Edwards considers options that the Calvinist mainstream rarely entertains.

Still, Edwards is a staunch Calvinist. Understanding those things Arminians can have in common with him and appreciate in him, as well as those
issues in his thought that provide a stark contrast to Arminianism, opens us
to new possibilities. Engaging with Edwards through a Reformed Arminian
lens automatically leads Arminians or non-Calvinists to ask questions like the
following: Is it possible to be an Arminian, yet be broadly Reformed, bene-
fitting from the beauty of Reformed theology while remaining untethered to
the undesirable deterministic and particular-grace aspects of Calvinism? Is it
possible to be an Arminian—truly affirming libertarian free will, the freedom

[16] See, e.g., F. Leroy Forlines and J. Matthew Pinson, *The Apologetics of Leroy Forlines*
(Gallatin, TN: Welch College Press, 2019); Matthew McAffee, "Forlinesean Eschatology: A
Progressive Covenantal Approach," in *The Promise of Arminian Theology: Essays in Honor of
F. Leroy Forlines*, ed. Matthew Steven Bracey and W. Jackson Watts (Nashville: Randall House
Academic, 2016), 141–70; F. Leroy Forlines, *Secularism and the American Republic: Rethinking
Thomas Jefferson on Church and State*, ed. Matthew Steven Bracey (Gallatin, TN: Welch College
Press, 2022). This is not meant to suggest that all Reformed theologians are Kuyperians.

of alternative choice—yet place the sovereignty and glory of God at the center of one's theology rather than the freedom and perfectibility of humanity?

Is it possible to affirm the *gratia universalis* and *gratia resistibilis* of the mainstream of the church catholic while still holding firmly to total depravity and the inability of fallen sinners to respond favorably to God or the gospel? Is it possible to be an Arminian while not asserting that prevenient grace universally undoes the effects of the fall?

Is it possible to be an Arminian yet articulate a robust Reformed doctrine of penal substitutionary atonement? Is it possible to be an Arminian while believing that union with Christ causes his active and passive obedience to be imputed to believers?

Is it possible to be an Arminian who affirms classic Reformed notions of progressive sanctification and postconversion sin? Is it possible to be an Arminian who does not feel compelled to affirm various iterations of entire sanctification and Christian perfection? Is it possible to be an Arminian who reads the Puritans and agrees with Word-based, ordinary-means-of-grace spirituality rather than decisionism on the one hand and higher-life or Holiness spirituality on the other? Is it possible to be an Arminian who articulates a Reformed doctrine of assurance of salvation while taking scriptural warning texts seriously and thus affirming the possibility of defection from Christ?

And this same interaction naturally leads to other questions by the Arminian who probes Edwards's thought—questions that get beyond the inner core of purely soteriological questions: Is it possible to be an Arminian who naturally agrees with Calvin on the noetic effects of sin and the inability to construct a robust natural theology and apologetic apart from special revelation? Is it possible to be an Arminian and believe that the noetic effects of sin prohibit human beings from understanding how to approach God in ecclesial practice and thus that practice must be warranted by Holy Scripture? Is it possible to be an Arminian who affirms the classic Reformed understanding of the sufficiency of Scripture and the ordinary means of grace? Is it possible to be an Arminian yet affirm covenantalism and inaugurated eschatology and not be a dispensationalist? Is it possible to be an Arminian yet affirm an Augustinian-Kuyperian vision of culture that H. Richard Niebuhr referred to as "Christ transforming culture" while still understanding that the noetic effects of human depravity demand a stark distinction—an antithesis—between a worldview and culture shaped by Scripture and the Christian tradition and a worldview and culture not shaped by them?[17]

All of these questions are uppermost in the minds of thoroughgoing Reformed Arminians. That is because they are in agreement with their fellow Arminians on how one comes to be in a state of grace. Yet they are in accordance with Calvinists on what it means to be in a state of grace. Furthermore, many of them wish to go even deeper and probe the implications of a Reformed understanding of creation, fall, redemption, and consummation for a full-orbed biblical theology, not only for ecclesiastical practice but also for thought and culture.

THE CONTRIBUTION OF THE PRESENT VOLUME

Arminians who interact deeply with the likes of Edwards, while eschewing his determinism and affirmation of particular and irresistible grace, will naturally be led to ask questions like these and seek answers. Many of these questions come to the fore in other chapters in this book. However, these chapters probe the narrower concerns of soteriology—what it means to be in a state of grace and how one comes to be in a state of grace.

Chapters 2 through 4 are highly appreciative of Edwards, emphasizing commonalities between him and the Reformed Arminian thrust that differs with what many Arminians popularly affirm. Thus Paul Harrison begins with a sketch of Edwards's life and ministry and an expression of deep appreciation for his preaching. Then he examines Edwards's approach to the way original sin causes humanity to be totally depraved in mind as well as in will and affections, showing its commonalities with Arminius and a Reformed Arminian understanding of human depravity and inability in salvation.

Kevin Hester probes Edwards's nuanced understanding of the nature of Christ's atonement. Edwards ultimately comes down on the penal substitutionary side of the debate, arguing that Christ fulfills the law on the sinner's behalf and suffers and dies to pay the penalty for sin. Christ takes on the Father's wrath for sin in the place and stead of the sinner. Hester also investigates Edwards's concomitant, and again nuanced, understanding of the imputation of the righteousness of Christ through faith alone in justification. He interacts

---

[17] See H. Richard Niebuhr, *Christ and Culture* (New York: Harper and Brothers, 1951).

with Edwards's thought from the vantage point of Reformed Arminianism, emphasizing the crediting of the active and passive obedience of Christ to the faithful in Edwards's own unique construction of that doctrine.

Barry Raper looks at the applications of Edwards's spirituality for the individual Christian and the church in our day. Focusing especially on Edwards's "The Distinguishing Marks of a Work of the Spirit of God," Raper offers a Reformed Arminian reading of Edwards that is appreciative of his Word-driven spirituality. That spirituality, as Raper explains, is concerned with privileging and promoting progressive sanctification and growth in Christ through the ordinary means of grace while being affirming of the sovereign work of the Spirit in "revivals of religion." Raper applies Edwards's spirituality to present-day concerns in personal and ecclesial piety.

The last three chapters critically interact with Edwards on the question of how one comes to be (and remain) in a state of grace. My chapter examines Edwards's preaching, which had as its centerpiece the free offer of the gospel. It then critically interacts with it from an Arminian perspective, questioning the consistency of such bold free-offer preaching with Edwards's view that God has two wills and two callings. While Edwards preaches the gospel like an Arminian, he affirms God's revealed will that all be saved and his secret will that only the elect be saved. Consistent with this principle is his belief in a universal calling that calls all people to repentance and makes hell hotter for them the more they resist, and a secret calling that comes only to the elect. Still, God purposefully withholds from the reprobate the grace necessary for conversion, all the while wooing them to himself and enlarging their punishment for their continued resistance to his calls.

Robert Picirilli's chapter critically examines Edwards's opposition to libertarian free will in the latter's classic *Freedom of the Will*. Picirilli pushes back on Edwards's philosophical arguments for his soft determinist or compatibilist conception of how God can determine every aspect of reality exactly as he wants it, including every "free" intention and decision human beings make. He also wades into the question of the relationship between divine foreknowledge and human free will. Picirilli asks whether Edwards is correct in asserting that everything that happens must, of necessity, occur, simply because God knows it will. In this connection, he also deals with two nondeterminist options that some non-Calvinists are open to (and disagrees with them): open theism, or what some have called limited omniscience, and Molinism.

In the last chapter, Matthew McAffee offers a nuanced critical treatment of Edwards's understanding of the certain perseverance of the saints. In this essay McAffee considers Edwards's defense of absolute perseverance based on God's sovereign determination, election, and effectual calling. He then engages it from a Reformed Arminian perspective. McAffee argues for an approach to perseverance that is based on persisting in union with Christ through faith alone. Yet the chapter also presents the Reformed Arminian understanding of the possibility of irremediably falling from that union—not repeatedly through sinning and failing to confess, but in a once-for-all defection from belief and hence from the union with Christ that provides believers the perfect righteousness through which they stand justified before God.

CONCLUSION

Jonathan Edwards is rightly considered one of the most influential theologians in history. A consideration of his thought in these key areas has great promise to help Arminians and Calvinists come together for dialogue in a way that is increasingly rare in our time. Such a consideration also brings with it hopeful possibilities for the Arminian theological community, giving a glimpse of new vistas for being both Arminian and Reformed. Yet these vistas are as old as Arminius himself, who considered himself a Reformed minister to his dying day and concurred enthusiastically with the Reformed confessions. He modeled what a Reformed theology can look like when shorn of determinism and particular grace. Interacting with Edwards will help us probe this balanced middle ground between the all-too-common caricatures of Reformed and Arminian thought.

Chapter 2

Jonathan Edwards: Reflections on His Life and Ministry

Paul V. Harrison

Almost everyone who attempts to narrate the life of Jonathan Edwards engages in hagiography. Edwards did indeed live as a saint. From his teenage years to his deathbed, he exemplified the deepest of commitments to virtue. This virtue, joined with his profound intelligence, resulted in an anointed ministry and a superb and expansive body of literature Christians will forever explore. This chapter will briefly survey some of the high points of his life and ministry with a focus on his biblical-theological preaching.

EARLY YEARS

Jonathan Edwards was born on October 5, 1703, to Timothy and Esther Edwards. Timothy was a Harvard graduate (though only after having apparently been expelled and readmitted) who served as pastor of the Congregational church in Windsor, Connecticut, for about sixty-four years (1694–1758). This was a solid home and one in which Jonathan would flourish.

One generation earlier, however, things were different. Timothy's mother, Elizabeth Tuthill Edwards, was wicked and perhaps insane. Three months into her marriage to Richard Edwards, she confessed that she was pregnant by another man. She involved herself in "repeated infidelities, rages, and threats of violence, including the threat to cut Richard's throat while he was asleep."[1] One of her sisters murdered her own child, and a brother killed another sister with an axe. Though Richard and Elizabeth had six children, of which Timothy was the oldest, Richard filed for divorce in 1688. Divorce was quite rare in those days, and the court refused the request. After more years of suffering, however, he filed a second time, and the court granted the divorce. He remarried and his life improved greatly.

Jonathan's mother, Esther, was the daughter of Solomon Stoddard, also a Harvard graduate and the institution's first librarian. Stoddard was pastor of the Congregational church in Northampton, Massachusetts, for around sixty years (1669–1729). For many years he was also one of New England's most influential ministers.[2] At Stoddard's funeral the preacher delivering the eulogy said, "There are sometimes men whom it pleases God to impart so much of His wisdom and grace, that under God they are accounted as shields of the Earth, the strength and glory of the places where they live."[3] Jonathan Edwards later recalled that "many looked on him [Stoddard] almost as a sort of deity."[4]

In Timothy and Esther Edwards's home in Windsor, Connecticut, Jonathan grew up as one of eleven children. All his siblings were girls, each of whom grew to at least six feet tall. As some put it, he had sixty feet of sisters.

At age twelve Jonathan went off to Yale College in New Haven, Connecticut, to study for the ministry, eventually earning both a B.A. and M.A. and serving as a tutor.[5] At around nineteen he penned seventy personal resolutions. A small sampling of these resolutions reveals the heart and piety of the young Edwards. The first states, "Resolved, That I will do whatsoever I think to be most to the glory of God, and my own good, profit, and pleasure, in the whole of my duration." Number five states, "Resolved, Never to lose one moment of

---

[1] George M. Marsden, *Jonathan Edwards: A Life* (New Haven: Yale University Press, 2003), 22.

[2] Patricia J. Tracy, *Jonathan Edwards, Pastor: Religion and Society in Eighteenth Century Northampton* (New York: Hill and Wang, 1980), 14.

[3] Tracy, *Jonathan Edwards, Pastor*, 14.

[4] Jonathan Edwards, *The Works of Jonathan Edwards with a Memoir by Sereno E. Dwight*, rev. Edward Hickman, 2 vols. (Edinburgh: Banner of Truth Trust, 1974), 1:cxxxiii.

[5] Iain Murray, *Jonathan Edwards: A New Biography* (Edinburgh: Banner of Truth Trust, 1987), 33. In his undergraduate work, Edwards finished first in his class.

time, but to improve it in the most profitable way I possibly can." Number six-teen states, "Resolved, Never to speak evil of any one, so that it shall tend to his dishonor, more or less, upon no account except for some real good." Number fifty-two states, "I frequently hear persons in old age say how they would live, if they were to live their lives over again: Resolved, That I will live just so as I can think I shall wish I had done, supposing I live to old age."[6]

In 1726 Jonathan accepted a call to assist his aged grandfather Stoddard in his pastoral labors at Northampton. The next year he married eighteen-year-old Sarah Pierpont, the daughter of the former pastor of the First Congregational Church in New Haven. The couple went on to have eleven children and enjoyed what Jonathan in his dying hours called an "uncommon union."[7]

When Stoddard died in 1729, Edwards, twenty-five years old at the time, assumed the mantle of pastor of the Northampton church, one of the largest in New England. In accord with the thinking of his day, he considered teaching and preaching his main responsibilities. Usually rising at four o'clock in the summer and five o'clock in the winter, he spent about thirteen hours a day in his study. He prayed and studied and wrote incessantly, seeking to know God and his truth and therefore to be able to present them to his people.

Edwards suffered from a weak physical constitution and addressed this by being especially careful about what he ate. He almost always appeared gaunt. He handed over the affairs of the household to Sarah, who ran things swim-mingly. He exercised regularly by chopping wood or riding his horse. On these rides he engaged in contemplation and would pin small pieces of paper on dif-ferent parts of his clothing as a reminder to write down certain thoughts when he returned home.

Reformed Arminians agree with much of Edwards's theology and practice. We rejoice in his commitment to Scripture, his Trinitarian theology, his under-standing of life-changing salvation entered through repentance and faith. We also have significant points of difference. As an eighteenth-century Congrega-tionalist, he was a thoroughgoing Calvinist, believing in unconditional elec-tion, limited atonement, irresistible grace, and the certain perseverance of the

---

6   Jonathan Edwards, "Resolutions," in *Letters and Personal Writings*, *The Works of Jonathan Edwards*, vol. 16, ed. George S. Claghorn (New Haven: Yale University Press, 1998), 753, 757.
7   Edwards, "On Sarah Pierpont," in *The Great Awakening*, *The Works of Jonathan Edwards*, vol. 4, ed. C. C. Goen (New Haven: Yale University Press, 1972), 467. *The Works of Jonathan Edwards* will hereafter be referred to as *WJE*.

saints. He also affirmed infant baptism. These disagreements do not keep us from valuing his contributions to the world.

A REVIVAL OF RELIGION

In 1734 revival broke out in Northampton in the wake of the death of two young people whose passing especially affected other youth. Edwards responded to this event by organizing home meetings across the town, beginning with the young people but eventually including adults. While the Northampton congregation sang only psalms in their corporate Sunday worship, in these meetings they began to sing the hymns of Isaac Watts. In December half a dozen people or so were converted. In particular, one young woman, known for being a "company-keeper," came to faith, and "the news of it seemed to be almost like a *flash of lightning*, upon the hearts of young people all over the town, and upon many others."[8]

Edwards narrated the effects of these conversions:

> And presently upon this, a great and earnest concern about the great things of religion and the eternal world became universal, in all parts of the town, and among persons of all degrees and ages. The noise among the dry bones waxed louder and louder. All other talk but about spiritual and eternal things was thrown by. All the conversation in all companies, and upon all occasions, was upon these things only; except so much as was necessary for people's carrying on their ordinary secular business. Other discourse, than of the things of God, would scarce be tolerated in any company. The minds of people were wonderfully taken off from the world: it was treated among us as a thing of very little consequence. Men seemed to follow their worldly business more as a part of duty, than from any disposition they had to it. The temptation now seemed to be

---

[8] Edwards, "The Preciousness of Time," in *Sermons and Discourses, 1734–1738*, WJE, vol. 19, ed. M. X. Lesser (New Haven: Yale University Press, 2001), 243.

on the other hand to neglect worldly affairs too much, and to spend too much time in the immediate exercises of religion.[9]

He went on to explain that "souls did as it were come by flocks to Jesus Christ. From day to day, for many months together, might be seen evident instances of sinners brought out of darkness into marvellous light, and delivered out of an horrible pit, and from the miry clay, and set upon a rock with a new song of praise to God in their mouths."[10]

Both church and town were deeply changed:

> The town seemed to be full of the presence of God: it never was so full of love, nor so full of joy; and yet so full of distress, as it was then. There were remarkable tokens of God's presence in almost every house. It was a time of joy in families on the account of salvation's being brought unto them; parents rejoicing over their children as newborn, and husbands over their wives, and wives over their husbands. The goings of God were then seen in his sanctuary [*Psalms 68:24*], God's day was a delight, and his tabernacles were amiable [*Psalms 84:1*]. Our public assemblies were then beautiful; the congregation was alive in God's service, everyone earnestly intent on the public worship, every hearer eager to drink in the words of the minister as they came from his mouth; the assembly in general were, from time to time, in tears while the Word was preached; some weeping with sorrow and distress, others with joy and love, others with pity and concern for the souls of their neighbors.[11]

By the time the revival died down, around three hundred people had made professions of faith, raising the church's communicant members to 620. The awakening had touched all segments of the town: rich and poor, young and old, men and women.

---

[9] Edwards, *A Faithful Narrative of the Surprising Work of God*, in *The Great Awakening*, *WJE*, 4:117.

[10] Edwards, 4:150–51.

[11] Edwards, 4:151.

Religious fervor usually subsides gradually. That is what happened in Northampton, but certain events especially contributed to a spiritual waning. A damper was put on things when a "poor weak man" attempted to cut his throat because of his spiritual struggles. Edwards wrote that by late May 1735, the Spirit seemed to be "gradually withdrawing." The spiritual movement came to a screeching halt on Sunday, June 1, 1735, when one of the town's leading citizens and Edwards's uncle, Joseph Hawley II, slit his throat and died. Apparently, having been surrounded with conversion but not having experienced it himself, he had fallen into a depressed state and had suffered terribly from sleeplessness. The coroner concluded that he had been delirious. In fact, after this incident "multitudes in this and other towns seemed to have it strongly suggested to 'em, and pressed upon 'em, to do as this person had done."[12]

Though when Edwards was young, he frequently complained in his diary of being "exceedingly dull, dry, and dead" or "dull for several days" or "decayed," he developed a rich devotional life, often rejoicing in Christ and experiencing the sweetness of knowing God. He recorded:

> Once, as I rid out into the woods for my health, *anno* 1737; and having lit from my horse in a retired place, as my manner commonly has been, to walk for divine contemplation and prayer; I had a view, that for me was extraordinary, of the glory of the Son of God; as mediator between God and man; and his wonderful, great, full, pure and sweet grace and love, and meek and gentle condescension. This grace, that appeared to me so calm and sweet, appeared great above the heavens. The person of Christ appeared ineffably excellent, with an excellency great enough to swallow up all thought and conception. Which continued, as near as I can judge, about an hour; which kept me, the bigger part of the time, in a flood of tears, and weeping aloud. I felt withal, an ardency of soul to be, what I know not otherwise how to express, than to be emptied and annihilated; to lie in the dust, and to be full of Christ alone; to love him with a holy and pure love; to trust in him; to live upon him; to serve and follow him, and to be totally wrapt

---

[12] Edwards, 4:206.

up in the fullness of Christ; and to be perfectly sanctified and made pure, with a divine and heavenly purity. I have several other times, had views very much of the same nature, and that have had the same effects.[13]

In 1740 revival fires began to burn again in New England, ignited this time by the itinerant evangelist George Whitefield and especially radiating out from Boston. The Church of England minister included Northampton in his circuit and preached there with good effect. By 1741 the effects of this second revival became evident in Northampton as some began to respond visibly, that is, bodily, to Edwards's preaching. There were outcries and faintings. People became physically weak in church meetings. Weeping became common.

In a letter to a fellow minister, Edwards explained the way that many young people who had come to his house for instruction were impacted by the recent revival movement: "Many seemed to be very greatly and most agreeably affected with those views which excited humility, self-condemnation, self-abhorrence, love and joy: many fainted under these affections."[14] Not unlike the revival in the mid-1730s, this movement resulted in the conversion and spiritual renewal of numerous individuals.

Many readers will be familiar with Edwards's sermon "Sinners in the Hands of an Angry God," which he preached during this time in the nearby town of Enfield. Speaking from Deut 32:35, "Their foot shall slip in due time," Edwards emphasized the impending judgment of God on impenitent sinners. While he preached, "there was a great moaning and crying out throughout the whole house." He was forced to stop and ask the people to be quiet, but the noise only increased with "shrieks and cries . . . piercing and amazing."[15] Such a tumult persisted that the sermon was never finished. Instead, the ministers present went down among the congregation to offer spiritual assistance to the convicted. Things finally settled down enough for the congregation to sing a song and for a preacher to offer a closing prayer.

Ministerial attitudes in New England toward the revivals varied, with some thinking they were the work of the devil and others concluding they were

---

[13] Jonathan Edwards, *Personal Narrative*, in *Letters and Personal Writings*, WJE, 16:801.

[14] Marsden, *Jonathan Edwards*, 217.

[15] Marsden, 220.

God-anointed. The various extravagances (fainting, etc.) of the movements provided fuel for critics, and Edwards felt forced to defend what he considered beyond doubt a work of God. In his "The Distinguishing Marks of a Work of the Spirit of God," he argued that certain behaviors sometimes attending revivals neither prove nor disprove the works to be genuinely from God. Among these behaviors were "effects on the bodies of men; such as tears, trembling, groans, loud outcries, agonies of body, or the failing of bodily strength." Likewise, he argued that, if people experienced "great impressions" on their imaginations and became involved in "great imprudences and irregularities in their conduct," these did not constitute proof that a revival of religion was not from God. Even if those impacted by such a revival "fall away into gross errors, or scandalous practices, it is no argument that the work in general is not the work of the Spirit of God."[16]

Positively, Edwards laid out the case from 1 John 4 that five things give evidence a work is from heaven:

> It raises the people's esteem of Jesus.
> It works against the interests of Satan's kingdom.
> It increases people's regard for Scripture.
> It leads people to truth.
> It operates as a spirit of love for God and man.[17]

Edwards's thinking on revivals remains relevant today.

EDWARDS, NORTHAMPTON, AND
THE HALFWAY COVENANT

For all the blessings Edwards and his people shared, events in 1744 drove a wedge between them. Several young men in the congregation, ranging from ages twenty-one to twenty-nine, secured books on medicine and midwifery and had for some years been talking about women in a lewd fashion. They even went so far as to mock and harass young women in the congregation. One of the

---

[16] Jonathan Edwards, "The Distinguishing Marks of a Work of the Spirit of God," in *The Great Awakening, WJE*, 4:230, 241.

[17] Edwards, 4:249–55.

roughest of the bunch, Timothy Root, called one of the books "the young folks' Bible." When the matter finally erupted in public, Edwards took steps to deal with it. His friend Samuel Hopkins recorded how things unfolded: He "chose a Number of Men, to assist their Pastor in examining into the Affair. Upon which Mr. EDWARDS appointed the time for their meeting at his House: and then read a Catalogue of the Names of young Persons, whom he desired to come to his House at the same time. Some were the accused, and some Witnesses; but it was not then declared of which Number any particular Person was."[18] This, of course, cast aspersions on all included on the list, and soon the whole church and town were abuzz over the matter. The church eventually worked its way through the ugly matter as best they could, but Hopkins reported that, because of Edwards's mishandling the matter, the pastor's influence was never the same again.

Remember that Edwards had followed his Grandfather Stoddard's sixty-year pastorate. A theological powerhouse himself and a dominant personality throughout New England, Stoddard had led his congregation and many others into some theological anomalies. In Congregational church practice, members were taught to have their children baptized, along the lines of the Israelites' having their infant sons circumcised. In the course of time, however, many of these baptized children grew into adulthood without ever having experienced conversion themselves. They in turn had children and wanted them to be baptized. What was to be done? It was decided that such adults, if they lived morally upright lives and would "own" the covenant, could have their children baptized, though the parents still could not vote or partake of the Lord's Supper. Since 1662 almost the whole of New England had embraced this position that came to be called derisively "the Halfway Covenant." Stoddard was a chief influence in the popularity of this approach.

Stoddard, however, came to be dissatisfied with this plan, feeling that it did not go far enough. For about the last thirty years of his pastorate, he also allowed and encouraged church attenders who were unconverted to participate in the Lord's Supper. He maintained that the supper was designed by God to be a "converting ordinance." God would use the emblems of Jesus's sacrifice

---

[18] Samuel Hopkins, *The Life and Character of the Late Reverend Mr. Jonathan Edwards, President of the College of New-Jersey. Together with Extracts from His Private Writings & Diary. And Also Seventeen Select Sermons on Various Important Subjects*, 2nd ed. (Northampton: Printed by Andrew Wright, 1804), 59.

to bring conviction to souls and usher them into his kingdom. For part of his biblical defense, he used the pattern of the Israelites' broad participation in the Passover as a backdrop for his understanding of communion.

When Edwards assumed the church's leadership in 1729, he merely carried on existing practice. Over the course of time, however, he struggled with his inherited ecclesiology, and around 1746 he concluded that not only was his grandfather's *extension* of the Halfway Covenant wrong, but the *covenant itself* was against Scripture. In making public his new views in 1749, he confessed:

> I have formerly been of his [Stoddard's] opinion, which I imbibed from his books, even from my childhood, and have in my proceedings conformed to his practice; though never without some difficulties in my view, which I could not solve: yet, however, a distrust of my own understanding, and deference to the authority of so venerable a man, the seeming strength of some of his arguments, together with the success he had in his ministry, and his great reputation and influence, prevailed for a long time to bear down my scruples.[19]

In announcing his new understanding of the Scripture, Edwards said that he entered into this debate "with the greatest reluctance that ever I undertook any public service in my life" but that "my doing this appeared to me very necessary and altogether unavoidable."[20]

Edwards anticipated that his people would not go along with him, especially on the point of baptism, and he was right. He eventually lectured on the subject to his congregation, but few of them attended. He wrote a book on the subject, but they scarcely read it. When all was said and done, the Northampton church overwhelmingly voted to dismiss their pastor, with only twenty-three men siding with him. One who observed the preacher during this time wrote, "I never saw the least symptoms of displeasure in his countenance the whole week, but he appeared like a man of God, whose happiness was out of the reach

[19] Jonathan Edwards, "An Humble Inquiry into the Rules of the Word of God, Concerning the Qualifications Requisite to a Complete Standing and Full Communion in the Visible Christian Church," in *Ecclesiastical Writings*, *WJE*, vol. 12, ed. David D. Hall (New Haven: Yale University Press, 1994), 169.

[20] Edwards, 12:170.

of his enemies, and whose treasure was not only a future but a present good, overbalancing all imaginable ills of life, even to the astonishment of many, who could not be at rest without his dismission."[21]

After Edwards was dismissed and had preached a compassionate and kind farewell sermon on July 1, 1750, the congregation had the audacity to ask him to continue to preach for them since they were struggling to fill the pulpit. This he did for some time.

LATER LIFE AND MINISTRY

In 1751 Edwards was called to be a missionary to the Mohican Indians in Stockbridge, Massachusetts. So he and his large family moved about fifty miles west, and America's greatest theologian became the teacher in this backwoods place. Interestingly, however, these six years or so were some of the most productive of his life. He was able to devote himself to writing and so produced some of his most influential works.

Edwards's time in Stockbridge came to a close when his son-in-law, Aaron Burr, Sr. (Edwards's daughter Esther's husband and the father of the American vice president), died in 1757. Burr served as Princeton's second president from 1748 until his death at age forty-one. The board of Princeton called Edwards to succeed him, but the preacher-theologian did not want the position. He called a council of his trusted friends, who unanimously recommended that he take the post. On their urging he accepted the presidency and moved to Princeton in January 1758, leaving his family in Stockbridge for the time being.

Smallpox was then quite a danger, and the new college president had been exposed to the disease on his trip from Stockbridge. So on February 23 he and some of his family were inoculated against the disease. The others did fine, but Edwards contracted smallpox on the roof of his mouth. He died on March 22, 1758, at the age of fifty-four.

When it became clear to him that he would not survive, he called his daughter Lucy to his side and said,

> Dear Lucy, it seems to me to be the Will of God that I must
> shortly leave you & therefore give my kindest Love to my dear

---

[21] Marsden, *Jonathan Edwards*, 361.

Wife & tell her, that the uncommon Union that has so long subsisted between us has been of such a Nature as I trust is Spiritual and therefore will continue forever: and I hope she will be supported under so great a trial & submit chearfully to the Will of God; And as to my Children you are now like to be left Fatherless which I hope will be an Inducement to you all to seek a Father who will never fail you; & as to my Funeral I would have it be like unto Mr Burrs, and any additional Sum of Money that might be expected to be laid out that way, I would have it disposed of to charitable uses.[22]

In one account of the hours just before Edwards's death, some in the room, thinking their conversation could not be heard by him, were lamenting the terrible impact his passing would have. But the dying preacher-theologian did hear them and said, "Trust in God and ye need not fear." William Shippen, a Philadelphia physician who had overseen Edwards's inoculation, wrote to Sarah,

And never did any mortal man more fully and clearly evidence the sincerity of all his profession, by one continued, universal, calm, cheerful resignation, and patient submission to the divine will, through every stage of the disease, than he; not so much as one discontented expression, nor the least appearance of murmuring through the whole. And never did any person expire with more perfect freedom from pain;—not so much as one distorted hair—but in the most proper sense of the words, he really fell asleep. Death had certainly lost its sting, as to him.[23]

---

[22] Letter from William Shippen to Sarah Pierpont Edwards, March 22, 1758, in *Correspondence by, to, and about Edwards and His Family, WJE Online*, vol. 32, ed. Jonathan Edwards Center, http://edwards.yale.edu/archive?path=aHR0cDovL2Vkd2FyZHMueWFsZS5lZHUvY2dpLWJpbi9uZXdwaGlsby9zZWxlY3QucGw/d2plby4zMQ=; Marsden, *Jonathan Edwards*, 494.

[23] Marsden, 494.

EDWARDS'S LEGACY OF THEOLOGICAL PREACHING

Edwards's primary legacy is usually thought of as having been the greatest theologian and philosopher in American history.[24] It is amazing and instructive, however, that his biblical and theological labors flourished in the context of pastoral ministry in a local congregation. One of the most enduring things he left the church is his theological preaching, and ministers today have a great deal to learn from him.

Arguably, outside of Scripture there are no better sermons than Edwards's. Among the many excellent sermons Edwards preached, one of his best is "The Excellency of Christ," preached in August 1736. Edwards chose Rev 5:5–6 as his text: "Weep not: behold, the Lion of the tribe of Judah, the Root of David, hath prevailed to open the book, and to loose the seven seals thereof. And I beheld, and, lo, in the midst of the throne . . . stood a Lamb as it had been slain" (KJV). Focusing on Jesus's identity as Lion and Lamb, Edwards asserted, "There is an admirable conjunction of diverse excellencies in Jesus Christ." He explained, "There do meet in Jesus Christ infinite highness and infinite condescension"; "infinite justice and infinite grace"; "infinite glory and lowest humility"; "infinite majesty and transcendent meekness"; "infinite worthiness of good, and the greatest patience under sufferings of evil"; "absolute sovereignty and perfect resignation"; "self-sufficiency, and an entire trust and reliance on God."[25]

While most know him only for his sermon "Sinners in the Hands of an Angry God," the Yale edition of his works fills twenty-six large volumes. No American theologian has made a more significant impact on Christianity than Edwards, and his preaching was no small part of that.

Godliness

What made Edwards a powerful preacher? First, his genuine godliness gave force to his words. From his youth he pursued God relentlessly. Of the seventy resolutions he penned as a teenager, the first read, "*Resolved*, That I will do whatsoever I think to be most to the glory of God, and my own good, profit,

---

[24] This section is adapted from Paul V. Harrison, "Preaching with Jonathan Edwards," *Pulpit* (Fall 2018), https://nafwb.org/site/preaching-with-jonathan-edwards/.

[25] Edwards, "The Excellency of Christ," 19:565–71.

and pleasure, in the whole of my duration." Number 5: "*Resolved*, Never to lose one moment of time, but to improve it in the most profitable way I possibly can." Number 19: "*Resolved*, Never to do any thing, which I should be afraid to do, if I expected it would not be above an hour before I should hear the last trump."[26]

Indispensable to Edwards's preaching was the time he spent in prayer, meditation, and Bible study. The beauties of nature reminded him of the Creator. Thunder and lightning made him mindful of God's majesty and sovereignty. An informed conscience guided his lifestyle. He devoted himself to his wife and eleven children. He made anonymous gifts to the needy. In short, he lived in the self-conscious spotlight of God and his Word. Such living adds much to a preacher's words.

Preparation

Second, Edwards's sermons reflected careful preparation. He recognized that the scriptural requirement to be "apt to teach" (1 Tim 3:2, KJV) meant he had to give himself tirelessly to study. He began most days at four or five in the morning, often spending up to thirteen hours of the day in study. One can preach only what one knows, so Edwards worked to know much about God and Scripture. This was not knowledge for its own sake but to deepen his relationship with God and to share his findings with his flock. That sharing generally took the form of extended sermons, written word for word, which he would quote and read to his people. He followed the pattern of preaching in his day: explanation of the text, development of the doctrine there, and an extended application. He usually prepared three sermons, each an hour long, every week. Around 1,200 of these works have survived.

One can hear the objections being voiced: "Nobody should study that long." "People won't listen to that kind of preaching today." "Others have preached with power who didn't take such pains in study." Personally, I relate to these objections and agree somewhat. However, when much intellectual slothfulness abounds and is evident in our pulpits, we need to be pulled back in the direction of more study. A seasoned minister once told me preaching was the easiest part of pastoring. Edwards would not have agreed.

---

[26] Edwards, "Resolutions," 16:753.

Scripture-Centered

Third, the sermons of Jonathan Edwards were powerful because of their heart-searching, scriptural focus. He always took a text and trained his attention on what God was saying. What did he mean? What did the text teach about God and humanity? How did it apply to life? For example, in his sermon on Luke 17:32, "The Folly of Looking Back in Fleeing out of Sodom," Edwards said, "Some in Sodom may seem to carry a fair face, and make a fair outward show; but if we could look into their hearts, they are every one altogether filthy and abominable." Drawing from Gen 19:23, he warned, "It seems to have been a fair morning in Sodom before it was destroyed."[27]

His application focused on those still in their sins:

> Sodom is the place of your nativity. . . . You are the inhabitants of Sodom. . . . Remember Lot's wife. For she looked back as being loath utterly and forever to leave the ease, and pleasure, and plenty that she had in Sodom; and having a mind to return to them again. Remember how she came off. And remember the children of Israel in the wilderness, who had a mind to go back again into Egypt. . . . You must be willing forever to leave all the ease, and pleasures, and profits of sin, to forsake all for salvation; as Lot forsook all, and left all he had to escape out of Sodom.[28]

This kind of heart focus was how Edwards always preached.

Logic

Fourth, Edwards's sermons were powerful because they pressed his listeners with unrelenting logic. While Edwards had no qualms about his hearers experiencing emotion, as long as biblical truth alone influenced their affections, his driving objective was leading his people to grapple with truth. Acts 18:4 says Paul "reasoned in the synagogue every Sabbath." Edwards followed Paul's

---

[27] Jonathan Edwards, "The Folly of Looking Back in Fleeing out of Sodom," in *WJE*, 19:325, 328.

[28] Edwards, 19:330–31.

example and was always pressing his congregants to think, believing that clear thinking would reveal truth and impress it on people's hearts.

For example, in his sermon on 1 Kgs 18:21, where Elijah challenges the people torn between two opinions, Edwards put forth the following doctrine: "Unresolvedness in religion is very unreasonable." He stated:

> There are but two things that God offers to mankind for their portion: one is this world with the pleasures and profits of sin, together with eternal misery ensuing; the other is heaven and eternal glory, with a life of self-denial and respect to all God's commandments preceding. Many continue as long as they live without coming to any settled determination in their own minds which of these to choose. They must have one or the other, and can't have both; but they are always held in suspense, never make their choice.[29]

Edwards believed that when a preacher speaks from his core beliefs, when he stakes his soul and all he has on the truth of his message, and when what he says is indeed properly aligned with the truth of Scripture, there is inherent power in the words.

Edwards proceeded to show how unreasonable it was to follow such a course of indetermination. It is unreasonable because religion is the thing most important to us: "It makes an infinite odds [difference] to us." It is unreasonable because the issues of choosing God or not are fully within our ability to understand: "God has made us capable of making a wise choice for ourselves." Additionally, "'Tis a glorious opportunity that God puts into our hands, that we may determine for ourselves. . . . God sets life and death before us."[30]

Edwards continues:

> The things among which we are to make our choice, are but few in number. There are but two portions set before us. . . . If there were many terms of the offer that are made, many things of near or equal value, one of which we must choose, a

---

[29] Edwards, "The Unreasonableness of Indetermination in Religion," in *WJE*, 19:96.
[30] Edwards, 19:98–99.

continuing long in suspense and undetermined would be more excusable; there would be more reason for our long deliberating, before we could fix. But there are but two. There are but two states in another world, in one or the other of which we must be fixed to all eternity.[31]

He concludes, "Their delaying to [come to a determination] is unreasonable, because they know not how soon their opportunity of choosing for themselves will be at an end. Their opportunity will continue no longer than life. When once life is past, they will no more have the offer made them. The sentence will be then past: the matter will be issued."[32]

Oratory

Fifth, power accompanied Edwards's preaching because of his delivery. Unlike his contemporary George Whitefield, Edwards was not known for being dramatic. In fact, he almost always carried a full manuscript to the pulpit and read most of it to his congregation. But as counterintuitive as it may seem, his deliberate, thoughtful delivery carried power.

His friend Samuel Hopkins described Edwards's sermon delivery as "easy, natural, and very solemn. He had not a strong, loud voice; but appeared with such gravity and solemnity, and spake with such distinctness, clearness, and precision; his Words were so full of Ideas, set in such a plain and striking Light, that few Speakers have been so able to demand the Attention of an Audience as he." Hopkins added that the preacher's words often revealed "a great degree of inward fervor, without much noise or external emotion."[33]

Boldness

Finally, Edwards's sermons were powerful because he spoke them boldly as the truth of God. He maintained that when one listened to Scripture rightly presented, he heard, as it were, the voice of God. In this connection he insisted that real reliance on God and His Word meant that everything, even longstanding

---

[31] Jonathan Edwards, 19:99.
[32] Edwards, 19:101.
[33] Samuel Hopkins, "Memoirs of President Edwards," in *The Works of President Edwards in Four Volumes* (New York: Leavitt, Trow & Company, 1844), 1:32.

church tradition, had to be evaluated in light of Scripture. He wrote, "Surely 'tis commendable for us to examine the practices of our fathers, we have no sufficient reason to take practices upon trust from them. Let them have as high a character as belongs to them; yet we may not look upon their principles as oracles. . . . He that believes principles because they affirm them, makes idols of them."[34]

As mentioned previously, Edwards inherited Halfway Covenant practices and went along with them for many years on the force of his grandfather's arguments and reputation. Yet Edwards later concluded that the practices were unbiblical. This laid him "under an inevitable necessity publicly to declare and maintain" his new position.[35] This stand took courage, for, as he wrote to a friend, "this will be very likely to overthrow me, not only with regard to my usefulness in the work of the ministry here, but everywhere."[36] His congregation, in fact, did turn on him and dismissed him. The point for us, however, is that Edwards's preaching carried power because he boldly presented God's truth even when it contradicted tradition.

Edwards helps us see the truth about preaching. In God's hands, sermons can be used to transform souls. When a preacher speaks from his core beliefs, when he stakes his soul and all he has on the truth of his message, and when what he says is indeed properly aligned with the truth of Scripture, there is inherent power in the words.

---

[34] Edwards, "An Humble Inquiry," 12:168.
[35] Edwards, 12:170.
[36] Jonathan Edwards, "Letter to the Reverend Thomas Foxcroft," in *WJE*, 16:283–84.

Chapter 3

Edwards on Original Sin and Depravity

Paul V. Harrison

INTRODUCTION

One of Jonathan Edwards's most important works was *Original Sin.*[1] Published just after Edwards died, it is a response to John Taylor (1694–1761). A heterodox Nonconformist minister from Norwich, England, Taylor had written *The Scripture-Doctrine of Original Sin Proposed to Free and Candid Examination* in 1740.[2] In this essay Taylor took traditional orthodoxy to task, and Edwards felt the responsibility to set the record straight.

Taylor handled the subject in such a manner that nearly all the basic teachings of Calvinism came into play. Edwards believed that the principles Taylor espoused struck at the very roots of biblical Christianity:

---

[1] The full title is *The great Christian doctrine of original sin defended; evidences of it's [sic] truth produced, and arguments to the contrary answered. Containing, in particular, a reply to the objections and arguings of Dr. John Taylor, in his book, intitled, "The Scripture-doctrine of original sin proposed to free and candid examination," &c.*

[2] Taylor's book went through several editions and elicited responses from David Jennings (1691–1762), Isaac Watts (1674–1748), and John Wesley (1703–91).

> I stand ready to confess to the forementioned modern divines,
> if they can maintain their peculiar notion of *freedom*, consist-
> ing in the *self-determining power of the will*, as necessary to
> *moral agency*, and can thoroughly establish it in opposition to
> the arguments lying against it, then they have an impregnable
> castle, to which they may repair, and remain invincible, in all
> the controversies they have with the reformed divines, con-
> cerning *original sin*, the *sovereignty* of grace, *election, redemp-
> tion, conversion*, the *efficacious operation* of the Holy Spirit,
> the nature of saving *faith, perseverance* of the saints, and other
> principles of the like kind.[3]

Specifically, the issue of original sin was not one of peripheral significance. "I
look on the doctrine as of *great importance*," Edwards wrote.[4]

A SUMMARY OF EDWARDS'S THOUGHT

Evidence of Original Sin

Edwards divided his work into four parts. First, he examined the evidence for
original sin both from "observation and experience" and from the perspective
of Scripture. He included some of the main assertions of Taylor and his followers. Part two analyzed in detail critical Scripture texts involved in the controversy. Among others, Edwards considered Genesis 1–3; John 3 (especially
verse 6); Rom 3:9–24; Rom 5:6–21; and Eph 2:3. He especially scrutinized the
Romans passages because they are critical to the subject and because Taylor
had written an exposition of that book.[5] Edwards's next section, the briefest of
the four, deals with how Scripture presents the redemption of Christ relative to

---

[3] Jonathan Edwards, *Original Sin*, in *The Works of Jonathan Edwards*, vol. 3, ed. Clyde A.
Holbrook (New Haven: Yale University Press, 1970), 376.

[4] Edwards, *Original Sin*, in *WJE*, 3:103.

[5] John Taylor, *A Paraphrase with Notes on the Epistle to the Romans. To Which Is Prefix'd, a
Key to the Apostolic Writings, or an Essay to Explain the Gospel Scheme, and the Principal Words
and Phrases the Apostles Have Used in Describing It* (Dublin: Printed by R. Reilly, for John
Smith at the Philosophers Heads on the Blind-Quay, 1746).

humanity's condition and needs. Finally, he handled the various objections to the doctrine of original sin.

For Edwards, empirical evidence was not lacking to demonstrate humanity's universal infection with sin:

> If a particular tree, or a great number of trees standing together, have blasted fruit on their branches at a particular season, yea, if the fruit be very much blasted, and entirely spoiled, it is evident that something was the occasion of such an effect at that time; but this alone don't prove the nature of the tree to be bad. But if it be observed, that those trees, and all other trees of the kind, wherever planted, and in all soils, countries, climates, and seasons, and however cultivated and managed, still bear ill fruit, from year to year, and in all ages, it is a good evidence of the evil nature of the tree: and if the fruit, at all these times, and in all these cases, be very bad, it proves the nature of the tree to be very bad.[6]

Becoming more personal in his analysis of humanity's sin problem, he lamented the condition of the "Christian" community. The Reformation had burnished the corroded church, "but how is the gold soon become dim! . . . To what a prodigious height has a deluge of infidelity, profaneness, luxury, debauchery, and wickedness of every kind, arisen! The poor savage Americans are mere babes (if I may so speak) as to proficiency in wickedness, in comparison of multitudes in that the Christian world throngs with."[7]

Original Sin Results in Human Depravity

Scripture likewise underscores man's depraved nature, Edwards emphasized. He cited Prov 20:6, "Most men will proclaim every man his own goodness: but a faithful man who can find?"(KJV), Matt 7:13–14, "Enter ye in at the strait gate: for wide is the gate and broad is the way that leadeth to destruction. . . .(KJV),

---

[6] Edwards, *Original Sin*, 3:191.
[7] Edwards, 3:183.

and other passages, concluding that "these things clearly determine the point, concerning the tendency of man's nature to wickedness."[8]

Edwards characterized Arminianism as "denying an original, innate, total corruption and depravity of heart."[9] In its place he believed that the principles he laid out in his *Freedom of the Will* "obviate some of the chief objections of Arminians against the Calvinistic doctrine of the *total depravity and corruption of man's nature*, whereby his heart is wholly under the power of sin, and he is utterly unable, without the interposition of sovereign grace, savingly to love God, believe in Christ, or do anything that is truly good and acceptable in God's sight."[10]

Michael McClymond and Gerald McDermott emphasize Edwards's understanding of depravity as "invincible necessity."[11] His doctrine of this "inherent" human depravity, like that of the Reformed Confessions, was that it was "a propensity that is *invincible* or a tendency which really amounts to a fixed, constant, unfailing *necessity*."[12] Depravity is not total in the sense that humanity is as sinful as it could be, since God, through his common grace or "merciful influences," has put "restraints" on sin.[13] Instead, depravity is so extensive and complete in humanity that the human intellect and affections are utterly dead in sin and blinded by sin. Thus even sinners' good deeds are idolatrous. God has implanted the knowledge of himself in every human being. Yet because of their total depravity, no one can please God or desire God apart from the light of grace. They have a "dreadful stupidity of mind, occasioning a sottish insensibility" of the truth God has given them.[14]

Thus Edwards, in keeping with traditional Calvinism, posits that total depravity results in a total spiritual inability to do anything spiritually good or to respond to the preaching of the gospel without efficacious divine grace. Indeed, humanity is in a "state of total corruption and depravity" which can

---

[8]   Edwards, 3:167.

[9]   Jonathan Edwards, *Freedom of the Will*, vol. 1, *WJE*, ed. Paul Ramsey (New Haven: Yale University Press, 1957), 373.

[10]   Edwards, 1:432.

[11]   Edwards, *Original Sin*, 3:124; on the themes in this paragraph, see Michael McClymond and Gerald McDermott, *The Theology of Jonathan Edwards* (New York: Oxford University Press, 2012), 348.

[12]   Edwards, 3:123, 125.

[13]   Edwards, 3:136–37.

[14]   Edwards, 3:157.

be counteracted only by the "opening of the eyes of the blind" that comes in conversion.[15]

Cause and Effect

A consistent aspect of Edwards's thinking is that every effect has a cause, and that this is true in both the physical world and the spiritual world: "The natural dictate of reason shews, that where there is an effect, there is a cause, and a cause sufficient for the effect; because, if it were not sufficient, it would not be effectual: and that therefore, where there is a stated prevalence of the effect, there is a stated prevalence in the cause: a steady effect argues a steady cause."[16]

Such logic, in Edwards's thought, applies to everything, including the individual acts of the human will. The freedom to choose this or that, as asserted by Arminians, is simply inconsistent. He stated, "On the whole, it is clearly manifest, that every effect has a necessary connection with its cause, or with that which is the true ground and reason of its existence. And therefore if there be no event without a cause, as was proved before, then no event whatsoever is contingent in the manner that Arminians suppose the free acts of the will to be contingent."[17]

When Edwards applied this cause-and-effect determinism to the universal propensity to sin, he sought a root cause sufficient for the effect. He found this cause in the person of Adam, citing Rom 5:12: "By one man sin entered into the world, and death by sin; and so death passed upon all men, for that all have sinned" (KJV).

Like many before him, Edwards understood that Adam's plunge into sin submerged his offspring along with him. He wrote, "God dealing with Adam as the head of his posterity, . . . and treating them as one, he deals with his posterity as having *all sinned in him*." Thus, just as God removed his "vital gracious influence" and "spiritual communion" from Adam, "the common head," he also "withholds the same from all the members, as they come into existence; whereby they come into the world mere flesh, and entirely under the government of natural and inferior principles; and so become wholly corrupt,

---

[15] Jonathan Edwards, "A Treatise on Grace," in *Writings on the Trinity, Grace, and Faith, WJE*, vol. 21, ed. Sang Hyun Lee (New Haven: Yale University Press, 2003), 161.

[16] Edwards, *Original Sin*, 3:121.

[17] Edwards, *Freedom of the Will*, 1:216.

as Adam did."[18] Note that in Edwards's thought, sin is passed along not simply because all humanity naturally sprang from their first parent but because Adam was the appointed "head" or representative of the race.

The Imputation of Guilt

Where some would concede humanity's inherited corruption but seek to avoid the imputation of guilt, Edwards understood the one to be inseparable from the other: "The guilt a man has upon his soul at his first existence, is one and simple: viz. the guilt of the original apostasy, the guilt of the sin by which the species first rebelled against God."[19] To Edwards, the apostle Paul's teaching in Rom 5:12 could not be more clear: "The doctrine of original sin is not only here taught, but most plainly, explicitly, and abundantly taught." The conclusion to be drawn is that "in the eye of the Judge of the world, in Adam's first sin, *all* sinned."[20]

This brings us to the heart of the problem and the reason why the doctrine of original sin is often rejected: how can it be right and just that one man sins and another thereby becomes guilty? In this case, of course, the *entire race* becomes guilty before God on the basis of Adam's wicked choice. To make sure we feel the depth of the difficulty, we should note that the guilt of original sin, according to Edwards, immediately adheres to Adam's offspring. This means that while infants may seem sweet and innocent, we should not be deceived by such appearances: "A young viper has a malignant nature, though incapable of doing a malignant action, and at present appearing a harmless creature."[21]

Imputation and Infant Damnation

Calvinists have often struggled with the principle of imputed sin and guilt, especially when it comes to infants. Some cave in under the moral and intellectual pressure of condemning babies to hellfire and abandon their principles, thus making an exemption for infants from the damning effects of Adam's sin.

---

[18] Edwards, *Original Sin*, 3:383.

[19] Edwards, 3:390.

[20] Edwards, 3:346.

[21] Edwards, 3:423. This is reminiscent of Augustine's thought on infants: "In the branch they have not yet committed any evil, but they are ruined in their root." In *Nicene and Post-Nicene Fathers*, First Series, ed. Philip Schaff, 14 vols (Peabody, MA: Hendrickson, 1994), 6.455.

Charles Hodge, for example, while holding a hard line on unconditional election, yet concluded that "all who die in infancy are saved."[22]

Others maintain that Adam's sin infects and ultimately results in the damnation of some infants. Yet, hiding behind God's sovereignty and the secrets
of his will, they make no effort to explain how this could be just. Calvin himself took this approach. Commenting on why God destroyed all of Sodom,
including infants, he raised the question often asked from that text: "What had
infants done, to deserve to be swallowed up in the same destruction with their
parents?" Calvin replied that the question had an "easy" answer, "namely, that
the human race is in the hand of God, so that he may devote whom he will to
destruction." Likewise, God may show mercy to whom he will: "Again, whatever we are not able to comprehend by the limited measure of our understanding, ought to be submitted to his secret judgment."[23]

When faced with the harsh implications of original sin, Edwards was not
content to hide behind mystery. He concluded that whatever God does is right,
and since infants clearly were born with a corrupt and guilty nature, it must be
just and holy in those cases where God condemns them. This hard conclusion
was not to be shunned but embraced as coming from the Lord, and as the ultimate Christian rationalist, Edwards set about to explain how God could be just
to establish such circumstances. In doing so, Edwards plowed new theological
ground.

The Justice of Imputation

So again, how can it be just for Adam to sin and his progeny to be held accountable? John Taylor had presented his argument in these words:

> But that any Man, without my Knowledge or Consent, should
> so represent me, that when he is guilty I am to be reputed
> guilty, and when he transgresses I shall be accountable and
> punishable for his Transgression, and thereby subjected to the
> Wrath and Curse of God; nay further, that his Wickedness
> shall give me a *sinful Nature*, and all this before I am born, and

---

[22] Charles Hodge, *Systematic Theology*, 3 vols. (1982; repr., Grand Rapids: Eerdmans), 1:26.
[23] John Calvin, *Commentaries on the First Book of Moses Called Genesis*, vol. 1 of Calvin's
Commentaries (1998; repr., Grand Rapids: Baker), 1 (part 1), 513.

consequently while I am in no capacity of knowing, helping
or hindering what he doth; surely any one, who *dares* use his
Understanding, must clearly see this is unreasonable, and altogether inconsistent with the Truth, and Goodness of God.[24]

At one level, Edwards simply argued that, whether one likes it or not, the
connection between Adam and his posterity exists. God "deals with them
together, or as one." If he "orders the consequences of Adam's sin, with regard
to his posterity's welfare, even in those things which are most important, and
which do in the highest degree concern their eternal interest, to be the same,
with the consequences to Adam himself, then he treats Adam and his posterity as in that affair one." No matter how difficult this seems, "fact obliges us to
get over the difficulty." We do this "either by finding out some solution, or by
shutting our mouths, and acknowledging the weakness and scantiness of our
understandings," just as we do in many other instances where "undeniable"
facts of divine creation and providence are "attended with events and circumstances, the manner and reason of which are difficult to our understandings."[25]

When confronting the options of shutting his mouth or "finding out some
solution," the master theologian not surprisingly chose the latter. His answer
was that Adam's offspring are not held responsible for *his* sin. His sin, in reality,
was *their* sin. An identity existed between Adam and humanity at large so that
each person in fact sinned when Adam sinned. The language Edwards used to
stress this identity was most often that of a tree and its branches. He explained
that, in each step of his dealings with Adam "in relation to the covenant or
constitution established with him," God viewed Adam's "posterity as being one
with him." Even though he "dealt more immediately with Adam, it yet was as
the head of the whole body, and the root of the whole tree; and in his proceedings with him, he dealt with all the branches, as if they had been then existing
in their root."[26]

He explained further:

---

[24] John Taylor, *The Scripture-Doctrine of Original Sin Proposed to Free and Candid Examination*, 3rd ed. (London: J. Waugh, 1750), 109.

[25] Edwards, *Original Sin*, 3:395.

[26] Edwards, 3:389.

Some things, being most simply considered, are entirely distinct, and very diverse; which yet are so united by the established law of the Creator, in some respects and with regard to some purposes and effects, that by virtue of that establishment it is with them as if they were one. Thus a tree, grown great, and an hundred years old, is one plant with the little sprout, that first came out of the ground, from whence it grew, and has been continued in constant succession; though it's now so exceeding diverse, many thousand times bigger, and of a very different form, and perhaps not one atom the very same: yet God, according to an established law of nature, has in a constant succession communicated to it many of the same qualities, and most important properties, as if it were one. It has been his pleasure, to constitute an union in these respects, and for these purposes, naturally leading us to look upon all as one. So the body of man at forty years of age, is one with the infant body which first came into the world, from whence it grew; though now constituted of different substance, and the greater part of the substance probably changed scores (if not hundreds) of times; and though it be now in so many respects exceeding diverse, yet God, according to the course of nature, which he has been pleased to establish, has caused, that in a certain method it should communicate with that infantile body, in the same life, the same senses, the same features, and many the same qualities, and in union with the same soul; and so, with regard to these purposes, 'tis dealt with by him as one body.[27]

Imputation and Personal Identity

Edwards's thinking on this point is hard to categorize. At points he seems to embrace a federal headship view of the connection between Adam and the human race. He was our "head." Still, Edwards stresses the union between Adam and his seed. Calvinists regularly stress such a union, but Edwards was not following the usual lines of argument. He meant something more than

---

[27] Edwards, 3:397–98.

what is commonly meant by Reformed theologians. In explaining himself, Edwards launched into what Clyde Holbrook called "one of the most creative pieces of reasoning to be found in the treatise"[28] and what John Gerstner called a "bizarre philosophical doctrine of identity."[29]

Edwards examined what it is that constitutes personal identity. At times siding with John Locke and thinking it to be individual consciousness, his more mature reflection, represented in his treatise *Original Sin*, based identity simply in the will of God. I will summarize his thought and then present his own words on the subject.

The ongoing personal identity of an individual is the result of God's sustaining will. When God constitutes a person, that individual continues throughout life to be that same person because God sustains him or her in that identity. No created thing continues to exist because of its own nature, as though it contained within itself the inherent power to maintain existence. In fact, if God were to cease willing the existence of anything, at that moment it would dissolve into nothingness. All things continue to exist only because God wills for them to do so. This will for something or someone to continue to exist is different from God's original (creative) will for something to come into existence only in that the one precedes the other. The willing and power of God are the same. In other words, God's sustaining work regarding creation is really no different than his original creative work. Therefore, when an individual is the same person at one moment that he was the moment before, it is only because God wills it. Identity ultimately exists because God wills it.

In the case of Adam's posterity, our identity, according to the will of God, was one with Adam. We were one moral whole, so that when Adam sinned, we sinned. We were one with him. Here are the words of Edwards:

> And with respect to the identity of created substance itself, in the different moments of its duration, I think, we shall greatly mistake, if we imagine it to be like that absolute independent identity of the first being, whereby "he is the same yesterday, today, and forever." Nay, on the contrary, it may be

---

[28] Clyde A. Holbrook, in Edwards, 3:55.

[29] John H. Gerstner, *The Rational Biblical Theology of Jonathan Edwards*, 3 vols. (Powhatan, VA: Berea, 1992), 2.333. McClymond and McDermott use the term "original metaphysic" to refer to Edwards's schema. See *Theology of Jonathan Edwards*, 351.

demonstrated, that even this oneness of created substance, existing at different times, is a merely *dependent* identity; dependent on the pleasure and sovereign constitution of him who worketh all in all. This will follow from what is generally allowed, and is certainly true, that God not only created all things, and gave them being at first, but continually preserves them, and upholds them in being.[30]

Edwards concluded, "Therefore the existence of created substances, in each successive moment, must be the effect of the *immediate* agency, will, and power of God."[31] This is "altogether equivalent to an *immediate production out of nothing*, at each moment."[32]

Edwards then applied this logic to the case of Adam and his offspring, insisting that no one can give a "solid reason" why God, "who constitutes all other created union or oneness, according to his pleasure, and for what purposes, communications, and effects he pleases," could not "establish a constitution whereby the natural posterity of Adam, proceeding from him, much as the buds and branches from the stock or root of a tree, should be treated as one with him, for the derivation, either of righteousness and communion in rewards, or of the loss of righteousness and consequent corruption and guilt."[33]

In a footnote Edwards argued that God justly could have so tied the mass of humanity together into a "moral whole" had they all existed in various parts of the earth when Adam lived and was tested. From this he concluded that what God could have done in respect to *place*, he did in respect to *time*.[34]

With this foundation, Edwards made final application of his insights:

> Let us see how the consequence of these things is to my present purpose. If the existence of created substance, in each successive moment, be wholly the effect of God's immediate power, in that moment, without any dependence on prior existence, as much as the first creation out of nothing, then what exists

[30] Edwards, *Original Sin*, in 3:399–400.
[31] Edwards, 3:401.
[32] Edwards, 3:402.
[33] Edwards, 3:405.
[34] Edwards, 3:405–6.

at this moment, by this power, is a *new effect;* and simply and absolutely considered, not the same with any past existence, though it be like it, and follows it according to a certain established method. And there is no identity or oneness in the case, but what depends on the *arbitrary* constitution of the Creator; who by his wise sovereign establishment so unites these successive new effects, that he *treats them as one,* by communicating to them like properties, relations, and circumstances; and so, leads us to regard and treat them as one. When I call this an arbitrary constitution, I mean, that it is a constitution which depends on nothing but the divine will; which *divine will* depends on nothing but the *divine* wisdom. In this sense, the whole course of nature, with all that belongs to it, all its laws and methods, constancy and regularity, continuance and proceeding, is an *arbitrary* constitution. In this sense, the continuance of the very being of the world and all its parts, as well as the manner of continued being, depends entirely on an arbitrary constitution. . . . All is constantly proceeding from God, as light from the sun. "In him we live, and move, and have our being."[35]

Holbrook's analysis of Edwards's thought on this subject is intriguing. He states, "Edwards, of course, was not arguing for a universal identity between Adam and posterity; what he had established by his metaphysical excursion was the basic principle that in certain respects, degrees, and for various purposes, God made identical those things which in other respects were not one." This statement, however, is hard to understand, for on one hand he says that Edwards was not suggesting "a universal identity" but on the other that he established God's ability to make "identical" things otherwise distinct.[36]

Edwards's conclusions, of course, completely transform how one understands original sin. In fact, with this understanding of identity between Adam and the race, is it even proper to say that Adam's sin was imputed to humanity? Gerstner answered in the negative: "It is not a doctrine of imputation—mediate

<hr>

[35] Edwards, 3:402–4.
[36] Edwards, 3:57–58.

or immediate."[37] Yet Edwards repeatedly affirmed the imputation of Adam's sin to the race.

Examining the various facets of Edwards's thought, we should conclude that he did in fact adhere to the imputation of Adam's sin to the race. We might note, for example, his repeated assertions that God "treated" Adam and his posterity as one. It seems that while he maintained the fascinating idea that God could have actually *made* them one, he concluded that God only *treated* them as such.

With that said, Edwards's words surely point to an intriguing connection between Adam and his offspring. For example, the New England theologian did, in fact, understand humanity actually to play a role in Adam's fall. He stated that the "first existing of a corrupt disposition in their hearts" should not be seen as "sin belonging to them, distinct from their participation of Adam's first sin." Rather it is "as it were the *extended pollution* of that sin, through the whole tree, by virtue of the constituted union of the branches with the root; or the inherence of the sin of that head of the species in the members, in the consent and concurrence of the hearts of the members with the head in that first act."[38] This assertion of "consent and concurrence" takes the edge off the doctrine of the imputation of Adam's sin, for with such an understanding, our intuitive sense of justice is satisfied: we inherit Adam's sin and guilt because, to at least some extent, we ourselves willed to sin in the Garden. Again, this stands on the brink of not being imputation at all.

Before leaving this fascinating subject, we may note as an aside what Edwards said about Christ's relation to Adam and his identification with the race. Jesus's human nature is usually understood to be free from sin on the basis of the virgin birth. But how does Edwards's view of the race's identification with Adam fit? The answer is that in the will of God, he did not ordain that Jesus be included in humanity's identification with Adam.[39]

Human Inability to Do Good

A major component of Edwards's view of fallen humanity is the inability of humans to do good. Laden with a wicked nature and a taste for evil, humanity

---

[37] Gerstner, *Rational Biblical Theology*, 2:328.
[38] Edwards, *Original Sin*, 3:391.
[39] Gerstner, *Rational Biblical Theology*, 2.327.

inevitably embraces sin and is unable to do otherwise. Such a conclusion was common theological fare for Calvinists, but nothing seems to have rattled the theological cage of Taylor and his followers as much as this idea. Responsibility, the English minister insisted again and again, extends only as far as ability: "If I have no Power, or, which is all one, no sufficient Power to do my Duty, then it is evident, with all equitable and honest Judges, that I have no Duty to do. For no Man can be obliged to do, nor can any reasonable Being expect he should do what he has not sufficient Power to do."[40]

All theologians feel the barb of this argument. If this principle holds sway, however, Calvinistic thought *in toto* falls to the ground.[41] Edwards, therefore, gave it special attention.

Recognizing some validity to the argument, the Northampton pastor, following ideas developed before his time, asserted that the principle holds only in certain cases. Abilities and inabilities, he said, were of two kinds, natural and moral. Each is just as real as the other, the difference being in the kind of abilities or inabilities they describe, the one dealing with spiritual matters and the other physical. He explained:

> Some seem to disdain the distinction that we make between *natural* and *moral* necessity, as though it were altogether impertinent in this controversy: "That which is necessary (say they) is necessary; it is that which must be, and can't be prevented. And that which is impossible, is impossible, and can't be done: and therefore none can be to blame for not doing it." And such comparisons are made use of as the commanding of a man to walk who has lost his legs, and condemning and punishing him for not obeying; inviting and calling upon a man, who is shut up in a strong prison, to come forth, etc. But in these things Arminians are very unreasonable. Let common sense determine whether there be not a great difference between those two cases; the one, that of a man who has

[40] Taylor, *Scripture-Doctrine of Original Sin*, 63.

[41] In my opinion, this principle is the foundational theological/philosophical issue between Calvinism and Arminianism (as well as liberalism). Though the proposition is often not explicitly referenced, from a theological point of view, its acceptance or rejection determines one's understanding of original sin, depravity, sin, election, grace, and atonement.

offended his prince, and is cast into prison; and after he has lain there a while, the king comes to him, calls him to come forth to him; and tells him that if he will do so, and will fall down before him, and humbly beg his pardon, he shall be forgiven, and set at liberty, and also be greatly enriched, and advanced to honor: the prisoner heartily repents of the folly and wickedness of his offence against his prince, is thoroughly disposed to abase himself, and accept of the king's offer; but is confined by strong walls, with gates of brass, and bars of iron. The other case is, that of a man who is of a very unreasonable spirit, of a haughty, ungrateful, willful disposition, and moreover, has been brought up in traitorous principles, and has his heart possessed with an extreme and inveterate enmity to his lawful sovereign; and for his rebellion is cast into prison, and lies long there, loaded with heavy chains, and in miserable circumstances. At length the compassionate prince comes to the prison, orders his chains to be knocked off, and his prison doors to be set wide open; calls to him, and tells him, if he will come forth to him, and fall down before him, acknowledge that he has treated him unworthily, and ask his forgiveness; he shall be forgiven, set at liberty, and set in a place of great dignity and profit in his court. But he is so stout and stomachful, and full of haughty malignity, that he can't be willing to accept the offer: his rooted strong pride and malice have perfect power over him, and as it were bind him, by binding his heart: the opposition of his heart has the mastery over him, having an influence on his mind far superior to the king's grace and condescension, and to all his kind offers and promises. Now, is it agreeable to common sense, to assert and stand to it, that there is no difference between these two cases, as to any worthiness of blame in the prisoners, because, forsooth, there is a necessity in both, and the required act in each case is impossible? 'Tis true, a man's evil dispositions may be as strong and immovable as the bars of a castle. But who can't see, that when a man, in the latter case, is said to be "unable" to obey the command, the expression is used improperly, and

not in the sense it has originally and in common speech? And
that it may properly be said to be in the rebel's power to come
out of prison, seeing he can easily do it if he pleases; though by
reason of his vile temper of heart which is fixed and rooted, 'tis
impossible that it should please him?[42]

Edwards illustrated the matter further by comparing a natural inability to
fly like a bird with a moral inability of a loving son to murder his father.[43] Both
are absolute but spring from different realms. He concluded that God cannot
justly hold people responsible to do what they lack the natural ability to do, but
that he can be just in condemning people for not doing what only their moral
inability keeps them from doing.

A critical aspect of Edwards's analysis is his agreement with his Arminian
opponents that the principle of blaming individuals only as far as their abilities
extend, were it to be proven, would also apply conversely in the realm of praise.
If a person is necessarily virtuous with no choice but to be holy, then he is not
to be credited and praised for his good behavior. What is true for blame is also
true for praise. If necessity empties bad choices of blame, then it empties good
ones of praise.

This principle, if it be true, does seem to cut both ways, but this is where
Edwards especially showed the principle to be flawed. Is not Jesus necessarily
good and holy? he asked. Does not his nature guarantee his acting rightly? Yet
who would deny that he is to be praised for his goodness?[44] To my knowledge,
this argument awaits an adequate response from the Arminian side.

At root, Edwards argued that blame or praise is rightly posited in reference
to the nature or essence of a thing, not to how it comes to be in that condition.
If a being is evil, then he is blameworthy; if good, then praiseworthy.[45]

---

[42] Edwards, *Freedom of the Will*, 1:362–63.
[43] Edwards, 1:160.
[44] Edwards, 1:281. "His holy behavior was necessary . . . [and] his holy behavior was properly
of the nature of virtue, and was worthy of praise" (281).
[45] Edwards, 1:337.

AN ARMINIAN RESPONSE TO EDWARDS

Total Depravity and Inability

Arminians can agree with much of Edwards's thought. Traditional Arminianism agrees that humanity is totally depraved and thus unable to take one step toward God without the intervention of divine grace. Arminius stressed that all human "powers," whether of the intellect, the will, or the affections, are characterized by "utter weakness . . . to perform that which is truly good, and to omit the perpetration of that which is evil." The human intellect is "destitute" of the knowledge of God because of its "darkness." Thus it is, Arminius stated, "incapable of those things which belong to the Spirit of God."[46] William den Boer summarizes Arminius's view when he says that the fall, for Arminius, results in spiritual "ignorance and blindness, and the intellect judges the Gospel to be foolishness. The fallen intellect perverts the natural Revelation. The will is not only injured, but trapped, ruined and useless. It has lost its freedom and without the assistance of grace it is powerless."[47]

Yet this robust understanding of human depravity was not limited to Arminius. Indeed, the Remonstrants, Arminius's successors in the Netherlands, confessed in the Five Articles of the Remonstrance that "man has not saving grace of himself, nor of the energy of his free will, inasmuch as he, in the state of apostasy and sin, can of and by himself neither think, will, nor do anything that is truly good."[48]

In full agreement with Edwards, Robert Picirilli summarizes the modern Reformed Arminian view when he states:

> As Jer 17:9 affirms, "The heart is deceitful above all things, and desperately wicked." For these last two words some suggest incurably sick, an appropriate rendering.

---

[46] Jacobus Arminius, *The Works of James Arminius*, trans. James Nichols and William Nichols, 3 vols. (Nashville: Randall House, 2007), 2:192–93, Public Disputation 11, "On the Free Will of Man and Its Powers." All references to Arminius's *Works* in this chapter refer to the London edition translated by James Nichols and William Nichols unless otherwise indicated.

[47] William den Boer, *God's Twofold Love: The Theology of Jacob Arminius (1559–1609)* (Göttingen: Vandenhoeck and Ruprecht, 2010), 199.

[48] Five Articles of Remonstrance, in Philip Schaff, *The Creeds of Christendom* (New York: Harper and Brothers, 1877), 1:518.

This depravity is likewise total. Most interpreters of Scripture and the human condition will acknowledge that this does not mean that every individual is as evil as he is capable of becoming. It does mean, however, that every part of human nature is evilly affected by the fall, whether the mind, the desires, or the will. Fallen men are not able to understand spiritual things, are controlled by wicked passions, and make their choices under inclinations and influences that are contrary to the ways of God. Left to themselves, no persons will ever turn to God. . . .

So human beings continue to reflect the image of God, regardless how fallen, and are capable of great good as viewed from our flawed perspective. At the same time, they are estranged from their Creator. They do not know him and do not want to know him. They have declared their independence from him and love their sins. In their separation from God they cannot understand and do not find appealing the vision that God has for them. They are blind and deaf and dead, and (in full agreement with Luther and Calvin) in that condition they cannot by any act of their wills, by any volition or decision, turn themselves toward God.[49]

Inherited Sin and Guilt

Arminians heartily concur with Edwards that humanity indeed suffers from inherited sin, and this sin can be traced to Adam. However much one may sense an unfairness in this arrangement, two arguments compel such a conclusion. First, sin and death reign universally with no exceptions. Second, Scripture, especially Romans 5, speaks with such clarity as to settle the matter for believers.

Arminius certainly concurred with Reformed theologians on this point. On February 8, 1606, with controversy swirling about him, he delivered an oration entitled "On Reconciling Religious Dissentions among Christians." In that

---

[49] Robert Picirilli, *Free Will Revisited: A Respectful Response to Luther, Calvin, and Edwards* (Eugene, OR: Wipf and Stock, 2017), 94–95.

speech he stated, "Our very origin is tainted with the infection of the primitive offence of *the Old Adam*."[50]

Between 1603 and 1609, Arminius discussed various subjects in the divinity classes he taught at the University of Leiden. These discussions were put together into a document entitled *Disputations on Some of the Principal Subjects of the Christian Religion*. Disputation Eight contained the statement: "The *inwardly working* cause [of sin] is the original propensity of our nature towards that which is contrary to the divine law, which propensity we have contracted from our first parents, through carnal generation."[51]

Arminius would also agree with Edwards in assessing many of the devastating consequences attending the fall. He wrote that fallen humanity is in "a state of the deepest infelicity." He continued, "In this state, the free will of man towards the true good is not only wounded, maimed, infirm, bent, and weakened; but it is also imprisoned, destroyed, and lost. And its powers are not only debilitated and useless unless they be assisted by grace, but it has no powers whatever except such as are excited by Divine grace."[52]

---

[50] Arminius, *Works*, 1:454, Oration V, "On Reconciling Religious Dissensions among Christians."

[51] Arminius, *Works*, 2:162, Public Disputation 8, "On Actual Sins."

[52] Arminius, *Works*, 1.526, Public Disputation 11, "On the Free Will of Man and Its Powers." On the subject of inherited guilt, however, Arminius's position appears less clear. On the one hand, he said that "on account of" Adam's sin, "we have all been constituted sinners, and rendered (*rei*) obnoxious or liable to death and condemnation" (2:717, "Certain Articles to be Diligently Examined and Weighed"), and he states in his "Conference with Junius" that God imputed "the guilt of the first sin to all Adam's posterity, no less than to Adam himself and Eve, because they also had sinned in Adam" (3:224, "Friendly Conference with Junius"). Also, answering the question whether the "guilt of original sin" is "taken away from all and every one by the benefits of Christ?" Arminius replied that "deliverance from this guilt" is one of Christ's benefits. Therefore, "believers only are delivered from it" (2:65, "Nine Questions"). On the other hand, when discussing the spiritual condition of infants, on first glance he cited the opinions of Adrianus Borrius (1565–1630): "When Adam sinned in his own person and with his free will, God pardoned that transgression. There is no reason then why it was the will of God to impute this sin to infants, who are said to have sinned in Adam, before they had any personal existence, and therefore, before they could possibly sin at their own will and pleasure" (2:11–12, "Apology against Thirty-One Theological Articles"). However, it is difficult to know how to take this passage, since it comes from an answer to a series of false accusations from Arminius's and Borrius's detractors. They had falsely accused Borrius of saying, "Original Sin will condemn no man. In every nation, all infants who die without (having committed) actual sins, are saved," which Arminius stated Borrius denied ever having publicly said (2:10). A number of Arminius scholars see Arminius as not affirming Borrius's opinions here but simply quoting Borrius and stating that he is not guilty of heresy. John Mark Hicks, for example, says that Arminius "stops short of endorsing" Borrius's "premises and conclusions. . . . Arminius

While Arminius accepted much of the traditional understanding of how humanity acquires a sinful nature, I cannot find where he offers a rationale for this, other than that it was a part of the original covenant between God and Adam. For example, he asserted:

> The whole of this sin, however, is not peculiar to our first parents, but is common to the entire race and to all their posterity, who, at the time when this sin was committed, were in their loins, and who have since descended from them by the natural mode of propagation, according to the primitive benediction. For in Adam "all have sinned" (Rom. v, 12.). Wherefore, whatever punishment was brought down upon our first parents, has likewise pervaded and yet pursues all their posterity. So that all men "are by nature the children of wrath," (Ephes. ii, 3,) obnoxious to condemnation, and to temporal as well as to eternal death; they are also devoid of that original righteousness and holiness. (Rom. v, 12, 18, 19.) With these evils they would remain oppressed forever, unless they were liberated by Christ Jesus; to whom be glory forever.[53]

---

notes Junius' position to demonstrate that Borrius' opinion remains within the Reformed tradition. . . . At no point does Arminius endorse either position. Rather, he always affirms that infants bear the guilt of Adam's sin" (John Mark Hicks, "The Theology of Grace in the Thought of Jacob Arminius and Philip van Limborch: A Study in the Development of Seventeenth Century Dutch Arminianism, PhD diss., Westminster Theological Seminary, 1985, 24). See also Carl O. Bangs, *Arminius: A Study in the Dutch Reformation* (Nashville: Abingdon, 1971), 338–40; J. Matthew Pinson, *Arminian and Baptist: Explorations in a Theological Tradition* (Nashville: Randall House, 2015), 19; Pinson, *40 Questions about Arminianism* (Grand Rapids: Kregel Academic, 2022), 141. I myself am uncertain as to whether guilt is imputed by God to the race because of Adam's sin. It is noteworthy that the Free Will Baptist *Treatise* avoids committing its subscribers to the doctrine of inherited guilt, stating rather that Adam's posterity "inherit a fallen nature of such tendencies that all who come to years of accountability, sin and become guilty before God." *A Treatise of the Faith and Practices of Free Will Baptists* (Antioch, TN: National Association of Free Will Baptists, 2016), 45.

[53] Arminius, *Works*, 1:764, "Apology against Thirty-One Theological Articles." We should also note that Arminius believed in a natural headship theory related to Adam, which seems to make God less directly involved in the racial consequences of Adam's sin, at least in a judicial sense. See also F. Leroy Forlines, who like Arminius espouses the natural headship theory. Forlines argues that "sin is imputed to the race because the race by being in Adam was a part of Adam when he sinned, thus identified with him in his sin and the guilt of that sin." Yet Forlines goes on to say that "those who die in infancy will not escape hell because the guilt of Adam was

Fallen Humanity's Spiritual Abilities

Turning to the issue of fallen humanity's spiritual abilities, I conclude that it seems to be the intuitive dictate of human reason that one should not be held responsible to do what one lacks the ability to do. This is true in the physical realm, as Edwards admitted, but it also holds true in the spiritual realm. As stated previously, Edwards claimed that moral inabilities do not excuse moral failure. Where a lame man, suffering from a natural inability, cannot justly be required to walk, a sinful man, suffering from moral inability, can justly be expected to be holy. The distinction between natural and moral abilities, however, seems to fall short of giving Calvinists the relief they desire, for three reasons.[54]

First, Edwards's handling of the subject begs the question.[55] He assumes the absolute nature of moral inability. Were he to maintain this in an imaginary world where God's grace or the devil's influence is absent, this would be another matter. But he assumes such inability in our world, which is permeated both with spiritual powers urging humanity to sin and the gracious hand of God reaching out to sinners to offer them assistance and the ability to do what they could not do in and of themselves. Many a sinner under the gracious influence of God's Spirit has repented of sin. Many a godly person has succumbed to the allure of evil.

Consider Edwards's assertion that a morally upright father is unable to kill his son or that a virtuous woman cannot give away her chastity. He uses such illustrations to prove the existence of such moral inability. Yet to argue that while a father is loving his son he cannot kill him is to assume the answer in the question.

Edwards may assert the moral inability of godly people to commit evil, but one glance at David staring at Bathsheba convinces us otherwise. We may be

---

not imputed to them, but because the atoning work of Christ is applied to them." See Forlines, *Classical Arminianism: A Theology of Salvation* (Nashville: Randall House, 2011), 27, 239.

[54] On this subject see the comments of Perez Fobes (1742–1812), pastor at Raynham, Massachusetts, and vice president and professor at Brown University: "Whether this is, or is not a mere play on the word *can*, by shifting the idea of power from active to passive, I will not decide, but certain it is that, in the opinion of many, this method of removing the difficulty . . . tends more to puzzle and perplex the mind, than to reconcile texts of Scripture." In *Human and Divine agency united, in the salvation of men—considered, in a sermon, preached to the Congregational society in Berkley, A.D. 1795* (Providence: Printed by Bennett Wheeler, 1796), 9.

[55] See Picirilli, *Free Will Revisited*, 118–25.

told that hardened sinners will inevitably persist in evil and are unable to turn from it, but a look at the penitent thief on the cross tells us that people, through God's merciful dealings with them, can indeed do what they otherwise could not do. Yes, human beings left to their own sinful inclinations will sin, but when God's presence and work are considered, no such assumptions can hold.

Second, the distinction between "moral" and "natural" seems to be invalid. Is not the moral inability Edwards supposes based in nature? He himself wrote,

> When I use this distinction of moral and natural necessity, I would not be understood to suppose, that if anything comes to pass by the former kind of necessity, the nature of things is not concerned in it, as well as in the latter. I don't mean to determine, that when a moral habit or motive is so strong, that the act of the will infallibly follows, this is not owing to the nature of things.[56]

In Edwards's scheme of things, our moral ineptitude was built directly into our nature. The very inclination to good was missing from fallen humanity's psyche, and it could not be otherwise. This led Gerstner to quip, "We say, Edward's assertion notwithstanding, that in his thought moral inability is a natural inability."[57]

This distinction is also difficult to maintain scripturally. In Rom 1:19 Paul defends the justness of God's wrath on humanity by showing that "what can be known about God is evident among them, because God has shown it to them." Ignorance of God and his nature apparently would have excused them. Similarly, in Rom 2:15 the apostle links God's judgment on the Gentiles to their having "the work of the law . . . written on their hearts. Their consciences confirm this." Again, ability to discern God's laws seems inherently tied to responsibility. Jesus appears to assert the same principle when he tells the Pharisees, "If you were blind, you would not be guilty of sin" (John 9:41, NIV). Do these passages refer to natural or moral abilities? The two seem to blur.

Interestingly, Reformed theologians have commonly linked ability with responsibility and have done so based on Scripture. For example, John Owen

---

[56] Edwards, *Freedom of the Will*, 1:157–58.
[57] Gerstner, *Rational Biblical Theology*, 2:357.

(1616–1683), in his work on the Holy Spirit, compared humanity's spiritual ability before and after their fall into sin:

> We fell not from our first estate for want of power to obey, but by the neglect of the exercise of that power which we had. God made us upright, but we sought out many inventions. And in the latter way, as it belongs to the covenant of grace, there is, by virtue of that covenant, a supply of spiritual strength given in by the promise unto all them who are taken into it, enabling them to answer the commands for holiness, according to the rule of the acceptance of their obedience, before laid down. No man who is instated in the covenant of grace comes short or fails of the performance of that obedience which is required and accepted in that covenant merely for want of power and spiritual strength; for God therein, according to his divine power, gives unto us "all things that pertain unto life and godliness, through the knowledge of him that hath called us to glory and virtue."[58]

Owen added:

> It is true, this grace or strength is administered unto them by certain ways and means, which if they attend not unto they will come short of it. But this I say, in the careful, diligent, sedulous use of those means appointed, none who belong to the covenant of grace shall ever fail of that power and ability which shall render the commands of the gospel easy and not grievous unto them, and whereby they may so fulfil them as infallibly to be accepted. This the Scripture is plain in, where Christ himself tells us that "his yoke is easy, and his burden light," Matt. xi. 30; and his holy apostle, that "his commandments are not grievous," 1 John v. 3: for if they should exceed all the strength

---

[58] John Owen, *A Discourse Concerning the Holy Spirit*, in *The Works of John Owen*, ed. William H. Goold, 16 vols. (Edinburgh: Banner of Truth Trust, 1965; reprint ed. of Johnstone & Hunter, 1850–1853), 3:617.

which we either have or he is pleased to give unto us, they
would be like the Jewish ceremonies, a yoke which we could
not bear, and a law not only grievous but unprofitable. But, on
the contrary, our apostle expressly affirms (and so may we)
that "he could do all things," that is, in the way and manner,
and unto the end for which they are required in the gospel,
"through Christ that strengthened him."[59]

Third, the distinction between natural ability and moral ability fails to deal with the root issue, which perhaps can best be gotten at by asking the question, "Why is it unjust to hold one responsible for that which he lacks the natural ability to do?" While I cannot find where Edwards answers this question, the following response seems to be the best available: because the inability is absolute, because it is real, because the thing being required, all things considered, cannot be done. If this is the correct answer, then one finds no relief in stating that an inability is of a moral nature, when that inability is understood to be as absolute as a natural inability.

Arminius seemed consistently to have embraced the principle that responsibility extends only as far as ability. In discussing the covenant God made with Adam, he concluded that "God could prescribe obedience to him in all things for the performance of which he possessed suitable powers, or would, by the grace of God, have them in that state."[60]

In discussing how "our divines" can be charged with teaching such that "it follows from their doctrine *that God is the author of sin*," Arminius offered five reasons. The third reason is, "Because they teach, 'that God has either denied to man, or has withdrawn from man, before he sinned, grace necessary and sufficient to avoid sin:' Which is tantamount to this,—as if God had imposed a law on man which was simply impossible to be performed or observed by his very nature."[61] Arminius was explicit on this point in his important and insightful analysis of Romans 9:

---

[59] Owen, *Discourse Concerning the Holy Spirit*, 3:617.

[60] Arminius, *Works*, 2:369, Private Disputation 29, "On the Covenant into Which God Entered with Our First Parents."

[61] Arminius, *Works*, 2:715, "Certain Articles to be Diligently Examined and Weighed." The only "divine" he named is Calvin.

But, in order to a law's being just, it necessarily demands these two conditions,—that it be enacted by him who has the power of commanding;—that it be enacted for him who has the power or rather the ability to perform it . . . that is, who has power of such a kind as may be impeded by no intervening decree from performing, by its own act, what it can. Whence it appears that sin is a voluntary transgression of the law, which the sinner has committed by his own fault, because he could have avoided it:—I am speaking of the act itself. On account of a sin of this class, and with a sinner of this kind, God may rightfully be angry. But if this condition be taken away, God cannot rightfully be angry with a man for sin; nay, nor can the man commit sin. I say this for the sake of those who suppose that God can with any good reason be angry with transgressors of the law, even though they could not have obeyed it by the act itself, on account of the decree intervening: but they are much mistaken. For an action of this sort, which is unavoidable on account of the determination of some decree, does not deserve the name of "sin."[62]

It is important to remember that Arminius, like Edwards, believed that fallen humanity suffers from far-reaching spiritual inability. Arminius referred to unconverted man's "*utter inability to resist sin and to subject himself to the law.*"[63] The Dutchman, however, believed that this inability was transformed by grace. Fallen man was not left to himself and thereby deprived of the ability to hear and respond to God's call. In fact, if we were spiritually unable to believe the gospel, all things considered, we could not be held responsible for our unbelief: "Unless they [i.e., those who continue in unbelief] have the *ability to believe*, and, indeed, the *ability to will to believe*, they can not rightly be punished for their unbelief."[64]

---

[62] Arminius, *Works*, 3:504, "Analysis of the Ninth Chapter of St. Paul's Epistle to the Romans."

[63] Arminius, *Works*, 2:198, Public Disputation 12, "On the Law of God."

[64] Jacobus Arminius, *The Works of James Arminius*, vol. 3, trans. W. R. Bagnall (Auburn, ME: Derby and Miller, 1853), 3:485, "Examination of Perkins's Pamphlet."

In 1605 Arminius replied to several questions posed to him. The resultant brief document, entitled *Nine Questions*, includes the following question and Arminius's answer. Question: "Can God, now, in his own right, demand from fallen man faith in Christ, which he cannot have of himself, though God neither bestows on him, nor is ready to bestow, sufficient grace by which he may believe?" Answer: "This question will be answered by a direct negative. God cannot by any right demand from fallen man faith in Christ, which he cannot have of himself, except God has either bestowed, or is ready to bestow, sufficient grace by which he may believe if he will."[65]

Though the basis of their thinking may not always be explicit, Arminians consistently maintain the line of thought that somehow ability and responsibility go hand in hand. God's requirement of just behavior by human beings in their relationships with each other springs from the justice of God himself, and this justice he does not and cannot abandon in his dealings with fallen man.

CONCLUSION

The theology of Jonathan Edwards stands as a reputable and lasting monument to a mind and heart devoted to God. Not content merely to spout the answers of his forebears, he often launched into uncharted waters and drew conclusions the church still rejoices in today.

While elucidating the joys of knowing Christ, he also exposed the harsh realities of the fall and its impact on humanity. With clear scriptural and logical proofs, he staved off the Pelagian tendencies of some of his contemporaries, and Arminians can rejoice in many of his insights. However, his *apologia* for Calvinism leaves the strong impression that God is misrepresented in such thought, and it has led the vast majority of the Christian community to reject his understanding of God's decreeing the damnation of the masses who suffer from an absolute inability to respond. At the same time, however, Edwards laid out formidable challenges that the Arminian community of faith continues to struggle with today.

---

[65] Arminius, *Works*, 2:66, "Nine Questions, Exhibited, by the Deputies of the Synod." Along these same lines, Arminius (*Works*, ed. Bagnall, 3:378, 380) argued, "If a man is ordained to commit sin, then he can not sin. For sin is a voluntary act, and the decree of God in reference to sin introduces a necessity of sinning." He expanded on this idea: "The necessity and inevitability of sinning excuses from sin, and frees from punishment, him who commits that act. I say *act*, and not *sin*, because an *act*, which one necessarily and inevitably commits, can not be called *sin*."

Chapter 4

The Atonement and Justification by Faith in Jonathan Edwards

Kevin L. Hester

INTRODUCTION

Jonathan Edwards was known as a champion and defender of the Reformed tradition during his day. His first published work was written against ideas he viewed as eminently dangerous to the advance of the gospel. He named these ideas Arminianism.[1] In that light, it might be surprising to find a modern-day Arminian interested in mining Edwards's thoughts from that very writing. Nevertheless, it is my contention that in the face of modern trends threatening to fray the threads of evangelical theology, Edwards's thought may serve as a lodestone to focus the contributions of his evangelical inheritors. Even though his writings bear witness to the traditional antipathy between Calvinistic and Arminian soteriology, I believe that if both sides are willing to look

---

[1] Michael McClenahan has demonstrated that especially in the area of justification, Edwards's primary Arminian opponent was Anglican Archbishop John Tillotson. While Edwards may occasionally refer to other ideas as "Arminian," Tillotson's writings informed Edwards's argumentation, especially in his *Justification by Faith Alone*. See McClenahan, *Jonathan Edwards and Justification by Faith* (Burlington, VA: Ashgate, 2012).

again at his contributions, we may yet find more agreement than disagreement. His thought moves beyond the strict confines of Calvinism in several areas, and these areas of his thought can serve as *foci* for a *rapprochement* that perhaps Edwards himself was unable to visualize.

Edwards was never a slave to Calvin or to his system of theological thought. He said, "I shall not take it at all amiss, to be called a Calvinist, for distinction's sake: though I utterly disclaim a dependence on Calvin, or believe the doctrines which I hold, because he believed them; and cannot justly be charged with believing everything just as he taught."[2] While Edwards viewed himself as squarely within the Reformed tradition, he was always careful to follow the text of Scripture wherever it would lead him even if this went beyond the usual theological constructions of his time. If modern-day Calvinists and Arminians will take a similar approach, we may find that Edwards provides more common ground than we could have ever imagined. McClymond and McDermott have argued convincingly that Edwards's thought allows him to serve as a "*bridge figure* between diverse and sometimes conflicting parties in the Christian world."[3] I believe that the rich images of the atonement found in Edwards's thought and his presentation of the role of initial and continuing faith in his concept of justification are two such areas where modern readers from the Arminian and Calvinist sides of evangelicalism can identify a shared theological vision.

The explosion of scholarship on Jonathan Edwards over the last half century was perhaps spurred, at least in part, by the work of Perry Miller, who saw in him a genius through whom distinctly early American contributions to philosophy and literature could be read.[4] It is noteworthy, however, that Miller engaged this central unifying factor of Edwards's theological thought unimaginatively and "bracketed" with negativity in an attempt to focus on what he saw as Edwards's more interesting contributions.[5] Despite Edwards's keen

---

[2] Jonathan Edwards, *The Freedom of the Will*, in *The Works of Jonathan Edwards*, vol. 1, ed. Paul Ramsey (New Haven: Yale University Press, 1957), 131.

[3] Michael J. McClymond and Gerald R. McDermott, *The Theology of Jonathan Edwards* (London: Oxford University Press, 2011), 22. While McClymond and McDermott are focused on the possibilities for bridging gaps among Eastern and Western Christianity, Protestantism and Roman Catholicism, and charismatic and noncharismatic Christianity, I argue that the same can be said for the relationship between Calvinism and Arminianism.

[4] Perry Miller, *Jonathan Edwards*, American Men of Letters Series (New York: William Sloane Association, 1949).

[5] Stephen R. Holmes, *God of Grace and God of Glory: An Account of the Theology of Jonathan Edwards* (Grand Rapids: Eerdmans, 2000), 18. For this negative opinion on Edwards's

The Atonement and Justification by Faith in Jonathan Edwards61

philosophical interest, he lived his life as a pastor and missionary who was fully engaged in Christian ministry. When we look for his thought, we find it in sermons and in theological treatises. His thinking on all subjects began in the inscrutable mysteries of God and manifested itself in the theoretical and practical applications of a pastor. I do not wish to neglect Edwards's contributions in other areas, but it must be remembered that "what Edwards had to say was explicitly and irreducibly theological."[6] It is only as a pastor and a theologian that his thought can be properly contextualized.[7]

The recognition of Jonathan Edwards's place among America's greatest theologians was perhaps slow in developing. His earliest theological commentators in the nineteenth century either pushed his theological ideas beyond his own limits, or they were moving toward an "Enlightenment liberalism" that had little desire to engage his more dogmatic method.[8] Nevertheless, since Miller's work, there have been several substantive studies of Edwards's theology

---

theology, see Miller, *Jonathan Edwards*, xiii and 328.

[6] Holmes, *God of Grace*, 30.

[7] Rhys Bezzant makes just this point in his article "The Gospel of Justification and Edwards's Social Vision," in *Jonathan Edwards and Justification*, ed. Josh Moody (Wheaton: Crossway, 2012): 71–94.

[8] Holmes, *God of Grace*, 27. For a discussion of the inheritors of Edwards's theology who moved beyond his thought, see Dorus Paul Rudisill, *The Doctrine of the Atonement in Jonathan Edwards and His Successors* (New York: Poseidon, 1971); Douglas A. Sweeney and Allen C. Guelzo, eds., *The New England Theology: From Jonathan Edwards to Edwards Amasa Park* (Grand Rapids: Baker Academic, 2006); Oliver Crisp, "The Moral Government of God: Jonathan Edwards and Joseph Bellamy on the Atonement," in Oliver D. Crisp and Douglas A Sweeney, eds., *After Edwards: The Courses of New England Theology* (New York: Oxford University Press, 2012); and Daniel W. Cooley and Douglas A. Sweeney, "The Edwardseans and the Atonement," in *A New Divinity: Transatlantic Reformed Evangelical Debates During the Long Eighteenth Century*, ed. Mark Jones and Michael A. G. Haykin; Reformed Historical Theology 49 (Gottingen: Vandenhoeck & Ruprecht, 2018). Particularly helpful in raising new questions on the nature of how Edwards's substitutionary atonement was later developed into a moral government view is S. Mark Hamilton, "Re-thinking Atonement in Jonathan Edwards and New England Theology," *Perichoresis* 15.1 (2017): 85–99. Oliver Crisp terms the atonement view of Edwards's successors as "Non-Penal Substitution," *International Journal of Systematic Theology* 9.4 (2007): 415–33. Most recently, Obbie Tyler Todd has distinguished Edwards's view of the atonement from the views of his followers by saying, "The Edwardseans co-opted one of Jonathan Edwards' most fundamental principles—God's glory displayed—in order to distance themselves from their progenitor. Instead of insisting upon the degree or amount of Christ's suffering as Edwards often did, his disciples believed that the exhibition of God's glorious attributes (i.e. justice, goodness) is the proper equivalent to hellish suffering which ultimately vindicates God's moral governance." "A Countervailing Atonement: The Meaning of Equivalence in the American Moral Governmental Theory of the Atonement," *Scottish Journal of Theology* 72 (2019): 375–84, 380.

as a whole produced and scores of others dealing with particular theological treatises or teachings.[9] These works have sought to demonstrate his unique contributions to theology and have discovered differing interpretive keys. Whereas Conrad Cherry focused on Edwards's perspective of faith, Holmes has highlighted Edwards's aesthetic and ontological understanding of sovereignty and grace.[10] The latest attempt by McClymond and McDermott to present Edwards's thought eschews highlighting one separate theme in favor of the image of a symphony, pointing out that, depending on one's perspective, different nuances emerge in his writing.[11] It is precisely because he is an "open-system" thinker that Edwards has been so notoriously difficult to pin down and why so many different versions of Edwards have appeared.[12] It is also the reason that he is helpful for us as a means of bridging some of the gap between Calvinistic and Arminian interpretations of the atonement and justification. Edwards never approached these theological questions with the idea that the answers had already been fully given. Indeed, his theology argued that God's work could never be exhausted. Therefore, Edwards was always looking for new ways to broaden understanding in his own work, willing to listen to disparate theological voices, and never afraid to pursue avenues of thought that tread perilously close to other theological traditions.

Despite Edwards's willingness to speculate, it is important to remember that he was at heart a Puritan and a Reformed theologian. This is especially vital given my thesis. I have no desire to pretend that Jonathan Edwards was not Reformed. His pedigree in the Calvinist tradition is, if not unassailable, still a nearly universal view.[13] This is especially true in his soteriology and in

---

[9] See Conrad Cherry, *The Theology of Jonathan Edwards: A Reappraisal* (Bloomington, IN: Indiana University Press, 1990 [1966]); Holmes, *God of Grace and God of Glory*; and McClymond and McDermott, *The Theology of Jonathan Edwards*.

[10] Cherry, *Theology of Jonathan Edwards*; Holmes, *God of Grace*. Others have argued for aesthetics, the Trinity, or apologetics as the central theme of his theology. See McClymond and McDermott, *Theology of Jonathan Edwards*, 9.

[11] McClymond and McDermott, 9.

[12] McClymond and McDermott, 9.

[13] One of the chief authors to question the truly Reformed character of Edwards's theology, at least in reference to justification, is Thomas A. Schafer, "Jonathan Edwards and Justification by Faith," *Church History* 20 (1951): 55–67; nevertheless, even he argues that Edwards "was deeply rooted in the Calvinistic Puritanism of both Old and New England," 64, n. 10. George Hunsinger is the most vocal critic of Edwards's perspective on justification, arguing that he fails, at least in principle if not in words, to uphold the Reformation dictum of justification

his presentation of the atonement. Nevertheless, he did not write as a mere Calvinist. "An independent spirit," Edwards was "both firmly rooted in the Reformed theological tradition and—perhaps as part of that identity—eager to embody *semper reformanda* according to *sola scriptura*."[14] He expressed an openness and a speculative awe of the beauty and mystery of God's work. It is in these shadows and margins, these carefully nuanced details, that Calvinists and Arminians may find grounds for greater understanding and mutual respect.

Neither should we deny that Edwards often argued against opponents whom he called "Arminians." It is, however, important for us to gauge as closely as possible against whom and against what teachings he aimed in his writings. In Edwards's New England, the term "Arminianism" was a byword, a catchall used to designate enemies old and new of a particular Reformed understanding first expressed at the Synod of Dort in 1619. Arminianism, named for Jacob Arminius, is used to refer to his teachings and those of his Dutch Reformed followers called the Remonstrants who were responding to Theodore Beza's strict interpretation of Calvin's thought. In distinction from later Calvinist teaching, Arminius and his followers are known to have taught universal provision for the atonement, freedom of the will when assisted by prevenient grace, God's free grace as resistible by God's decree, conditional election based on God's foreknowledge of faith, and in some cases the possibility of apostasy following true conversion. While these views proved to be quite popular in England among certain Puritan and Nonconformist groups before and during Edwards's lifetime, "there was probably not, in 1734, an avowed Arminian in the Puritan pulpits of New England."[15] Against what and whom, then, was Edwards arguing?

While there are no named opponents in Edwards's work on "Justification by Faith Alone," he states in his preface that members of the "new fashioned divinity" (Arminians) have accosted traditional interpretations of justification for their "nice speculation, depending on certain subtle distinctions," preferring instead a "plain and direct" approach to the doctrine.[16] Michael McClenahan

---

by faith alone. "Dispositional Soteriology: Jonathan Edwards on Justification by Faith Alone," *Westminster Theological Journal* 66 (2004): 107–20.

[14] Jonathan Huggins, "Jonathan Edwards and Justification: Embodying a Living Tradition," *Journal of Reformed Theology* 8 (2014): 201.

[15] Schafer, "Jonathan Edwards and Justification by Faith," 55.

[16] Jonathan Edwards, "Justification by Faith Alone," in *Sermons and Discourses, 1734–1738*, *WJE*, vol. 19, ed. M. X. Lesser (New Haven: Yale University Press, 2001), 205, 237.

has demonstrated that at least one of Edwards's primary Arminian targets was Anglican Archbishop John Tillotson.[17] Edwards takes Tillotson's primary assertion to be that there is some merit in the faith and life of the believer that is in some sense made acceptable by grace before God. Thus, as Cherry says, Edwards was arguing against a form of neonomianism that presented a "new kind of obedience and the gospel as a new kind of law [wherein] the grace sufficient for salvation is viewed as conditional on the human performance of faith."[18] Edwards's response is driven by his pastoral concern to ensure that grace remains grace and to establish the forensic character of justification.[19]

A similar neonomian "understanding of faith and grace" is also implied in Edwards's *Freedom of the Will*.[20] Nevertheless, the authors against whom he is writing form a motley assortment. They include the English Anglican Daniel Whitby; Thomas Chubb (a deist); and Isaac Watts, the English nonconformist known more for his psalmody. Where Whitby and Chubb are concerned, the ideas being refuted are tied to a view that would better be termed Pelagianism than Arminianism, since both authors argue for an unfettered will unhampered in any way by original sin and depravity and with no more assistance of grace than what may be found in natural ability and the examples of the saints. Chubb's deism could not rightly be termed Arminianism. As for Whitby, his "denial of the imputation of Adam's sin to the rest of mankind . . . carried him beyond the . . . Arminian position."[21] Watts expressed a similar perspective on the unfettered will in his *Essay on the Freedom of Will in God and the Creature*, though his views are less clear and potentially clouded by questions related to his theological positions on the Trinity and other doctrines.[22]

It is best to conclude that if Edwards is dealing with a theological system as a whole, it is not one that would be readily identifiable as Arminianism today. This Arminian is quick to reject the Pelagianism and nascent Deist and Socinian perspectives that troubled Edwards and would reject them together with him. Most modern evangelical Arminians have little sympathy for such

---

[17] Michael McClenahan, *Jonathan Edwards and Justification by Faith* (Burlington, VA: Ashgate, 2012).

[18] Cherry, *The Theology of Jonathan Edwards*, 187.

[19] McClenahan, *Jonathan Edwards and Justification by Faith*, 53, 139.

[20] Cherry, *Theology of Jonathan Edwards*, 189.

[21] Paul Ramsey, "Introduction," in *Freedom of the Will*, in *WJE*, 1:82.

[22] Ramsey, "Introduction," 1:94. Ramsey notes that Edwards retained great respect for Watts, "hesitating to even call him an Arminian."

shallow views of the effect of original sin as found in the authors against whom Edwards wrote. The theological position of modern Arminians is found more fully stated in Edwards than in his opponents. The same was most likely true in his time and after, for "in the eighteenth century there was probably more in common between Edwards's defense of orthodoxy and the restored Arminianism of Arminius which emerged with new strength and warmth . . . than between the latter and some of the 'Arminians' whom Edwards opposed."[23] If one must identify that theological system, the term "Arminianism" is not now, if it ever was, the proper term.

At the same time, there were tendencies in Edwards's family, his congregants, and the church culture at large that troubled him, and he also referred to these as "Arminian." In a letter from 1749, Edwards identified his sister's son, Joseph Hawley III, one of his congregants and opponents at Northampton, whom he described as "a man of lax principles in religion, falling in in some essential things with Arminians."[24] Another example of the Arminian tendencies Edwards opposed may be seen in the Robert Breck affair. Between 1733 and 1734, Breck was presented for ordination, and questions were raised about his suitability as a candidate. As in most ecclesio-political squabbles, hard evidence is difficult to come by. It is clear, though, that part of what certain individuals found objectionable were "Arminian" tendencies, despite Breck's objections to the contrary. These tendencies seem to have included his opinion that "it was ridiculous to say God would damn the heathen who had never heard of Christ" and that he had affirmingly quoted the deist Thomas Chubb saying, "A person might be saved out of love of virtue itself, even without any faith or knowledge of Christ."[25] While Edwards was not immediately involved in the affair, he did sign and support the move to block the ordination and would later write the defense of the association's decision.

If the "Arminian" tendencies that so troubled Jonathan Edwards were occurring outside the context of an Arminian theological system, and if, as it has been shown, they were present in Reformed churches from the period, is

---

[23] Cherry, *Theology of Jonathan Edwards*, 3.

[24] Cherry, 4. He also mentions his fear that the "younger generation will be carried away with Arminianism, as a flood."

[25] George M. Marsden, *Jonathan Edwards: A Life* (New Haven: Yale University Press, 2003), 177. It is this debate that many scholars think was the instigation for Edwards's preaching of the sermons that would eventually be published as "Justification by Faith Alone."

it really appropriate to see this cultural shift in light of Arminianism? Rather, it would seem best to conclude with Schafer that the expressions that Edwards found objectionable had more to do with a "native American variety of human self sufficiency" than a theological shift toward Arminianism.[26] Given this conclusion, modern interpreters of Edwards should be more interested in the content of his theological thought and its prospects for furthering discussion, understanding, and mutual respect rather than reading modern soteriological grievances into the labels he employed. It is with this interest and hope in mind that we now turn to Edwards's thought.

EDWARDS ON THE ATONEMENT

Edwards's view of the atonement is enigmatic. He says that it is the "great Christian doctrine of Christ's satisfaction . . . [that] is, as it were, the center and hinge of all doctrines of pure revelation."[27] Though it fills such an important role in his theological thought, there is little systematic discussion of it throughout his writings. This fact has puzzled interpreters. Holmes says, "It is something of a surprise here to find how little systematic treatment is offered by Edwards; the doctrine is everywhere assumed, certainly, but not often discussed at any length; and the two major discussions that are present in the corpus are interesting partly because they disagree."[28] It has also provided room for a great deal of speculation on whether Edwards had a thoroughgoing position or whether his views changed over time. Schafer raised this question in his study of justification in Edwards, saying,

> In view of . . . Edwards' discourse on justification and its prominence among his first publications, the almost total lack of emphasis on the doctrine in the great works of his last twenty years . . . [indicates that] there are important elements in Edwards' religious thought which cause the doctrine of

---

[26] Schafer, "Jonathan Edwards and Justification by Faith," 55.

[27] Edwards, "Controversies" Notebook, in *WJE Online*, vol. 27, ed. Jonathan Edwards Center, Part IV "Efficacious Grace," http://edwards.yale.edu/archive?path=aHR0cDovL2Vkd2FyZH MueWFsZS5lZHUvY2dpLWJpbi9uZXdwaGlsby9nZXRRvYmplY3QucGw/Yy4yNjo2LndqZW8=.

[28] Holmes, *God of Grace*, 142.

justification to occupy an ambiguous and somewhat precarious place in his theology.[29]

Nevertheless, Jonathan Edwards's writings assert (even if not as strongly as some would like) that the atonement was the centerpiece of God's work in the world.[30] It was the wellspring of his theological thought and is sprinkled throughout his sermons, treatises, and especially *The Miscellanies*. Edwards teaches that while God existed before creation, humanity came to know him only in the unfolding of redemption. The story of God is ultimately the story of God's redemption of humanity. Creation and consummation are subsumed in the atonement. In a letter to the trustees of the College of New Jersey, Edwards laid out his plan for a new work of theology in progress that he called "A History of the Work of Redemption." In this work he planned to outline "the great work of redemption by Jesus Christ; which I suppose is to be the grand design of all God's designs, and the *summum* and *ultimum* of all the divine operations and degrees; . . . beginning from eternity and descending from thence to the great work and successive dispensations of the infinitely wise God in time . . . till at last we come to the general resurrection, last judgment, and consummation of all things."[31]

Not only did Edwards see the atonement as the central purpose of God in creation, but he also viewed it as central to our experience of God. Rather

---

[29] Schafer, "Jonathan Edwards and Justification by Faith," 57. Numerous authors have come to the defense of Edwards on this point in order to reclaim his place in the Reformed tradition. See Jeffrey C. Waddington, "Jonathan Edwards's 'Ambiguous and Somewhat Precarious' Doctrine of Justification," *Westminster Theological Journal* 66 (2004): 357–72; and Jonathan Ray Huggins, "Jonathan Edwards on Justification by Faith Alone: An Analysis of His Thought and Defense of His Orthodoxy," Master's Thesis, Reformed Theological Seminary, 2006. We will note other questions about Edwards's Reformed credentials as it relates to justification by faith in the role that faith plays in uniting the believer to Christ.

[30] Brandon James Crawford has defended Edwards's place in the Reformed tradition through his focus on how Edwards viewed the atonement in Reformed covenantal categories. Though Edwards may have pressed the boundaries of these covenants, sometimes seeing the covenant of grace and the covenant of works as one basic covenant, the covenantal love demonstrated among the Trinity and manifested to humanity is the centerpiece of God's glory as manifested in the atonement. See Brandon James Crawford, "Divine Love as the Organizing Principle of Jonathan Edwards's Doctrine of the Atonement," *Journal of the Evangelical Theological Society* 62.3 (2019): 563–81.

[31] Edwards, "To The Trustees of the College of New Jersey," in *Letters and Personal Writings*, WJE, vol. 16, ed. George S. Claghorn (New Haven: Yale University Press, 1998), 727–28; McClymond and McDermott, *Theology of Jonathan Edwards*, 183.

than simply focusing on the work of Christ alone, Edwards viewed the entire process of redemption from within a Trinitarian framework.[32] The basis for the atonement lay in the eternal decrees of God and an "inter-Trinitarian covenant of redemption."[33] The Father, the Son, and the Holy Spirit are all intimately involved in the process of redemption and in the application of redemption to the human person. Edwards viewed the Trinity as functioning economically in this way in the "covenant of redemption" but also saw it based in an ontological reality. This "relationship of order and beauty" in God serves as the ontological basis for "God's inter-Trinitarian decision to glorify Himself in this way."[34]

In the very first sermon Edwards ever preached, this was also his primary assertion. Speaking on 1 Cor 1:29–30, Edwards argued that all the blessings we experience come from God, and the greatest of these, redemption, is a work of the Trinity. He said that

> in this verse is shown our dependence on each person in the Trinity for all our good. We are dependent on Christ the Son of God, as he is our wisdom, righteousness, sanctification, and redemption. We are dependent on the Father, who has given us Christ, and made him to be these things to us. We are dependent on the Holy Ghost, for 'tis of him that we are in Christ Jesus; 'tis the Spirit of God that gives us faith in him, whereby we receive him, and close with him.[35]

The Father's purpose in the atonement was to glorify himself and his Son and, through the Spirit, to provide a bride for his Son. This bride, the church,

---

[32] Crawford states, "Christ's historical work finds its origin in the eternal love existing between the members of the Trinity, which found expression in eternity past in the Covenant of Redemption. In it the Father expresses his love for the Son, the Son expresses his love for the Father, and together Father and Son express their love for the Son's bride." "Divine Love," 567. On Edwards's understanding of the economic Trinity, see also Kyle Strobel, "By Word and Spirit: Jonathan Edwards on Redemption, Justification, and Regeneration," in *Jonathan Edwards and Justification*, ed. Josh Moody (Wheaton: Crossway, 2012), 45–70.

[33] McClymond and McDermott, *Theology of Jonathan Edwards*, 245.

[34] Holmes, *God of Grace*, 134. Holmes is basing his argument here on Edwards's *Miscellanies* 1062. Holmes also provides a very interesting discussion of Christ as the foundation of God's purposes of election wherein Christ is himself the "object of election."

[35] Jonathan Edwards, "God Glorified in Man's Dependence," in *Sermons and Discourses, 1730–1733*, WJE, vol. 17, ed. Mark Valeri (New Haven: Yale University Press, 1999), 201.

would exist "for the adequate displays of his unspeakable and transcendent goodness and grace."[36]

In order to secure this bride, God's eternal decrees would have to deal with the problem of humanity's sin. At the fall, humanity had lost its first estate and had placed itself in a position of enmity with God. God's holiness must be satisfied if reunion were ever to be possible. The fall, therefore, serves as the most immediate cause of the need for the atonement. When Adam sinned, all humanity sinned with him. Because of this, all humanity stands guilty before God and corrupt in their natures. All humanity is "naturally and morally one entity" with Adam.[37] They were incapable of desiring God or satisfying his divine justice. The need for the atonement in Edwards is found in two traditional components. There is the Adamic guilt that passed to the human race and the individual guilt that arises from an inability to keep the law of God.[38] While Edwards discussed both components in his theology, he did not starkly divide the two concepts as has come to be customary in many theological treatments. This seems to arise from the way in which he grounds the union between Adam and his progeny and the fact that the fall has worked corruption in the will and nature of all individuals.

As Cherry says, "Edwards insists that sin is a Fall of the race in Adam (the continuity of guilt being maintained by the direct power of God) and not simply a series of separate human acts. It is a corruption of heart that reaches deep into the human subject, a corruption to be estimated primarily by comparing the selfishness of man with the overflowing love of the infinite God."[39] This corruption does not simply flow from the imputation of an alien guilt to us as in some components of the Reformed (federal) tradition, but it is a direct

---

[36] Jonathan Edwards, *The Miscellanies*, in *WJE*, vol. 23, ed. Douglas A. Sweeney (New Haven: Yale University Press, 2004), 178–79. See also Crawford, "Divine Love," 565–67.

[37] Crawford, "Divine Love," 570. Jonathan Hill sees Edwards's understanding of the imputation of guilt and of righteousness as consistent with the participatory model of the atonement proposed as Pauline by adherents of the New Perspective even while he recognizes that Edwards's language typically reflects the "Calvinistic penal substitution model." "'His Death Belongs to Them': An Edwardsean Participatory Model of Atonement," *Religious Studies* 54 (2018): 196 n. 18.

[38] While he recognizes traditional federalist language in Edwards, S. Mark Hamilton argues that Edwards ultimately presents an "*Augustinian Realist* ontology" that is operative in his understanding of both humanity's union with Adam and the union of Christ with the Elect. "Jonathan Edwards on the Atonement," *International Journal of Systematic Theology* 15.4 (2013): 397, 410–11.

[39] Cherry, *Theology of Jonathan Edwards*, 201.

result of our own actual sin through our union with Adam. Edwards sees a real connection between our sin and corruption and the sin of Adam in the fall. In his treatise on *Original Sin*, Edwards quotes Stapferus's *Theologica Polemica* approvingly and makes use of the image of a tree to argue that Adam's posterity is one with him as the root of the tree is one with the branches. The whole of humanity, therefore, is rightly seen as one organic unit and one moral person sinning in Adam. In this way,

> if we consider the *morality* of the action, and what *consent* there is to it, it is altogether to be maintained, that his posterity committed the *same* sin, both in number and in kind, inasmuch as they are to be looked upon as consenting to it. For where there is consent to a sin, there the same sin is committed. Seeing therefore that Adam with all his posterity constitute but *one moral person*, and are united in the same covenant, and are transgressors of the same law, they are also to be looked upon as having, in a moral estimation, committed the same transgression of the law, both in number and in kind.[40]

Images of this nature, coupled with Edwards's hesitancy to embrace specific terms associated with traditional covenantal theology, led Perry Miller to argue that Edwards discarded the traditional view of Adam's federal headship of the human race. McClymond and McDermott disagree, saying that while Edwards was indeed a covenantalist in his basic approach, he "reconfigured" the Reformed tradition of seeing a "covenant of works as a foil for a postlapsarian covenant of grace."[41] Instead, on the one hand, Edwards believed that the initial covenant of works had never been abrogated and was still ongoing. Adam (and humankind with him) failed God's moral law by breaking the covenant of works, and we fulfill his act by continuing to break this covenant.[42]

---

[40] Jonathan Edwards, *Original Sin*, in *WJE*, vol. 3, ed. Clyde A. Holbrook (New Haven: Yale University Press, 1970), 381. Italics in the original.

[41] McClymond and McDermott, *Theology of Jonathan Edwards*, 248. For a discussion of traditional federal theology, see David A. Weir, *The Origins of the Federal Theology in Sixteenth-Century Reformation Thought* (New York: Oxford University Press, 1990).

[42] This has important implications for Edwards's understanding of Christ's active and passive obedience, which we will soon see.

Christ, on the other hand, as the second Adam, accomplishes the requirements of this covenant of works. Edwards says that this was "the covenant that we had broken, and that was the covenant that must be fulfilled."[43] Thus Christ was subject to three laws—the moral law, the ceremonial law, and the mediatorial law—and as a result, Christ's atoning work begins at the fall. His appearances in the Old Testament, his incarnation, his death, and his current mediatorial service are all components of God's redemption of the world through Christ, and all are necessary for the atonement.

While Christ works to accomplish the atonement in all his labors since the fall, his office of mediator is ultimately fulfilled in the incarnation. Having broken the covenant of works, the human race sinned against an infinite being. God's justice therefore demanded an infinite recompense. Finite beings were incapable of making satisfaction by suffering in this fashion, and their corruption rendered them unable to fulfill the covenant. In the incarnation the infinite took up the capacity to suffer, and the uncorrupted faithfully fulfilled the righteous demands of God's covenant of works. In this way the God-man serves as the mediator who both suffers for the sin of Adam and keeps the covenant of works.

Grounding sin in a violation of the covenant of works, Edwards was able to see "the whole life of Jesus as redemptive, not just his death, and to insist on the rationality—or appropriateness—of the atonement."[44] Edwards used this principle to assert that the atonement includes the imputation of what has traditionally been referred to as the active and the passive obedience of Christ. Though Edwards used the term "passive obedience" often, he cautioned against the use of the term if it is thought to imply that Christ's suffering is not in and of itself an aspect of his active obedience in his fulfillment of the inter-Trinitarian covenant of redemption wherein he is elected to the role of mediator.[45] Edwards said,

---

[43] Jonathan Edwards, *A History of the Work of Redemption*, in *WJE*, vol. 9, ed. John F. Wilson (New Haven: Yale University Press, 1989), 309.

[44] Holmes, *God of Grace*, 146.

[45] Edwards used the term "passive" obedience in *The Miscellanies*, in *WJE*, vol. 13, ed. Harry S. Stout (New Haven: Yale University Press), 378; see also Edwards, "Justification by Faith Alone," 19:193, 195.

The distinction of active and passive obedience in this case
is utterly improper, for all obedience is active. All obedience,
considered under the notion of obedience, is active; and considered under the notion of obedience, 'tis righteousness. 'Tis
contrary the obedience there [is] in suffering. So far as 'tis
in obedience, 'tis active; if considered as obedience, 'tis considered [as] act. Indeed, the sufferings of Christ may be considered under a twofold consideration: either as a part of his
obedience [or] a part of his righteousness, [and] so it is meritorious; or as properly his suffering, and so it is a satisfaction
or propitiation for sin.[46]

Edwards did not like to separate the concepts of active and passive obedience, preferring instead to see all aspects of the atonement as Christ's obedience
to the Father.[47] He outlined the way that the atonement has both positive and
negative aspects. "Christ's sufferings did more than release believers from the
penalty against sin that would have sent them to hell. Christ did not suffer only
to satisfy God's anger and justice. His sufferings were also positive and meritorious acts that purchased happiness in heaven."[48] Edwards argued, therefore,
that what Christ accomplishes in the "believer's justification implies, not only
remission of sin, or acquittance from the wrath due to it, but also an admittance
to a title to that glory that is the reward of righteousness, in inseparable unity."[49]

---

[46] Jonathan Edwards, "Paper on Justification," in *Documents on the Trinity, Grace
and Faith, WJE Online*, vol. 37 ed. Jonathan Edwards Center, http://edwards.yale.edu/
archive?path=aHR0cDovL2Vkd2FyZHMueWFsZS5lZHUvY2dpLWJpbi9uZXdwaGlssby9n
ZXRvYmplY3QucGw/Yy4zNToxMy53amVv.

[47] This is why Edwards was hesitant to speak strongly of Christ's passive obedience. He
believes that Christ's suffering was a fulfillment of the inter-Trinitarian Covenant of Redemption and the Covenant of Works demonstrated by his active obedience in suffering according to
the will of the Father. For the best discussion on Edwards's understanding of active and passive
obedience, see Ryan Hurd, "Jonathan Edwards's View of that Great Act of Obedience: Jesus's
Laying Down His Life," *Westminster Theological Journal* 78 (2016): 271–86.

[48] McClymond and McDermott, *Theology of Jonathan Edwards*, 251. Gerstner also notes the
way that Edwards seems to always couple the positive and negative components of the atonement. John Gerstner, *The Rational Biblical Theology of Jonathan Edwards*, 3 vols. (Powhatan,
VA: Berea and Ligonier, 1992), 2:414.

[49] Robert W. Jensen, *America's Theologian: A Recommendation of Jonathan Edwards* (New
York: Oxford University Press, 1988), 60.

The concept of divine justice drives the primary images of God's atonement as worked in Christ. This justice is demonstrated through the means by which God works in Christ to remove guilt and to impute righteousness.[50] Both elements of justice require satisfaction. Christ works to fulfill the principles of distributive and commutative justice. Distributive justice deals with the allocation of benefits and burdens, in this case the burden of God's punishment on humanity for sin. Commutative justice deals with the proper apportionment of goods, in this case what God purchases for the redeemed through all aspects of his obedience, including the active and the passive. Edwards "makes of Christ's satisfaction both the payment of a debt which merits a reward (commutative justice) and an expiation which forms the basis for the forensic justification of the sinful elect (distributive justice)."[51]

Edwards's primary understanding of the atonement was therefore presented along the lines of Anselm's satisfaction view with the inclusion of some positive aspects that are traditionally soft-pedaled in the tradition. Edwards said that the infinite "demerit of sin" demanded "infinite suffering" and in respect to Christ "the blood which he spilled, his life which he laid down" was the price with which he "purchased" the Church of God, paying for "the demerit of the sins of mankind."[52] While Holmes sees no evidence that Edwards was aware of Anselm's position directly, the concept of satisfaction was deeply tied to the Reformation tradition and can be found in Calvin.[53] Cherry also sees Edwards falling into the Anselmic tradition of a forensic understanding of the atonement, arguing that in Edwards the "imputation of Christ's righteousness is developed according to Christ's two major functions in relation to divine

---

[50] Hurd, "Jonathan Edwards's View of That Great Act of Obedience," 277–78.

[51] Dorus Paul Rudisill, *The Doctrine of the Atonement in Jonathan Edwards and His Successors* (New York: Poseidon Books, 1971), 19. Hamilton prefers the terms "retributive" and "rectoral" justice. S. Mark Hamilton, "Jonathan Edwards, Anselmic Satisfaction and God's Moral Government," *International Journal of Systematic Theology* 17.1 (2015): 49. Hurd, with a focus on active and passive obedience, prefers the terms "penal" and "preceptive." "Jonathan Edwards's View of that Great Act of Obedience," 280 n. 60.

[52] Jonathan Edwards, "The Sacrifice of Christ Acceptable," in *Sermons and Discourses: 1723–1729, WJE*, vol. 14, ed. Kenneth P. Minkema (New Haven: Yale University Press, 1997), 452.

[53] Holmes, *God of Grace*, 145 n. 66. For Calvin, see his *Institutes of the Christian Religion*, 2.17.4. John Calvin, *Institutes of the Christian Religion*, 2 vols., trans. Henry Beveridge (Grand Rapids: Eerdmans, 1994), 1:455–56.

justice. Christ by his righteousness both satisfies the punitive demands of the law for sin and positively fulfills the law in order to achieve the atonement."[54]

Edwards generally followed a penal substitution model of the atonement. He often used the words *sacrifice, substitute,* and *satisfaction* in his discussions of the atonement.[55] If one uses J. I. Packer's definition of penal substitution, then Edwards checks all the boxes.[56] While there has been significant recent debate, "evidence strongly suggests Edwards' adherence to a version of the penal substitution theory of the atonement, that is, the theory according to which Christ willingly assumes the legal responsibility for the sin(s) of human beings . . . and by his substitutionary death pays their compensatory debt in order to satisfy God's retributive justice."[57] The complexity of Edwards's view of the atonement arose not simply from its basic forensic character but from the fact that, in his understanding, "the doctrines of imputation and justification

---

[54] Cherry, *Theology of Jonathan Edwards*, 93.

[55] Crawford, "Divine Love," 573.

[56] Packer outlines the basic characteristics of the penal substitution view of the atonement as (1) God's justice demands retribution, (2) the atonement is necessitated by God's desire and God's character, (3) the atonement includes judgment that is substitutional in nature, and (4) Christ's sacrifice has infinite value. See J. I. Packer, "What Did the Cross Achieve? The Logic of Penal Substitution," *Tyndale Bulletin* 25 (1974), 3–46.

[57] S. Mark Hamilton, "Jonathan Edwards on the Atonement," *International Journal of Systematic Theology* 15.4 (2013): 394–415, 395. Other proponents of the position that Jonathan Edwards held to a satisfaction view of the atonement include Crisp, "Moral Government of God," 78–90; Crawford, "Divine Love;" and Chris Woznicki, "The Coherence of Penal Substitution: An Edwardsean Defence," *Tyndale Bulletin* 70.1 (2019), 95–115. It should be mentioned that S. Mark Hamilton has withdrawn from his previous conclusion to state instead, "I am no longer convinced that we can make definitive claims about his [Jonathan Edwards's] adherence to the penal substitution model." "Re-Thinking Atonement in Jonathan Edwards and New England Theology," *Perichoresis* 15.1 (2017): 98. Hamilton's newfound doubts about Edwards seem more driven by his own questions on the moral character of the penal substitution model and its absence in Edwards's historical followers. It seems to me that Hamilton overlooks the federal language Edwards used, the complexity of his focus on the active and passive obedience of Christ, and his Reformed emphasis on union with Christ in the atonement, which are best understood according to the penal substitution model. While he discusses Edwards's federalism in another article and concludes that Edwards instead follows an "Augustinian realism," Hamilton fails to recognize that the adoption of a realist ontology does not necessarily mean the rejection of all other federal elements, even though he questions whether the "realist component of Edwards' penal substitution [may simply be] a robust doctrine of union with Christ." See Hamilton, "Jonathan Edwards on the Atonement," 412.

are subsumed under the doctrine of union with Christ, which he frames in relational, affective terms."[58]

While the forensic understanding of the atonement seems to be primary in Edwards's thought, it is not the only image Edwards used for Christ's work in the atonement. He often made use of mercantile images that are also found in Anselm. Christ

> has bought [eternal life] for us. If we had not sinned, God would have given us eternal life upon the account of our obedience. But by our sin we have lost it and Christ alone can redeem it, seeing divine justice must be satisfied and it would not have been just with God to let sin go unpunished. Christ so loved the offender that, rather than he should die, He would pay all that justice demanded, and [that] He has done, so that justice is paid and everlasting life is purchased and is to be received, without any money or price, by those that will come to Christ for it.[59]

Notice that even with the mercantile imagery, the concept of penal substitution looms large in the background. In fact, mercantile images provide Edwards with yet another way to expound Christ's satisfaction for sins and his meriting salvation for the elect through his obedience. Edwards therefore laid stress on the holiness of God but was also interested in God's role as governor and sovereign.

This emphasis led Edwards to include some images of the atonement that are clearly more governmental in nature. His statements in this regard are strong enough to trouble some commentators in the Reformed tradition. Reflecting on *Miscellanies* 306, John Gerstner inquired how Edwards could say, "If God did not punish sin, nobody could charge God with any wrong" and asserted that "pure governmentalism follows fast."[60] What Gerstner failed to see is that the apparent governmentalism here is driven not by any inherent need

---

[58] Crawford, "Divine Love," 580; see also Strobel, "By Word and Spirit," 45–70.

[59] Jonathan Edwards, "Life through Christ Alone," in *Sermons and Discourses 1720–1723*, *WJE*, vol. 10, ed. Wilson H. Kimnach (New Haven: Yale University Press, 1992), 525.

[60] Gerstner, *Rational Biblical Theology*, vol. 2, 435–36.

to punish or not punish sin. God will of his own ontological character of love move to provide the atonement together with its consequential punishment. Holmes notes that Edwards had "no problems with the governmental theory" and sees the same references as "pure governmentalism" but notes that this is "not the most important metaphor for the atonement in his writings."[61] It is remarkable, however, that in the most direct inheritors of his system, Edwards's governmental focus would come to take center stage in the theological expression of the atonement in the group known as the Edwardseans.[62]

As Holmes notes, this governmental tendency is not really a rejection of the satisfaction theory of the atonement, but it is based rather in an aesthetic ontology of beauty that Edwards saw as rooted in the nature of God and demonstrated in all God's works.[63] This means that there is present in Edwards an aesthetic image of the atonement as well. The incarnation, Christ's life, and his death bring all things into harmony in the atonement.[64] Edwards linked together the nature of God, the grace of God, and his holy justice in the atonement worked by Christ. There is no debate over which of the moral attributes of God is primary. Instead, all the attributes together motivate God's decrees to accomplish his will in a way that brings beauty and order. The word used most often by Edwards to describe this process was "fit." He used it to speak of the beautiful ordering of God's nature and his acts. It speaks to the atonement and the relationship established between the believer and Christ. "Edwards highlighted the aesthetic, rational, and personal aspects of the passion," and he described the horrors of the cross as the beauty of God in redemption.[65] Edwards said,

> From things being thus as has been observed, it comes to pass
> that whenever the saints behold the beauty and amiable excel-
> lency of Christ as appearing in his virtues, and have their souls
> ravished with it, they may behold it in its brightest effulgence,

---

[61] Holmes, *God of Grace*, 145 n. 65.

[62] See Rudisill, *Doctrine of the Atonement*. See also Douglas A. Sweeney and Allen C. Guelzo, eds., *The New England Theology: From Jonathan Edwards to Edwards Amasa Park* (Grand Rapids: Baker Academic, 2006) especially part three, "The Moral Government of God: Edwardseans and the Atonement" 133–48.

[63] Holmes, *God of Grace*, 20–21, 90–92, and especially 144–45.

[64] Jenson, *America's Theologian*, 125.

[65] McClymond and McDermott, *Theology of Jonathan Edwards*, 252.

and by far its most full and glorious manifestation, shining forth in a wonderful act of love to them, exercised in his last sufferings, wherein he died for them. They may have the pleasure to see all his ravishing excellency in that which is the height, and, as it were, the sum of its exhibited and expressed glory, appearing in and by the exercise of dying love to them; which certainly will tend to endear that excellency, and make that greatest effulgence of it the more ravishing in their eyes. They see the transcendent greatness of his love shining forth in the same act that they see the transcendent greatness of his loveliness shining forth, and his loveliness to shine in his love; so that 'tis most lovely love. Their seeing his loveliness tends to make them desire his love, but the sight of his loveliness brings satisfaction to this desire with it, because the appearance of his loveliness as they behold it, mainly consists in the marvelous exercise of his love to them. It being thus, his excellency both endears his love, and his love endears his excellency; and the very beholding his excellency, as thus manifested, is an enjoying of it as their own. And while the saints have the pleasure of these views, they may also have the additional pleasure of considering that this lovely virtue is imputed to them. 'Tis the lovely robe, and robe of love, with which they are covered. Christ gives it to them, and puts it upon them, and by the beauty of this robe recommends 'em to the favor and delight of God the Father, as well as of all heaven besides."[66]

Love is the motivating factor of the redemption in Edwards's aesthetic images of the atonement. Love motivates both the covenant of redemption and the sufferings of Christ, and the redeemed return the love they receive to their redeemer. In his sacrifice Christ demonstrated the love of God fully, and his love flows into the redeemed through the manifold graces of his Spirit. In a

---

[66] Jonathan Edwards, "Christ's Example. The Excellency of Christ. The Righteousness of Christ," The Miscellanies, in WJE, vol. 18, ed. Ava Chamberlain (New Haven: Yale University Press, 2000), 494–95.

sermon on Ps 1:3, Edwards waxed poetic on the nature and benefits of the love demonstrated in the atonement and its beauty as it unfolds in the Christian life.

> As the waters of a river run easily and freely, so the love of Christ. [He] freely came into the world. [He] laid down his life and endured those dreadful sufferings.
> His blood was freely shed: blood flowed as freely from his wounds as water from a spring.
> All the good things that Christ bestows on his saints come to 'em as freely as water runs down in a river.
> The chief and most excellent things that Christ bestows are the influences of his Spirit on their hearts, to enlighten and sanctify and comfort.
> These all come freely from Christ, like the waters of a river.
> Christ willingly gives his people, that look to him and trust in him, light and life in their souls.
> Christ is like a river in the great plenty and abundance of his love and grace.
> The love of Christ is great, [and he has] done great things from love.[67]

The final image of the atonement we will consider is one that brings together the love of Christ, the justice of the Father, and the sin of humanity. It recognizes the need to satisfy God's justice and God's desire to work redemption. To accomplish the atonement, Christ serves as our advocate before the Father. He takes up our suffering, and his merits are granted to us, for God sees us in him. Edwards used the analogy of a client and a patron to describe the atonement. Christ serves as our patron, and we are his clients. Christ as God is sufficient to meet our needs, and, in the incarnation, he takes up our needs as his own. Christ therefore unites himself to us and to our cause. In our union with him, his merits become ours. Because we are not equal to Christ in the union, his status, reputation, and merits give us, his clients, a better claim to the patron's

---

[67] Jonathan Edwards, "Christ is to the Heart Like a River to a Tree Planted by It," in *Sermons and Discourses, 1743–1758, WJE,* vol. 25, ed. Wilson H. Kimnach (New Haven: Yale University Press, 2006), 602–3.

friend (the Father). Christ as our patron becomes willing to suffer for us in our place out of his great love. Our "fit" response as clients is concurrent love.[68]

In all the images of the atonement that Edwards used, he always came back to the loveliness of the sacrifice of Christ, which satisfied the justice of God and purchased heaven for us. His life and his death are given to us as we are united to him. Christ's life for us and his suffering on our behalf are the material cause of the atonement. We turn now to a discussion of the instrumental condition of the atonement.

JUSTIFICATION BY FAITH

Edwards taught that the believer is justified by his faith in Christ alone. Faith is not a work, nor does it merit salvation. While Edwards was arguing in "Justification by Faith" against an "Arminian" neonomianism, he never downplayed the role that faith plays in the union. Faith, for Edwards, is the active uniting of the believer with Christ and includes the embracing of his offer of salvation and the forsaking of one's sin.[69] It is a "closing with Christ" that provides the imputation of Christ's suffering for our sin and the promise of heaven that had been purchased by his obedience to the covenant of works. Through faith all that is Christ's is viewed in common. In similar aesthetic language to what he used in describing the atonement, Edwards argued that faith is "fit" to unite the believer to Christ. This faith is not a moral fit because there is nothing in humanity that can be morally acceptable to God. It is instead naturally fit because the soul, in exercising faith, recognizes the ontological good in God and the beauty in God's grace in Christ.

Though justification comes ultimately as a result of Christ's work, the believer's union with Christ through faith is a secondary ground for justification. George Hunsinger says, "For Edwards' doctrine of justification by faith, Christ is the prime though not the exclusive ground of righteousness in the saints, and that salvation is, in some sense, given as a reward for their inherent holiness, loveliness, and obedience, so long as we see that the reward is not given directly but only indirectly through the primary ground in Christ."[70] Edwards

---

[68] Edwards, *The Miscellanies*, 23:713–16.

[69] Edwards, 18:216.

[70] George Hunsinger, "Dispositional Soteriology: Jonathan Edwards on Justification by Faith Alone," *Westminster Theological Journal* 66 (2004): 111.

thus distinguished his view by defining the "Arminian" position of faith as an obedience that God sees as deserving justification. He roundly rejected this neonomianism, yet his view of the active role faith plays in salvation resonates with later Arminian thought. Modern Arminians join Edwards in rejecting a neonomianism that grounds justification in the merit of faith. They assert that the exercise of faith is not even possible without the prevenient grace of God. The will, enabled and ennobled, may choose Christ, but there is nothing meritorious in the choosing. Faith is simply the means of the believer's union with Christ. Justification always rests on the merits of Christ alone, but union with Christ is founded on faith.

Edwards spoke of faith as the uniting of the believer with Christ. He did not like the term "instrument" of justification because it lacks the necessary active elements. He argued that the term had often been misunderstood, saying that "it was not intended that faith was the instrument wherewith God justifies, but the instrument wherewith we receive justification; not the instrument wherewith the justifier acts in justifying, but wherewith the receiver of justification acts in accepting justification."[71] Faith is a condition of justification, but Edwards argued that there are different degrees of conditionality. Not wanting to embrace a salvation by works, he distinguished between a cause and a condition. While Christ's work in the atonement is the cause of justification, there are other noncausal conditions of justification. Specifically, Edwards argued that faith is a noncausal condition of justification. However, he did not strictly confine the idea of a noncausal condition of justification to faith:

> Though faith be indeed the condition of justification so as nothing else is, yet this matter is not clearly and sufficiently explained by saying that faith is the *condition* of justification; and that because the word seems ambiguous both in common use, and also as used in divinity: in one sense, Christ alone performs the condition of our justification and salvation; in another sense, faith is the condition of justification; in another sense, other qualifications and acts are conditions of salvation and justification too. . . . And there are many other things besides faith which are directly proposed to us, to be pursued

---

[71] Edwards, "Justification by Faith Alone," 19:153.

or performed by us, in order to eternal life, as those which, if they are done or obtained, we shall have eternal life, and if not done or not obtained, we shall surely perish. And if it were so, that faith was the only condition of justification in this sense, yet I don't apprehend that to say that faith was the condition of justification, would express the sense of that phrase of Scripture of being "justified *by* faith."[72]

Faith functions "fitly" to accomplish salvation by bringing about the believer's union with Christ. It is not simply a means but an active uniting in which the believer accepts Christ and turns away from his sins. This action brings about the imputation of Christ's active and passive obedience. Yet it is more than simply a judicial union. Although God does reckon our sins punished and the law fulfilled in Christ, the judicial union is logically dependent on the actual union. Christ offers the union and the believer accepts. As in the case for all personal relationships, a union is mutual. In the case of the offer of salvation, the acceptance establishes the union. Edwards said,

God don't give those that believe, an union *with*, or an interest *in* the Savior, in reward for faith, but only because faith is the soul's active uniting with Christ, or is itself the very act of unition, on their part. God sees it fit, that in order to an union's being established between two intelligent active beings or persons, so as that they should be looked upon as one, there should be the mutual act of both, that each should receive the other, as actively joining themselves one to another. God in requiring this in order to an union with Christ as one of his people, treats men as reasonable creatures, capable of act, and choice; and hence sees it fit that they only, that are one with Christ by their own act, should be looked upon as one in law: what is real in the union between Christ and his people, is the foundation of what is legal.[73]

---

[72] Edwards, 19:153.
[73] Edwards, 19:158.

The believer's union with Christ is therefore seen as naturally "fit." Edwards sees the aesthetics of the relationship between the redeemer and the redeemed as one that is not only organic in nature but also reciprocally relational:

> All will allow that union with Christ, a real union, is, accord-
> ing to the gospel constitution, the condition of partaking of his
> benefits, and, I trust what none will deny, that there is a natural
> fitness in it that persons should be united to Christ, or be in
> Christ, in order to their being looked upon as his, belonging
> to him, interested in him, and so partaking with him; and that
> it would be naturally unfit that they should be looked upon
> as relatively in him or belonging to him if not really united
> to him, as if their souls or minds were not united to him; and
> that this is a requisite condition on account of the natural fit-
> ness of it; and that divine wisdom appoints it on that account.
> And yet I suppose no one will imagine that this in the least
> detracts from the freedom and sovereignty of divine grace in
> appointing the way of obtaining an interest in Christ and his
> benefits.[74]

From an Arminian perspective, God no doubt works in prevenient grace not only to enable belief but also to show the object of belief as beautiful and "fit." God's work need not render the will indifferent; it need only allow for the possibility of rejection. Of course, this Edwards was unwilling to grant.

Though he taught that the believer is justified by faith alone, he did not limit this faith to the initial conversion experience. Rather, he believed that saving faith would necessarily find its fulfillment in Christian obedience. Edwards has therefore been charged with taking up a Roman Catholic perspective of salva-tion.[75] His case is not helped by the way in which he often spoke of inherent

---

[74] Edwards, "Justification, Natural Fitness," 23:196.

[75] Shafer raises this question in "Jonathan Edwards and Justification by Faith," 59; see also Gerald R. McDermott, "Jonathan Edwards on Justification by Faith—More Protestant or Catholic?" *Pro Ecclesia* 17 (2008): 92–111; Anri Morimoto, *Jonathan Edwards and the Catholic Vision of Salvation* (University Park, PA: Penn State University Press, 1995); and Hunsinger, "Dispositional Soteriology." Douglas A. Sweeney does the best job in answering these charges. Drawing from heretofore unpublished works, he demonstrates that Edwards's emphasis on holy living was a pastoral address to a growing secular culture and the cold faith of some

righteousness or inherent merit that is "fitly" rewarded by God. We have seen how Edwards argued that there were other noncausal conditions of justification. These things, usually associated with sanctification in Protestant thought, were collapsed into justification in his view. Whereas he was concerned with neonomianism from the "Arminian" side, he was also concerned with antinomianism on the Calvinist side. His experiences in Northampton with the Halfway Covenant had led him to a firmer ecclesiology and an approach to justification that focused not on the moment of conversion but on the believer's ultimate approval by the Father: "So that not only the first act of faith, but after-acts of faith, and perseverance in faith, do justify the sinner; and that, although salvation is in itself sure and certain after the first act. For the way wherein the first act of faith justifies, is not by making the futurition of salvation certain in itself, for that is as certain in itself by the divine decree, before the first act of faith, as afterwards."[76] This "persevering faith" is the source of the believer's assurance as it is lived out in fear and trembling before God.[77]

We have seen that Edwards strove to place Christ's life and work within the context of the Trinitarian covenant of redemption. He is amazed at the beauty of God's work and its design.[78] The aesthetic ontology of the Trinity is manifested in the union the believer enjoys with Christ through faith. This union brings the two together through a free offer and an active acceptance. In this way, Christ's righteousness and death are not simply imputed but are real in the life of the believer as he or she is really united to Christ. The provision of the atonement and its application are not easily separated. They are one in the decrees of God, and they are one in the life of the believer. Edwards moved both within his Reformed tradition and beyond it in his understanding of the atonement. Nevertheless, he was always concerned with the biblical evidence and was willing to follow his speculation to new planes. It is here that Edwards can speak to us today.

---

congregants. It was an attempt to preach the whole counsel of God rather than an abandonment of Protestant ideals. Thus Edwards was catholic without being Catholic. Douglas A. Sweeney, "Justification by Faith Alone? A Fuller Picture of Edwards's Doctrine," in *Jonathan Edwards and Justification*, ed. Josh Moody (Wheaton: Crossway, 2012): 129–54.

[76] Edwards, "Perseverance, in What Sense Necessary to Salvation," 18:356.

[77] Edwards, 18:356.

[78] For a classic introduction to Edwards's aesthetics, see Roland André Delattre, *Beauty and Sensibility in the Thought of Jonathan Edwards: An Essay in Aesthetics and Theological Ethics* (New Haven: Yale University Press, 1968).

IMPLICATIONS

Edwards's View of the Atonement and the Trinity

While there are many implications that could be drawn from the broad view of the atonement presented in Edwards's writings, we will focus on four particular elements. One thing that Edwards brings to the fore is his Trinitarian framework for the atonement.[79] Too often in modern evangelical circles, the forensic view of the atonement seems to set the justice of the Father against the love demonstrated in the Son. If discussed at all, the Spirit seems an afterthought associated only with the application of the atonement. This sets up a potentially heretical division in the will and purpose of the Trinity. If Christ is loving, so is the Father. If the Father is holy, so also is the Son. Edwards's vision of the covenant of redemption between the members of the Godhead speaks to the unified will in God and the economy of redemption employed for the purpose of the atonement. The Father is not simply the Judge but the Lover who elects his Son for the purpose of redemption. The Son demonstrates his love in the passion and his justice in fulfilling the covenant of works that was broken by Adam. The Spirit, in Augustinian terms, is the love that unites the Father and the Son and the uniting principle of the believer with Christ. The Spirit calls us to love, and the inherent grace that comes to us through the Spirit allows us to satisfy God's justice.

If evangelicals would employ a similar Trinitarian framework in our discussions of the atonement, perhaps we could find fuller expression, as did Edwards, for the love of God. This is the second thing we should take away from this study. A strictly forensic understanding of the atonement highlights, rightly, God's holiness and justice. This is a biblical theme and should not be given up. At the same time, while Christ's suffering on the cross is the apex of the atonement, it is only one moment in the unfolding work of God to redeem a people for God's name. The incarnation, Christ's life, and his sufferings were

---

[79] Stephen H. Daniel does something similar to what I am proposing in his discussion of Edwards's Trinitarian theology. While he is not focusing upon the Trinitarian economy in the atonement, he expresses ways that Edwards's thought on the Trinitarian economy of revelation can contribute to an evangelical conversation and challenge to postmodern and even deconstructionist theology. See Stephen H. Daniel, "Postmodern Concepts of God and Edwards's Trinitarian Ontology," in *Edwards in Our Time: Jonathan Edwards and the Shaping of American Religion*, eds. Sang Hyun Lee and Allen C. Guelzo (Grand Rapids: Eerdmans, 1999).

all motivated by love. When we see Christ on the cross, let us see the justice of God, but let us also look beyond it to Christ's love for the Father and His love for us:

> In his last sufferings were also the highest manifestations and fruits of his love to God, for his offering up himself under those sufferings was an act of love and obedience to God and regard to his glory. God was the being to whom he offered up that sacrifice, and the gift was a gift of love to God. This sacrifice was offered in a twofold flame, viz. the flame of God's wrath, and yet (wonderful mystery) the flame of his own love to God.[80]

To discuss the atonement outside love is not only unbiblical (Rom 5:8; 1 John 4:9; John 15:13) but also drives a wedge between theology and worship and fails to allow the suffering of Christ to fulfill its role as the ultimate picture of loving sacrifice.

Edwards and Models of the Atonement

Presenting a fuller picture of the atonement in this way may help the modern evangelical church to defuse recurring modern attacks on the satisfaction view of the atonement.[81] Steve Chalke's assertion that the view is an example of cosmic child abuse comes immediately to mind, as does N. T. Wright's denial of imputation.[82] Recently, Chris Woznicki has successfully employed what he calls an "Edwardsean" model to explain how Christ's death by the will of the Father

---

[80] Edwards, "Christ's Example," 18:490.

[81] Josh Moody makes this same point and in his essay allows Edwards's voice to speak to a number of modern issues including the nature of justification by faith in light of interfaith dialogue, the new perspective on Paul, and the relationship between saving and sanctifying faith. Josh Moody, "Edwards and Justification Today," in *Jonathan Edwards and Justification*, ed. Josh Moody (Wheaton: Crossway, 2012): 17–44.

[82] Steve Chalke and Adam Mann, *The Lost Message of Jesus* (Grand Rapids: Zondervan, 2004); N. T. Wright, *Justification: God's Plan and Paul's Vision* (Downers Grove: IVP, 2009). George Hunsinger argues that Edwards's perspective on Paul and the law provides expert exegesis and "meticulous examination" that would prove a helpful guide to scholars dissatisfied with the views of E. P. Sanders and James Dunn. See also Hunsinger, "Dispositional Soteriology," 107.

is not an act of violence[83] and to defend the philosophical coherence of the penal substitution view of the atonement.[84]

If the non-necessity of the punishment of sin is understood to be the core of the governmental theory of the atonement, then neither Edwards (despite some ambiguity, as we have seen) nor Reformed Arminianism, as it has come to be known, are willing to go this far. Noted Reformed Arminian theologian F. Leroy Forlines often sought to clarify this distinction and differentiate his view of the atonement from governmental models expressed in Wesleyan theology.[85] The satisfaction view of the atonement was thus emphasized in his work but never precluded aspects of God's sovereign economy in salvation. In fact, Forlines ultimately argued that the satisfaction view of the atonement can be understood rightly only against the backdrop of God's sovereign government. In an image borrowed from Arminius's "The Priesthood of Christ," Forlines envisioned a divine council between the justice, mercy, and wisdom of God. He said,

> The justice of God demanded that the penalty of sin be paid. The love of God was interested in saving man, but it had to submit to the justice of God. The wisdom of God came forth with a plan that would satisfy both holiness and love. Through the incarnation and the substitutionary death of Christ, love could fulfill its desire to save, and holiness could hold to its insistence that sin be punished.[86]

---

[83] Chris Woznicki, "The Son in the Hands of a Violent God? Assessing Violence in Jonathan Edwards's Covenant of Redemption," *Journal of the Evangelical Theological Society* 58 (2015): 583–97.

[84] Chris Woznicki, "The Coherence of Penal Substitution: An Edwardsean Defence," *Tyndale Bulletin* 70.1 (2019): 95–115. For a fuller treatment and a similar philosophical defense, see William Lane Craig, *The Atonement* (New York: Cambridge University Press, 2018).

[85] F. Leroy Forlines, *The Quest for Truth: Theology for Postmodern Times* (Nashville: Randall House, 2001). Forlines provided an extended argument against the governmental theory of the atonement on pages 198–208 of this volume. See also his "Study of Paul's Teachings on the Believer's Death to Sin and Its Relationship to a New Life" (unpublished M.A. Thesis, Winona Lake School of Theology, 1959). In this work Forlines argued that the death of believers in union with Christ, as outlined in Romans 6, is best understood as a penal death rather than moral death.

[86] Forlines, *Quest for Truth*, 187.

Love and justice come together in Christ's sacrifice. Inasmuch as governmental aspects of the atonement are kept subservient to a penal substitution model and flow out from its center, they demonstrate the fully Trinitarian nature of redemption without violence to the divine person or biblical teaching on the doctrine.

Edwards's view of the atonement and his numerous images of it can help us in other ways as well. While the satisfaction view of the atonement is the primary image found in Scripture, it is not the only biblical image. Nor is it the only helpful image in understanding what God has done to restore a lost and broken humanity. For example, Romans 5 presents several images of the atonement, all of which speak to what Christ has done for us. The forensic view is primary (see "expiation" in 3:25 and sacrifice concepts throughout chapter 5), but Paul also uses a participationist model (vv. 1–5). Paul refers in several places throughout the chapter to Christ's mediatorial role in a reconciliation motif. A redemption/ransom view is prominent and fits in well with the following chapter's emphasis on the slavery to sin from which we have been freed. A rescue model lies behind the picture of Christ's death outlined in verses 7–8. I am simply arguing that modern evangelicals should be willing to be as broad as Edwards and as broad as Paul in outlining the story of redemption. We should, like Edwards, always maintain the priority of the satisfaction view while being willing to entertain additional analogies. This will allow us to paint a fuller picture of Christ's atonement, equip us to tell a multilayered story of personal relationships,[87] and enable us to view the gospel story from all angles of the multifaceted jewel it is.

Edwards and Imputation

It is this understanding of the atonement as a reconciliation of persons through the believer's union with Christ that will help the modern reader reflect on the numerous biblical images of union with Christ. It is through Christ that we

---

[87] On the importance of considering the personhood of God and the personhood of humanity for outlining the theology of the atonement, Forlines said, "It is important for us to remind ourselves that atonement is designed to settle a conflict between persons—God and man. We must see sovereignty as personally administered by one who thinks, feels, and acts. . . . Man is personal. Sin is an experience of the human personality in conflict with a personal God. Atonement is designed to resolve this conflict and to form the foundation for restoring holiness as the experience of human personality." Forlines, *Quest for Truth*, 184.

are ultimately united to the Father. This union both requires and provides the imputation of righteousness. Leaving aside questions of the natural or federal headship of Adam and Edwards's hesitancy to embrace traditional nomenclature, Edwards is clear on his view of Christ's atonement, insisting that it works positively and negatively, perfectly paying the penalty of human sin and providing a perfect righteousness that fulfills the requirements of God's moral law. Both these aspects of righteousness are imputed to the believer through faith.

The question of imputation has continued to be a major point of contention between Arminianism and Calvinism. Wesley's denial of imputation is well known, and his theological sway among Arminians has led many to assume that all Arminians reject Reformed concepts of imputation. This is certainly not the case. Arminius himself was traditionally Reformed in his view.[88] Early Arminian Baptists Thomas Helwys[89] and Thomas Grantham[90] taught the imputation of both the active and passive obedience of Christ to the believer. This Arminian General Baptist tradition has continued its emphasis on the satisfaction view of the penal substitutionary atonement including the imputation of Christ's death and his active obedience in distinction from traditional Wesleyan Arminianism. Noted Reformed Arminian theologians Robert E. Picirilli

---

[88] Against his accusers Arminius asserted that faith was not meritorious but served only as the "instrument through which one is imputed the merits of Christ." The language here is eerily reminiscent of Calvin and accords well with Edwards's later perspective, as we have seen. Jacob Arminius, *The Works of James Arminius*, 3 vols., trans. James Nichols and William Nichols (Nashville: Randall House, 2007), 2:51. On Arminius's traditional Reformed perspective on the imputation of the active and passive obedience of Christ, see J. V. Fesko, *Beyond Calvin: Union with Christ and Justification in Early Modern Reformed Theology (1517–1700)* (Göttingen: Vandenhoek and Ruprecht, 2012), 277, 282.

[89] Helwys said "that justification of man . . . only consists in the obedience and righteousness of Christ." Quoted in Goki Saito, "An Investigation into the Relationship between the Early English General Baptists and the Dutch Anabaptists," PhD diss., Southern Baptist Theological Seminary, 1974. See "Appendix B: Translation of Latin *Synopsis of the Faith of the True English Christians Church at Amsterdam*," 198.

[90] Thomas Grantham said, "The whole righteousness of Christ, active and passive, is reckoned as ours through believing" in his *Christianismus Primitivus, or The Ancient Christian Religion* (London: Francis Smith, 1678), Book 2, 62, 68. For a discussion of the soteriological positions of Helwys and Grantham and some reflection on their historical importance, see J. Matthew Pinson, *Arminian and Baptist: Explorations in a Theological Tradition* (Nashville: Randall House, 2016), 57–128.

and F. Leroy Forlines both championed the concept.[91] Most recently, J. Matthew Pinson has clearly articulated this position.[92]

Lately, some Wesleyan Arminians have begun teaching the imputation of what has classically been called the passive obedience of Christ (though most still deny any imputation of Christ's active obedience). Perhaps this shift has partly resulted from the sway of Thomas Oden, who taught a full-orbed doctrine of imputation.[93] Others see the shift as a partial, though complicated, response to N. T. Wright's new perspective on Paul.[94] Regardless, this question has important ramifications for theological distinctions on the nature of perseverance and apostasy and the role of faith in justification.

Pinson rightly captures the heart of the theological distinctions between Reformed Arminians and Wesleyan Arminians when he says, "These two systems agree on *how one comes to be* in a state of grace, but disagree on *what it means to be* in a state of grace."[95] While both Arminian groups hold to the possibility of apostasy, Reformed Arminianism's belief in the imputation of the righteousness of Christ necessitates that such apostasy can be committed only when the condition for union with Christ (faith) is severed. Unlike Wesleyan Arminians who hold that one's righteousness before God is dependent on

---

[91] Robert E. Picirilli, *Grace, Faith, Free Will, Contrasting Views on Salvation: Calvinism & Arminianism* (Nashville: Randall House, 2002), 164. Picirilli's use of the concept of imputation is an important component to his argument that "faith," understood biblically, is not a work. See 177–81 of this work. See also Forlines, *Quest for Truth*, 192–97. For Forlines the concept of imputation directly links the headship of Adam and of Christ and undergirds Forlines's satisfaction view of substitutionary atonement. This he defines as a major corollary of what he calls "Classical Arminianism." He says, "On atonement, Classical Arminianism is strongly committed to the penal satisfaction view. Justification is based on the imputation of the death and righteousness of Christ—that and that alone, nothing more and nothing less. The condition for receiving this justification is faith in Jesus Christ as Lord and Savior—that and that alone, nothing more and nothing less. We are saved by Christ alone on the condition of faith alone." *Quest for Truth*, xviii. See also Jesse F. Owens, "Forlines's Theology of Atonement and Justification," in *The Promise of Arminian Theology: Essays in Honor of F. Leroy Forlines*, eds. Matthew Steven Bracey and W. Jackson Watts (Nashville: Randall House, 2016), 81–100.

[92] J. Matthew Pinson, *40 Questions About Arminianism* (Grand Rapids: Kregel, 2022); see especially question 11, "Do Arminians Affirm the Imputation of Christ's Righteousness in Justification?", 97–111.

[93] Thomas C. Oden, "A Calm Answer," *Books and Culture* 7, no. 2 (2001): 13.

[94] Pinson demonstrates this connection clearly in his *40 Questions About Arminianism*, 97–98.

[95] Pinson, *40 Questions About Arminianism*, 97. Emphasis his. By "how one comes to be in a state of grace," Pinson means the active expression of repentance and faith in Christ alone, enabled by the preregenerating (or prevenient) grace of God.

sanctification, Reformed Arminians agree with Edwards (and Calvinists generally) that it is Christ alone who can provide the believer's righteousness before God. In Reformed Arminianism, then, a believer's assurance of salvation is a result of the imputation of Christ's active and passive obedience at the moment of faith rather than a reflection on the believer's inherent righteousness at any given moment.

The other theological contribution affected by the concept of imputation is the recognition of human faith as an active expression of the human will in the process of justification. While this is an active willing, it is not meritorious in regard to salvation. Edwards's discussion of faith provides a basis for *rapprochement* on this point as well, as we shall soon see.

Edwards and Justification by Faith

Just as Edwards speaks strongly to the modern evangelical scene on the atonement, he also speaks to the ongoing struggle among Calvinists and Arminians regarding justification by faith. He viewed himself as contributing to this debate. Nevertheless, on several points, I believe his writings can provide clarity and common ground for discussion. While Edwards strongly disagreed with the Arminian perspective that grace is resistible and was not above using the term "irresistible," he preferred to speak of grace as efficacious. While Arminians would not agree with Edwards on the ends of the efficacy of grace, they certainly embrace the concept that God's grace is necessary and efficacious in enabling individuals to come to a point where they may either accept or reject God's free offer of salvation. However, this was not Edwards's point. He preferred the term "efficacious" to demonstrate the active role of the person in "choosing" Christ. Edwards thus escapes the extreme fatalism so often seen in modern Calvinist treatises on this subject. We are not simply channels for God's grace but are active participants with it. Thus Edwards's point here provides a basis for ongoing discussion among modern Calvinists and Arminians. When both sides can agree that grace is necessary, faith is active, and conversion is not passive, we have a fruitful platform for discussion.

Edwards is also helpful for promoting the discussion of faith between Calvinists and Arminians. The repeated accusation Calvinists level at Arminians always seems to revolve around their claim that in the Arminian system, faith is (at least in some sense) a work. Edwards helps us here to see that though faith is active, it is not a human work by which believers merit salvation. Any merit associated with faith is entirely rooted in the imputation of Christ's righteousness. Faith is, as Edwards said, an active willing enabled by Christ. It is the union of the believer with Christ that brings salvation. Faith does not bring redemption; union with Christ does. Faith is simply the means of that union. As a means of union—or in Edwards's words, a "closing with Christ"—faith is not a work. Rather, it is an acceptance of Christ's sacrificial love. It is not an action through which Arminians believe that the individual merits salvation before God. Calvinists and Arminians would do better to discuss more substantive theological issues than whether or not faith constitutes a work.

Edwards himself was clear on this point. Building on a discussion of Rom 4:5, he argued that "the faith referred to cannot mean the same thing as a course of obedience or righteousness. In fact, *faith is equated with believing* on him that justifies the ungodly."[96] It is this faith that is "reckoned" as righteousness. It is not true righteousness in itself, because it is no "work" in itself. God's grace is free even if humanity comes to it by faith. Edwards saw faith as a "uniting act" and demonstrated that God's grace is not robbed when "the true Christian has an active part whereby he or she comes into union with Christ."[97]

Edwards's basis for redemption in one's union with Christ should also help Arminians see the assurance of salvation in a new light. While some brands of Calvinism may have another problem (antinomianism, for instance), some brands of Arminianism tend to struggle with a difficulty in establishing a strong theological basis for the assurance of salvation. Whereas I do not believe that Edwards's charge of neonomianism holds for the Arminian conceptions of salvation, in some branches of Arminianism, it does impact their belief in apostasy. Some Arminians argue that the presence of sin in the life of a believer means that the believer is not in a state of grace. In such a system, one's salvation is essentially kept by works. This certainly runs against Edwards's assertion that salvation at all times is based only on the work of Christ and appropriated by us through our union with him in faith, as Reformed Arminians posit. Thus salvation, including perseverance, is not our work but God's, and our assurance of salvation should rest in his power rather than in our frailty.

---

96 Huggins, "Jonathan Edwards and Justification," 180.
97 Huggins, 184.

Nevertheless, Edwards also provided another related lesson through the way he saw justification and sanctification as components of the same work of God. Justification can never be separated from sanctification. He pointed out that saving faith will necessarily result in holy living.[98] Christian obedience is required. While works have no merit outside our union with Christ, the grace at work in the believer aids in both willing and doing what God requires. Active, saving faith is a faith that necessarily perseveres in good works as the natural outgrowth of one's union with Christ. Legalism is ruled out because our actions can never be holy without Christ. Neonomianism fails because faith is not a work but the means of one's union with Christ, and there is no such thing as salvation that is not attended with holy living.

CONCLUSION

Jonathan Edwards lived his life committed to the love and justice of God demonstrated in the life and death of Christ. The beauty of Christ's sacrifices manifested themselves in numerous images of atonement that spoke to the "fitness" of God's work. This same "fitness" was manifested in the believer's union with Christ through faith and a life lived in humble obedience. On all these things Calvinists and Arminians agree, and if the modern evangelical church will speak these truths and live these lives, we may yet experience another "surprising work of God" in our own day.

---

[98] Huggins argues that for Edwards, justifying faith was the same fruit of grace that leads to what one might call sanctifying grace. Continuing or persevering faith is nurtured from the means of grace and Christian obedience. This obedience "does not bring justification, rather, it is an expression of faith" (187).

Chapter 5

Saints in the Hands of an Authentic Guide: Learning Piety from Jonathan Edwards

Barry Raper

When Jonathan Edwards is mentioned in Christian circles today, one often hears drastically different responses. One response is found among many in the "young, restless, and Reformed" movement: "Jonathan Edwards is my Homeboy!"[1] He is viewed by some, especially Calvinists, as the greatest theologian America has ever produced.[2] At the other end of the spectrum is a reaction that comes largely from ignorance: there are those who

---

[1] Collin Hansen was one of the first writers to draw attention to the resurgence of Reformed theology among young evangelicals in his essay "Young, Restless, and Reformed," in *Christianity Today*, September 22, 2006. Hansen's book, *Young, Restless, and Reformed: A Journalist's Journey with the New Calvinists* (Wheaton: Crossway, 2008), has on the book cover an illustration of a shirt with the picture of Edwards and the words "Jonathan Edwards is My Homeboy."

[2] John Piper, one of the most influential pastors and writers who continues to shape the Reformed movement, does not hide his admiration of Edwards. Concerning Edwards's impact on him, Piper states, "Alongside the Bible, Edwards became the compass of my theological studies. Not that he has anything like the authority of Scripture, but that he is a master of that Scripture, and a precious friend and teacher. One of my seminary professors suggested to us back in 1970 that we find one great and godly teacher in the history of the church and make him a lifelong companion. That's what Edwards has become for me. It's hard to overestimate what he has meant to me theologically and personally in my vision of God and my love for

associate Edwards only with his sermon "Sinners in the Hands of an Angry God." For these individuals, Edwards is caricatured as one of those "fire and brimstone" preachers.

It is possible, however, to suggest an approach to Edwards that is balanced, a middle ground where believers can interact critically with his entire corpus. The scope of his writings is impressive and can be beneficial for followers of Christ in the twenty-first century. Before considering a brief selection of the literature Edwards produced, it is appropriate to offer a few highlights of his life and the context of his ministry.

EARLY LIFE AND CONVERSION

Born on October 5, 1703, at East Windsor, Connecticut, Jonathan Edwards was the fifth of eleven children. His parents were Timothy and Esther Edwards. Timothy Edwards was the pastor of East Windsor's Congregational Church for more than sixty years. Solomon Stoddard, Esther's father, was an extremely influential pastor in Northampton, Massachusetts. Jonathan and his ten sisters grew up in a home shaped by pastoral ministry.[3]

Edwards's conversion to Christ most likely occurred in the spring of 1721. In his own personal narrative, looking back, he said about his encounter with the Word of God,

> [T]here came into my soul, and was as it were diffused through it, a sense of the glory of the divine being; a new sense, quite different from anything I ever experienced before. Never any words of Scripture seemed to me as these words did. I thought with myself, how excellent a Being that was; and how happy I should be, if I might enjoy that God, and be wrapt up to God in heaven, and be as it were swallowed up in him. . . . From about that time, I began to have a new kind of apprehensions and ideas of Christ, and the work of redemption, and the glorious

---

Christ." "The Pastor as Theologian: The Life and Ministry of Jonathan Edwards," http://www .desiringgod.org/resource-library/biographies/the-pastor-as-theologian.

[3] The biographical information on Edwards is taken from "Jonathan Edwards: Theologian of Revival," lectures delivered by Dr. Michael Haykin at The Southern Baptist Theological Seminary.

way of salvation by him. I had an inward, sweet sense of these things, that at times came into my heart; and my soul was led away in pleasant views and contemplations of them. And my mind was greatly engaged, to spend my time in reading and meditating on Christ; and the beauty and excellency of his person, and the lovely way of salvation, by free grace in him.[4]

The text that brought about this experience and response was 1 Tim 1:17: "Now to the King eternal, immortal, invisible, the only God, be honor and glory forever and ever. Amen." At least two things are worth noting from this testimony that would continue to be prominent in Edwards's thinking and spirituality. One is that his conversion was rooted in his encounter with Scripture; his life from that point forward was one marked by the Bible. Secondly, Edwards speaks of "an inward, sweet sense" that came into his heart. This description of God's work in the soul became a favorite expression in many of his writings.[5]

Marriage and Home Life

Edwards eventually married Sarah Pierpont on July 28, 1727. She was a great deal younger than he, yet from the outset he was impressed with her spiritual maturity. One example of this is found in the following comments concerning her:

> They say there is a young lady in [New Haven] who is beloved of that almighty Being, who made and rules the world, and that there are certain seasons in which this great Being, in some way or other invisible, comes to her and fills her mind with exceeding sweet delight, and that she hardly cares for anything, except to meditate on him—that she expects after a while to be received up where he is, to be raised out of the world and caught up into heaven; being assured that he loves her too well to let her remain at a distance from him always.

---

[4] Jonathan Edwards, *Personal Narrative* in *Letters and Personal Writings*, *The Works of Jonathan Edwards*, vol. 16, ed. George S. Claghorn (New Haven: Yale University Press, 1998), 792–93.

[5] Jonathan Edwards, *Personal Narrative*, 16:793.

There she is to dwell with him, and to be ravished with his love, favor and delight, forever. Therefore, if you present all the world before her, with the richest of its treasures, she disregards it and cares not for it, and is unmindful of any pain or affliction. She has a strange sweetness in her mind, and sweetness of temper, uncommon purity in her affections; is most just and praiseworthy in all her actions; and you could not persuade her to do anything thought wrong or sinful, if you would give her all the world, lest she should offend this great Being. She is of a wonderful sweetness, calmness and universal benevolence of mind; especially after those times in which this great God has manifested himself to her mind. She will sometimes go about, singing sweetly, from place to [place]; and seems to be always full of joy and pleasure; and no one knows for what. She loves to be alone, and to wander in the fields and on the mountains, and seems to have someone invisible always conversing with her.[6]

Though Edwards was physically attracted to Sarah, he was primarily attracted to her beauty of character. The two enjoyed a fruitful marriage and ministry together. As Michael Haykin states, "Sarah was so adept at managing the household affairs of the family that Jonathan was able to give himself unreservedly to all of the aspects of his ministry."[7] She would indeed be a busy woman in household management: Jonathan and Sarah were blessed with eleven children. On his deathbed he expressed his love for Sarah by telling two of his daughters that the union he enjoyed with Sarah was "an uncommon union which has been of such a nature, as I trust is spiritual, and therefore will continue forever."[8]

---

[6] Edwards, "On Sarah Pierpont," in *Letters and Personal Writings*, 16:789–90.

[7] Michael Haykin, *Jonathan Edwards: The Holy Spirit in Revival* (Webster, NY: Evangelical Press, 2005), 13.

[8] Samuel Hopkins, *Memoirs of the Rev. Jonathan Edwards, A.M.* (London: James Black, 1815), 188.

LEARNING FROM LOOKING BACK

Jonathan Edwards offers contemporary Christians a unique perspective. He is, without question, one of the most influential theologians in American history. Yet his theology was intricately intertwined with actual practice in and through a local church. He not only thought about the nature of the church but also was engaged in shepherding local congregations. Edwards also provides contemporary readers with a unique view into a crucial period of the church in American history. He witnessed firsthand the Great Awakening and all that followed in its wake, both authentic results and counterfeit ones. Coming from a context where spirituality was "in," Edwards has much to say to twenty-first-century American evangelicalism regarding authentic spiritual formation. In a culture where spirituality is often discussed but seldom defined, pastors can learn a great deal from Edwards, personally immersed as he was in an overly spiritualized context. How can a person judge what is authentic spirituality when "spirituality" takes on several different forms? Edwards can serve as a guide to help one answer this question.

In 1741 Edwards produced a lecture based on 1 John 4:1, "Beloved, do not believe every spirit, but test the spirits, whether they are of God" (NKJV). The address was entitled "Distinguishing Marks of the Work of the Spirit of God." A growing number of pastors in Edwards's day were opposed to some aspects of the revival. Edwards designed "Distinguishing Marks" to refute those who opposed the revival while at the same time warning against fanaticism and excesses. He also wrote the lecture for the purpose of demonstrating true tests of spirituality. Edwards stated:

> My design therefore at this time is to shew what are the true, certain, and distinguishing evidences of a work of the Spirit of God, by which we may proceed safely in judging of any operation we find in ourselves, or see in others.
>
> And here I would observe that we are to take the Scriptures as our guide in such cases: this is the great and standing rule which God has given to his church, to guide them in all things relating to the great concerns of their souls; and 'tis an infallible and sufficient rule. There are undoubtedly sufficient marks given to guide the church of God in this great affair of

judging of spirits, without which it would lie open to woeful delusion, and would be remedilessly exposed to be imposed on and devoured by its enemies: and what rules soever we may find in the Holy Scriptures to this end, we need not be afraid to trust to. Doubtless that Spirit that indited the Scriptures knew how to give us good rules, by which to distinguish his operations from all that is falsely pretended to be from him.[1]

It is worth pointing out at least two important aspects of this treatment of "judging" spiritual experience. First, this work evidently is the seminal form of a much larger and well-known treatise on the same subject, *Religious Affections*. Some of the same arguments are found in both expositions. The second distinguishing element surrounding "Distinguishing Marks" is that it was written in the same year in which Edwards preached "Sinners in the Hands of an Angry God." The Great Awakening was underway, and Edwards was not writing from a distance; he was a firsthand witness to the Awakening.

DISTINGUISHING MARKS OF AUTHENTIC SPIRITUALITY

In "Part One" of the address, Edwards spoke of nine marks that he characterized as "negative signs." He seemingly made these nine points, or signs, to solidify his position on true revival and to refute some of the growing opposition to the Great Awakening. The nine negative tests appear to have their basis in what some of the opponents of the revival were saying about this movement—experiences, in their estimation, that went against the norm. Also, it is important to emphasize that these nine marks, according to Edwards, cannot be used by either side of the revival as "proof" or "disproof." The terminology used by Edwards ("negative signs") could lead the modern reader astray. As Stephen Holmes states, "The negative sign is not as the name might suggest today, a disproof, but something that proves nothing."[10]

---

[1] Jonathan Edwards, "The Distinguishing Marks of a Work of the Spirit of God," in *The Great Awakening*, WJE, vol. 4, ed. C. C. Goen (New Haven: Yale University Press, 1972), 227–28.

[10] Stephen R. Holmes, "Religious Affections," in *The Devoted Life: An Invitation to the Puritan Classics*, ed. Kelly M. Kapic and Randall C. Gleason (Downers Grove: IVP, 2004), 288.

Take one sign as an example: both friend and foe of revival pointed to extraordinary outward displays of emotions and actions. Edwards suggested that when men and women exhibit strong emotional displays in worship, it neither proves nor disproves an authentic work of the Spirit. Edwards maintained that Scripture would allow for these types of reactions, provided they come within the bounds of the written Word. Holmes notes, "Edwards suggested the overzealous supporters and opponents of the revivals were both focusing on the same issues, and that in fact these things proved nothing either way; instead different questions needed to be asked."[11]

In the second part of the lecture, Edwards asked those different questions and laid down five signs given by the apostle John that constitute biblical tests of authentic spirituality. These signs are characterized as the "positive" signs of the work of the Spirit. The five signs are as follows: (1) a Christ-centered spirituality, (2) a sense of personal sin and desire for the kingdom instead of the world, (3) a Word-centered spirituality, (4) a growing conviction of truth, and (5) a genuine love for God.

Christ-Centered Spirituality

Edwards took the five signs or "Distinguishing Marks" in the order in which they appear in 1 John 4. Therefore, the first "test" discussed is from verses 2–3, where John speaks of the confession concerning Christ. In commenting on these verses, Edwards reasoned:

> So that if the spirit that is at work among a people is plainly observed to work after that manner, as to convince them of Christ, and lead them to Christ; more to confirm their minds in the belief of the story of Christ, as he appeared in the flesh, and that he is the Son of God, and was sent of God to save sinners, and that he is the only Saviour, and that they stand in great need of him; and seems to beget in them higher and more honorable thoughts of him than they used to have, and to incline their affections more to him; it is a sure sign that it is the true and right Spirit.[12]

---

[11] Holmes, 288.
[12] Edwards, "Distinguishing Marks," 4:250.

Here Edwards wedded both mind and heart in the confession of Christ. He argued that the Spirit is at work when people have their minds confirmed in the *biblical testimony* of Christ. Closely tied to this scriptural understanding and "higher and more honorable thoughts of him" is the work of the Spirit to "incline their affections more to him."

A Sensitivity to Sin

The next test of an authentic work of the Spirit is related to how the persons affected view personal sin. Edwards stated:

> So that we may safely determine, from what the Apostle says, that the spirit that is at work amongst a people, that is observed to work after such a manner as to lessen men's esteem of the pleasures, profits and honors of the world, and to take off their hearts from an eager pursuit after these things; and to engage them in a deep concern about a future and eternal happiness in, that invisible world, that the Gospel reveals; and puts them upon earnest seeking the kingdom of God and his righteousness; and convinces them of the dreadfulness of sin, the guilt that it brings, and the misery that it exposes to: I say, the spirit that operates after such a manner, must needs be the Spirit of God.[13]

This assessment is largely based on 1 John 4:4, where John says, "You are from God, little children, and you have conquered them, because the one who is in you is greater than the one who is in the world." In chapter 2, verses 15–17 of 1 John, the "world" has been defined as "the lust of the flesh and the lust of the eyes and the boastful pride of life" (NASB). The world is that which stands in opposition to God and his kingdom. Therefore, the logical conclusion is that the inbreaking of God's kingdom would bring about a definite stance against sin and a repudiation of the passing pleasures of this life. There is no genuine work of God's Spirit where there is not a sensitivity to sin and a genuine turning from it.

---

[13] Edwards, 4:251.

Word-Centered Spirituality

The third distinguishing mark is a high regard for the Bible as the Word of God. Edwards saw this in John's statement in 1 John 4:5–6: "They are from the world. Therefore what they say is from the world, and the world listens to them. We are from God. Anyone who knows God listens to us; anyone who is not from God does not listen to us." Edwards had already asserted that the only true grounds for assessing any spiritual work is the Bible. Once again he emphasized the centrality of the Scriptures in evaluating spirituality:

> 'Tis no valid objection against examples being made so much use of, that the Scripture speaks of the Word of God as the principal means of carrying on God's work; for the Word of God is the principal means nevertheless, as that is the means by which other means operate, and are made effectual: the sacraments have no effect but by the Word. And so it is that example becomes effectual; for all that is visible to the eye is unintelligible and vain, without the Word of God to instruct and guide the mind. 'Tis the Word of God that is indeed held forth and applied by example, as the Word of the Lord sounded forth to other towns in Macedonia and Achaia, by the example of those that believed in Thessalonica.[14]

It is the Word of God preached and lived out in experience that God uses to bring others into his kingdom. The Word of God is the "principal means of carrying on God's work." The Lord uses the example of believers and the sacraments, yet Edwards reminded the reader that "all that is visible to the eye is unintelligible and vain without the word of God to instruct and guide the mind."[15]

Conviction of Truth and Reality

There is a logical link between the third and fourth marks. Edwards maintained that if persons are led to value the Bible as the Word of God, then the work

---

[14] Edwards, 4:240.
[15] Edwards, 4:240.

of the Spirit will also bring about both deep conviction of truth and spiritual realities. He stated, "That spirit that operates in such a manner, as to cause in men a greater regard to the Holy Scriptures, and establishes them more in their truth and divinity, is certainly the Spirit of God." Edwards reminded pastors that when they observe the legitimate establishment of the truth of God's Word in their congregations, such a work can come only from God: "The Devil never would go about to beget in persons a regard to that divine Word, which God hath given to be the great and standing rule for the direction of his church in all religious matters and concerns of their souls, in all ages."[16]

Genuine Love for God

The final test Edwards employed from 1 John 4 was the "love" test. This test is obviously connected to every other test given in chapter 4. However, this test or mark of Christianity occupies more space in the apostle's writing than any other. The extended treatment of love, as a genuine sign of God's Spirit at work, enabled Edwards to state,

> Therefore this last mark which the Apostle gives of the true Spirit, he seems to speak of as the most eminent; and so insists much more largely upon it, than upon all the rest; and speaks expressly of both love to God and men; of love to men in the *1 John 4:7, 1 John 4:11*, and *1 John 4:12* verses; and of love to God in the *1 John 4:17, 1 John 4:18*, and *1 John 4:19* verses; and of both together in the two last verses; and of love to men as arising from love to God in these two last verses.[17]

Yet this love is not a vague, undefined sort of love. It is not simply the display of high emotions toward God or others. It is a love that grows out of God's self-disclosure in Christ through the Scriptures. "The Spirit excites to love on these motives, and makes *the attributes of God as revealed in the Gospel and manifested in Christ*, delightful objects of contemplation," Edwards wrote. It also leads the individual "to long after God and Christ, after their presence and

---

[16] Edwards, 4:253.
[17] Edwards, 4:256.

communion, and acquaintance with them, and conformity to them; and to live so as to please and honor them." This love calms contention between believers, providing a "spirit of peace and goodwill" and enabling acts of outward kindness and earnest desires of the salvation of others' souls. It causes a "delight in those that appear as the children of God and followers of Christ: I say when a spirit operates after this manner among a people, there is the highest kind of evidence of the influence of a true and divine spirit."[18]

In addressing the subject of love, Edwards warned about the presence of counterfeit love. There is a type of love that could be characterized as "self-love." However, love as defined by the apostle in chapter 4, according to Edwards, is

> a truly Christian love, thoroughly to distinguish it from all such counterfeits. It is love that arises from an apprehension of the wonderful riches of free grace and sovereignty of God's love to us in Christ Jesus; being attended with a sense of our own utter unworthiness, as in ourselves the enemies and haters of God and Christ, and with a renunciation of all our own excellency and righteousness. See vss. *1 John 4:9, 1 John 4:10, 1 John 4:11*, and *1 John 4:19*. The surest character of true divine supernatural love, distinguishing it from counterfeits that do arise from a natural self-love, is that that Christian virtue shines in it, that does above all others renounce and abase and annihilate self, viz. *humility*.[19]

PASSING THE TESTS IN PERSONAL LIFE

It is crucial to keep in mind that Edwards was not only concerned about legitimate scriptural tests, whereby he could judge what was happening around him. This external "proving" or "testing" was only half of his concern. He was equally focused on evaluating his own spiritual experience. He had already stated in the preface to "Distinguishing Marks": "My design therefore at this time is to shew what are the true, certain, and distinguishing evidences of a work of the

---

[18] Edwards, 4:256. Italics added.
[19] Edwards, 4:257.

Spirit of God, by which we may proceed safely in *judging of any operation we find in ourselves*, or see in others." In other words, the thought and theology in "Distinguishing Marks" and in *Religious Affections* were not only pastoral in nature but also intensely personal. As one examines Edwards's personal writings, it becomes clear that the "marks" of the Spirit of God were marks that Edwards knew not only in theory but also in personal practice.[20]

Delighting in Christ and the Word

For example, if Christ-centeredness is an indication of true spirituality, then Edwards is certainly a testimony to the possession of it. The combination of both mind and heart devoted to Christ is found in his *Personal Narrative*, where he talked about his own experience:

> From about that time, I began to have a new kind of apprehensions and ideas of Christ, and the work of redemption, and the glorious way of salvation by him. I had an inward, sweet sense of these things, that at times came into my heart; and my soul was led away in pleasant views and contemplations of them. And my mind was greatly engaged, to spend my time in reading and meditating on Christ; and the beauty and excellency of his person, and the lovely way of salvation, by free grace in him. I found no books so delightful to me, as those that treated of these subjects. Those words (*Song of Solomon 2:1*) used to be abundantly with me: "I am the rose of Sharon, the lily of the valleys." The words seemed to me, sweetly to represent, the loveliness and beauty of Jesus Christ. And the whole book of Canticles used to be pleasant to me; and I used to be much in reading it, about that time. And found, from time to time, an inward sweetness, that used, as it were, to carry me away in my contemplations; in what I know not how to express otherwise, than by a calm, sweet abstraction of soul from all the concerns of this world; and a kind of vision, or fixed ideas and imaginations, of being alone in the mountains, or some

---

[20] Edwards, "Distinguishing Marks." Italics added.

solitary wilderness, far from all mankind, sweetly conversing with Christ, and wrapt and swallowed up in God. The sense I had of divine things, would often of a sudden as it were, kindle up a sweet burning in my heart; an ardor of my soul, that I know not how to express.[21]

Once again it is instructive to see how his attention to Christ was directly tied to or mediated through his encounter with the Word of God. He stated, "And *my mind was greatly engaged*, to spend my time in *reading* and *meditating* on Christ; and the beauty and excellency of his person, and the lovely way of salvation, by free grace in him."[22] Therefore, Edwards's affection for Christ was one borne out of a proper, biblical understanding of Christ.

This Christ-centered life arose from a continual thirst for more of the Word that speaks of Christ. Contemporary readers will do well to remember *Resolution 28*, taken from his seventy *Resolutions*: "Resolved, to study the Scriptures so steadily, constantly and frequently, as that I may find, and plainly perceive myself to grow in the knowledge of the same."[23] Edwards was a man of the Book, and the Book points believers to look to Christ. In other words, to grow in the knowledge of the Scriptures is to grow in the knowledge of Christ. When believers delight in Christ, there will be a delight in the Scriptures. Edwards spoke of his love for the Word of God and how it nourished his soul: "I had then, and at other times, the greatest delight in the holy Scriptures, of any book whatsoever. Oftentimes in reading it, every word seemed to touch my heart. I felt an harmony between something in my heart, and those sweet and powerful words."[24]

Sense of Sin and Humility

There is also much evidence that Edwards took his personal sin seriously. Consider Resolution 12, "Resolved, if I take delight in it [solving a problem in

---

[21] Edwards, *Personal Narrative*, 16:793.

[22] Edwards, 16:793.

[23] Edwards, "Resolutions," 16:55. While some modern-day Christians frown on making resolutions, Edwards used resolutions to sharpen his spiritual life. These seventy resolutions were made 1722–1723 when he was only twenty-three years old. These goals were related to his personal piety.

[24] Edwards, *Personal Narrative*, 16:797.

divinity (theology), referring to Resolution 11] as a gratification of pride, or vanity, or on any such account, immediately to throw it by." Or Resolution 40, "Resolved, to inquire every night, before I go to bed, whether I have acted in the best way I possibly could, with respect to eating and drinking. *Jan. 7, 1723.*" He was fully aware of the danger Paul warns of in 1 Corinthians 9 about preaching to others without giving careful attention to personal discipline. Resolution 8 actually makes the sins of others an opportunity for humility in Edwards rather than a source of spiritual pride: "Resolved, to act, in all respects, both speaking and doing, as if nobody had been so vile as I, and as if I had committed the same sins, or had the same infirmities or failings as others; and that I will let the knowledge of their failings promote nothing but shame in myself, and *prove only an occasion of my confessing my own sins and misery to God.*"[25]

As Edwards grew closer to God, he also became more aware of the internal dimension of sin. The awareness of indwelling sin served to drive him further into a continual state of humility. In his *Personal Narrative*, he comments on this reality, "I have had a vastly greater sense of my own wickedness, and the badness of my heart, since my conversion, than ever I had before. It has often appeared to me, that if God should mark iniquity against me, I should appear the very worst of mankind." One should not conclude that the longer Edwards lived as a Christian, the more sin was manifested in his life. Yet his knowledge of the internal dimension and depth of sin was becoming greater. After an extended discussion of his heart, he stated, "It is affecting me to think, how ignorant I was, when I was a young Christian, of the bottomless, infinite depths of wickedness, pride, hypocrisy, and deceit left in my heart."[26] This increasingly greater sense of sin led Edwards to an increasingly greater awareness of the mercy and grace of God in Christ.

APPLYING EDWARDS'S TESTS TO ONE'S OWN LIFE

It is safe to assume that the five marks presented in "Distinguishing Marks" or the twelve presented in *Religious Affections* were not intended to be exhaustive, to say all that the Bible has to say about testing spiritual authenticity. However, the "tests" offered in "Distinguishing Marks" may serve as a foundation for us today when judging our own spiritual experience.

---

[25] Edwards, "Resolutions," 16:753–54, 756.

[26] These remarks came approximately eighteen or nineteen years after his conversion.

Like Edwards, Donald S. Whitney, in his book *Ten Questions to Diagnose Your Spiritual Health*, encourages believers to make a practice of diagnosing their own spiritual health. In the opening section, he suggests, "The English Puritans of 1550 to 1700 used to refer to ministers as 'physicians of the soul.' In our day, as in theirs, the timeless process of discerning one's spiritual health likewise involves questions and tests. My purpose . . . is to ask questions and suggest spiritual tests that can, by the help of the Holy Spirit, enable you to self-diagnose your spiritual health."[27]

Using the practice of questions, one may take Edwards's five marks and turn each into a tool to help diagnose/assess spiritual health. These marks would turn into questions such as, "Am I growing in my mind and heart as it relates to the person and work of Christ? Am I growing in my sense of personal sin and humility? Am I increasingly governed by God's Word? Do I have stronger convictions about the realities revealed in the Bible? Is my life displaying more love for God and others?"[28]

Every Christian would benefit from asking such questions. Pastors, who are called to be examples to their flocks, should also make it a consistent practice to monitor personal spiritual progress. For elders, by the very nature of the office, there is constant exposure to the Word of God. However, exposure to the Bible does not guarantee spiritual transformation. The nineteenth-century English preacher Octavius Winslow once remarked, "When a professing [Christian] man can read his Bible with no spiritual taste, or when he searches it, not with a sincere desire to know the mind of the Spirit in order to [walk] a holy and obedient walk, but with a merely curious, or literary taste and aim, it is sure evidence that his soul is making but retrograde movement in real spirituality."[29]

It is no wonder that Paul urged Timothy to *"pay close attention to your life and your teaching."*[30] While the public ministry of the Word is at the heart of Timothy's calling, it does not come divorced from the calling to grow in Christ. In fact, the passage in which this command is found (4:6–16) contains several

---

[27] Donald S. Whitney, *Ten Questions to Diagnose Your Spiritual Health* (Colorado Springs: NavPress, 2001), 13.

[28] The third question above is, almost verbatim, an actual heading to one of Whitney's chapters, yet it is the same idea of Edwards's test numbers three and four.

[29] Octavius Winslow, *Personal Declension and Revival of Religion in the Soul* (London: John F. Shaw, 1841), 14. This work was also quoted by Whitney, *Ten Questions*, 31–32.

[30] 1 Tim 4:16. Italics added.

imperatives that are aimed at Timothy's progression in godliness. Perseverance in these areas will ensure salvation for "both yourself and your hearers."

With such a high calling in view—to pursue Christ in a way that everyone can clearly see progress in godliness—believers could use the five tests from "Distinguishing Marks" both to monitor and to spur their progress. Therefore, these marks serve not only as the foundation of true spirituality but also provide the constant picture of the balanced and mature Christian. Followers of Christ must *continue* to progress in (1) Christ-centeredness, (2) hatred for sin, (3) Word-centeredness, (4) conviction of truth, and (5) love for God and others.

APPLYING THE TESTS TO ONE'S CONGREGATION

What would these tests/questions look like in a congregation? How could these tests/marks benefit ministry in a local church today? These questions could serve as a filter to help pastors and laity alike sift out what usually passes as infallible signs that God is really at work. Take congregational worship for example. We often hear a phrase like "the Spirit was really moving today" to describe an emotionally charged worship service. The following are just two examples of "signs" some might see as evidence that the Spirit is at work in our worship.

Raising Hands

Some argue that believers lifting their hands in worship is modeled and commanded in Scripture. The lifting of hands is certainly found frequently in the Psalter. When Paul instructs Timothy as to what is to take place within the congregation, he tells him, "I desire then that in every place the men should pray, lifting holy hands without anger or quarreling" (1 Tim 2:8, ESV). The word translated "holy" is the Greek word *hosios*. These "holy hands" are those that should be pure and clean, ones that reflect a life of piety toward God.[31] However, the emphasis in Paul's charge to Timothy seems to be not so much on the actual posture in prayer. Rather, given the context, the primary point seems to be that the lifting of hands is symbolic of the holy life the believer is living.

---

[31] Colin Brown, ed., *The New International Dictionary of New Testament Theology* (Grand Rapids: Zondervan, 1985), s.v. "holy."

When pastors look out over congregations and see hands raised in worship to God, it could be a genuine work of the Spirit, but we do not have a strong biblical basis for viewing this as the time when "finally" God is at work. On a personal level, I can remember a struggle I faced very early in the ministry. There were pastors and leaders I respected who were prone to raise their hands in corporate worship. The temptation existed for me, and sometimes I fell for it, to determine that I was not spiritual because I did not raise my hand. If pastors are not careful, this mentality can develop in our churches. It seems clear that this area would fall under Edwards's category of "negative" signs.

Space does not allow further discussion of contemporary examples of "negative" signs. However, numerous negative signs exist in the minds of people who fill the pews. Sometimes these ideas about spirituality have been embraced because pastors have communicated them from the pulpit. What these signs/marks are could be different for each congregation depending on such things as local church context, history, cultural trends, and leadership. It is crucial for pastors and their congregations to identify their particular negative signs and to move toward solid biblical tests for private and corporate spiritual experience.

Setting Aside Preaching

Consider one more example in corporate worship, this time under the category of positive signs. Occasionally, the contemporary "sign" that the Spirit of God is at work is when he is moving so powerfully that the preaching of the Bible is set aside or viewed as secondary. It is not uncommon to hear believers claiming an extraordinary movement of the Spirit, leading the service away from what had been planned into a more "direct" encounter with the Lord. This type of thinking is not unique to our current age—in fact, this development was sometimes seen in connection with revivals in the past. However, this setting aside of the Bible during times of revival came to be viewed as one of the primary ways Satan disrupted the genuine work of the Spirit.

In this regard, the Welsh revival of 1904 and 1905 provides a very instructive account. A key figure of this period was a young preacher named Evan Roberts. There were unusual claims that arose out of meetings Roberts held. He made it his practice to insist that everything done in each service was under the direct control of the Spirit. Iain Murray writes, "It was also the Spirit's leading,

Roberts believed, which accounted for his messages being short and few compared with time given to song, prayer and exhortations. Questioned on this, he would reply: 'Why would I teach when the Spirit is teaching?'"[32] This unmediated and supposed infallible communication to the people was a conviction embraced by Roberts that God was "bypassing the regular teaching ministry."[33] This "conviction" that defined Roberts's ministry did not end well. Evidence shows that eventually he suffered from some form of breakdown and also came to the conclusion, in looking back, that in many cases he had been deceived in making such bold claims.[34] Much damage had been done. As Murray notes, "Almost every possible feature of fanaticism was seen again: the supposition of immediate guidance, the claims to supernatural knowledge, the 'prayer of faith,' the allowance given to women to lead services, and not least, the practice of identifying 'converts' the instant they made a public 'decision.'"[35]

Upon reading Edwards, it seems safe to say that he would probably place the raising of hands in corporate worship under the category of *negative signs*. One could say with even greater confidence that Edwards would have judged Roberts's practice to fall squarely under the positive signs—*concluding positively that what was happening was not of the Spirit.* When preaching is set aside or is minimized in corporate worship in favor of a supposed "direct" encounter with God, then pastors and believers open themselves to nothing more than a version of Christian mysticism.

CONCLUSION

The "Distinguishing Marks" emerged within the context of revival. As Edwards witnessed many "spiritual" events and people, he found it necessary to go "to the law and the testimony" to have a solid basis for assessment. When forming a view of spirituality today, it is crucial for pastors and churches to follow the example set by Edwards, to allow the Bible to dictate what constitutes authentic spirituality, both for individuals and for local congregations. Sound theology

---

[32] Ian H. Murray, *Pentecost Today?: The Biblical Basis for Understanding Revival* (Carlisle, PA: Banner of Truth, 1998), 154–55.

[33] Murray, 154–55.

[34] Murray, 163.

[35] Murray, 161.

is needed to navigate life at all times, especially during a time when Americans are offered a "buffet" of religions and spiritual experiences.

It is also crucial to grasp that theology must include a proper understanding of revival. If persons believe that a revival brings with it manifestations of the Spirit that are different in "essence" rather than larger "measures" of what constitutes normal Christianity, then it is safe to say that the normal, ordained means of spirituality and growth for the church—the ordinary means of grace—will be set aside. Not only will God's means of spiritual transformation be dispensed with, but pastors and congregations will also open themselves up to discouragement and deceit. Discouragement will come as men and women try to "work up" a revival. The people will be deceived as the only infallible, objective guide on all spiritual matters has been exchanged for an unreliable subjective experience.

The tests offered by Edwards should be passed in congregational worship. However, true spirituality is the kind that exists outside the walls of the church. The New Testament has much to say concerning judging *the fruit of a person's life*. While Jesus warns us of having a judging spirit (Matt 7:1), it is equally clear that he expects his followers to inspect the lives that others live. Mere profession of Christianity does not guarantee possession of eternal life. The "proof" or evidences of true spiritual life are those that, in reality, cannot be hidden.

Another issue for personal and corporate assessment is time. The images used in the Bible of spiritual growth speak of a steady and somewhat slow process. There are genuine "spurts" of growth, but the tenor of Scripture points us to a journey—a long pilgrimage in which there are setbacks and victories.

Finally, even though times change, we can be grateful that Christ does not. Christians can be thankful also that the essence of Christianity and spiritual experience does not change. It is appropriate to close with a final quotation from Murray, linking once again revival and spirituality. He offers a timely reminder:

> This fact underlines an important lesson. The authenticity of any alleged revival is to be judged by the same tests by which the genuineness of all Christianity is to be tested. The normal mark of true grace consists in spiritual enlightenment producing love to God, reverence and obedience to Scripture, concern to serve Christ, personal holiness, compassion for

others and so on. If revivals consist of more of what Christians already possess, then these same characteristics of character and conduct will be eminent of every true revival. So it has proved. But where the priority of these things is passed by and other signs are introduced as proof of revival, perhaps 'miracles'—tongues, revelations, public confessions of sin, or forms of physical excitement—then mistaken assessments become a near certainty. . . . The question of proof is where the burden of proof must be laid. If the wrong things are treated as the important things then accurate discernment becomes a near impossibility. Things which are not the bedrock of normal Christianity never provide a safe test for the existence of revival, and where revivals have been claimed merely on the basis of unusual phenomena, subsequent events have almost invariably exposed the emptiness of the claim. In any alleged revival the greatest weight in the way of evidence *has to be put on those things which are always marks of the work of the Spirit.*[36]

"Jesus Christ is the same yesterday and today and forever."
Heb 13:8, ESV

---

[36] Murray, 31–32. Italics added.

Chapter 6

Ineffectual Grace in the Theology of Jonathan Edwards

J. Matthew Pinson

Jonathan Edwards adapted the traditional Puritan morphology of conversion to his Great Awakening revival preaching, emphasizing Spirit-wrought
awakenings and convictions in the lives of those being converted. This chapter
will probe Edwards's views on the Holy Spirit's role in bringing about spiritual
awakenings and convictions in the lives of those he never intends to convert.
It will note that Edwards's emphasis on such awakenings and convictions con-
trasts with the relative silence of contemporary Calvinism on the subject.

EDWARDS AND THE PURITAN
MORPHOLOGY OF CONVERSION

Timothy Edwards, Jonathan's father, bequeathed to his son a conception of
three main steps toward conversion, what scholars often refer to as the "Puritan morphology of conversion."[1] The first step toward conversion in this model
was conviction or awakening, or, as George Marsden puts it, "an awakening

---

[1] Stephen R. Yarbrough and John C. Adams, *Delightful Conviction: Jonathan Edwards and
the Rhetoric of Conversion* (Westport, CT: Greenwood, 1993), 8.

sense of a person's sad estate with reference to eternity."[2] This was the first, but insufficient, step toward conversion. "We must notice that usage," Marsden notes, "because 'awakening' is the most common term used for periodic outbreaks of religious enthusiasm in New England congregations." Yet, he stresses, an individual's awakening was "no guarantee of salvation."[3] The second step toward conversion was humiliation. Normally, according to this account, after their awakening and the enthusiasm that followed it, people would backslide into sin. This would make them aware of how terrible their sin was and of God's justice in eternally condemning them.[4] "Only then," Marsden says, "was one sufficiently prepared to reach the third step—if God graciously granted it—of receiving God's regenerating 'light,' or a 'new spirit created in them. . . . Unable to control God's grace, one could at best prepare oneself to be in a position to receive it. So the steps leading through the gradual process of conversion were steps of 'preparation.'"[5]

Edwards believed he himself had experienced conviction and awakening before his own conversion. He recalled seeking conversion after recovering from pleurisy as a young adult. But this seeking was not accompanied by the "kind of affection and delight" he had experienced during his first "awakening" as a child.[6] Yet, as Stephen Yarbrough and John Adams convincingly argue, there were differences between Edwards's morphology and that of the earlier Puritans. Edwards creatively adapted the typical Puritan morphology to fit his revival context. They quote his diary: "The reason why I, in the least, question my interest in God's love and favour is—1. Because I cannot speak so fully of my experience of the preparatory work, of which the divines speak: 2. I do not remember that I experienced regeneration, exactly in those steps, in which the divines say it is generally wrought."[7] Yet Yarbrough and Adams are quick to say, "Nevertheless, we go too far if, like David Laurence, we surmise that the difference between the expected preparatory pattern and Edwards' personal

---

[2] George Marsden, *Jonathan Edwards: A Life* (New Haven: Yale University Press, 2003), 26, citing Timothy Edwards's sermon on Acts 16:29–30, pp. 11–12, 1695, Washington University Library, cited in Kenneth Minkema, "The Edwardses: A Ministerial Family in Eighteenth-Century New England" (PhD diss., University of Connecticut, 1988), 82.

[3] Marsden, 26.

[4] Marsden, 27.

[5] Marsden, 28.

[6] Yarbrough and Adams, *Delightful Conviction*, 6.

[7] Yarbrough and Adams, 6.

experience 'eventually led him to reject the step-by-step model of conversion.'"[8] They explain that Edwards accepted the normal Puritan morphology as the ordinary or typical method of conversion.

Attendance to the Means of Grace

A key aspect of Edwards's doctrine of conversion is "seeking" or attendance to the means of grace. This process, as Conrad Cherry notes, "is itself also a means of grace. Seeking salvation is a means when it brings man to an awareness of his own helplessness and to a despair in his own strength."[9] While "intense seeking after faith—say through prayer—does not guarantee faith," it is nonetheless a means of grace. Edwards believed that it is mistaken to think that the more sinners attend to the means of grace in seeking after God, "the more they shall depend on it." Quite the contrary, Edwards argued: "The reverse is true: the more they do, or the more thorough they are in seeking, the less will they be likely to rest in their doings, and the sooner will they see the vanity of all that they do." Thus he urges sinners to seek salvation, utilizing the means of grace but knowing that "when you have done all, God will not hold himself obliged to show you mercy at last."[10]

While some scholars have said that Edwards leaned away from emphasis on the outward means of grace, Cherry correctly insists that, while safeguarding "the internals of grace in the immediate operation of the Holy Spirit," Edwards maintained that it "replaces neither the outward means of grace nor the human seeking through those means."[11] Sinners' seeking salvation through the means of grace "provides the framework within which God chooses to work by his Holy Spirit when converting man. . . . Hence means are not unnecessary, but it is the height of pride and 'vain self-flattery' for a man to believe that seeking salvation in the means will itself [without special grace] give him the salvation."[12]

---

[8]   Yarbrough and Adams, 8.
[9]   Conrad Cherry, *The Theology of Jonathan Edwards: A Reappraisal* (Garden City: Double-day, 1966), 61. All the quotations in this paragraph are from pp. 61–62.
[10]   Cherry, 61–62, citing Edwards's sermon "Pressing into the Kingdom of God."
[11]   Cherry, 61–62.
[12]   Cherry, 62.

Convictions and Awakenings

Thus, for Edwards, convictions and awakenings are the Holy Spirit's ordinary means of converting the elect. However, convictions and awakenings are not peculiar to the elect. The Holy Spirit convicts and awakens the reprobate as well. Jenson describes the normal process that Edwards believed God uses to convert the elect: converts "are first awakened with a sense of their miserable condition by nature, the danger they are in of perishing eternally, and that it is of great importance to them that they speedily . . . get into a better state."[13] Yet these awakenings and convictions are what Edwards referred to as "legal awakenings" or "legal convictions" or "legal strivings." He therefore contrasted them with the "evangelical," internal calling that God gives to his elect. These legal awakenings, convictions, and strivings of the Spirit cannot bring salvation. They can be only preparatory to salvation.[14]

Jenson explains that, for Edwards, the Holy Spirit "is here engaged in 'legal strivings' with natural religionists, wholly within the realm of that 'common grace' without which no creature can live at all."[15] However, as we will see later, the problem with this statement is that the way Edwards describes these legal awakenings, convictions, and strivings makes them more than just simple common grace that keeps the world spinning and allows sinners to perform morally good acts. Instead, Edwards portrays this grace as a careful, repeated, personal, gracious influence of the Holy Spirit, who is graciously giving the sinner repeated, special opportunities to be saved. Yet Jenson is correct in noting Edwards's distinction between this grace and the internal call God gives to the elect, that "divine and supernatural light" that dawns on them because of God's special—not common—regenerating grace. Edwards thus dichotomizes common and special grace, relating them, respectively, to the realms of nature and grace. Thus, as will be emphasized later, common grace is only the Holy Spirit assisting nature, whereas special, regenerating grace is a supernatural infusion of something that nature cannot provide.[16]

---

[13] Robert W. Jenson, *America's Theologian: A Recommendation of Jonathan Edwards* (New York: Oxford University Press, 1988), 63.

[14] Jenson, 63–64.

[15] Jenson, 64.

[16] See John E. Smith, "Religious Affections and the 'Sense of the Heart,'" in *The Princeton Companion to Jonathan Edwards*, ed. Sang Hyun Lee (Princeton, NJ: Princeton University Press, 2005), 106–7, 110–11.

EDWARDS'S VIEW OF THE SPIRIT'S
ACTIVITY TOWARD THE REPROBATE

Jonathan Edwards believed that conviction and spiritual awakening—the striv-ings of the Spirit—were necessary beginning steps in the conversion of the elect. Yet these steps were not peculiar to the elect. God also worked this way in the reprobate. The remainder of this essay will concern this activity of the Spirit with regard to the non-elect. I will call this "ineffectual grace" (a term I have never noticed in Edwards's writings). However, before we delve more deeply into Edwards's notion of ineffectual grace, it will be instructive to summarize his Calvinistic views on election and reprobation.

Edwards held to what today we would call single predestination. Thus, as Cherry puts it, Edwards's predestinarian views are "supralapsarian with regard to election and sublapsarian with regard to reprobation."[17] As Oliver Crisp explains, for Edwards, "God decrees creaturely eternal happiness antecedent to, and independently of, any foresight of good works pertaining to those crea-tures." But God's decree of reprobation is different: "It is *not* the case that God decrees creaturely eternal misery antecedent to, and independently of, any foresight of sinful works pertaining to those creatures." For Edwards, "in rep-robation, what a particular concrete individual has done is the crucial factor in their being damned," whereas what the individual has done has nothing to do with the decree of election. This is of course puzzling to Arminians, as to all non-Calvinists, especially considering Edwards's determinism. For unlike Arminians, who believe in what is often called "libertarian free will" (a term that seems to Arminians to be redundant), Edwards was a determinist. His views, as Crisp explains, "involved a version of theological determinism (the view that God determines all human action, but that all humans are free to the extent that they are not prevented from or coerced into some action)."[18]

This is what scholars often call "compatibilism" because it holds that divine determinism and human freedom are compatible. Yet, libertarians insist, the only way compatibilists can make divine determinism and human free-dom compatible is to redefine free will to mean, not *the ability to have chosen otherwise*, but rather *the ability to do what one wants to do*. In other words,

---

[17] Cherry, *Theology of Jonathan Edwards*, 56.
[18] Oliver D. Crisp, *Jonathan Edwards and the Metaphysics of Sin* (Hampshire, England: Ash-gate, 2005), 12–13.

Arminians believe that freedom is, by definition, the ability to have done some-thing other than what one did in fact do. Edwards, like other compatibilists, did not believe that individuals have such freedom. Thus compatibilists must redefine freedom as the quality of not being coerced (or at least, the Arminian would respond, not *feeling as though* one has been coerced)—the ability to do what one wants to do. Edwards simply believed that God, through regenera-tion, determined that the will of the elect would *want to* desire God.[19]

It is curious to Arminians why all Calvinists are not double predestinari-ans. If one is a divine determinist—if one accepts the compatibilist account of human freedom and divine determination of every detail of reality—then why engage in the mental gymnastics of making the decree of election anteced-ent to God's foresight of human faith, while making the decree of reprobation dependent on God's foresight of human sin? For the purposes of this chapter, however, it is enough to understand that Edwards has a deterministic account of God's relationship with his creation and thus believes that God has ordered his world in such a way that everything that comes to pass is divinely foreor-dained. This includes the fact that the Holy Spirit knows, at the moment that he is graciously convicting, awakening, and striving with the reprobate, that he will, by design, carefully withhold the grace necessary for salvation.

Reprobate People are Recipients of God's Offer of Mercy, God's Goodness, and Hope

Perhaps the best glimpse into Edwards's views on the conviction and awaken-ing that the Holy Spirit graciously gives elect and reprobate alike is his sermon on Luke 16:16, "Pressing into the Kingdom of God," which he preached in Feb-ruary 1735. In that sermon he gives several reasons why his hearers should be pressing into the kingdom. The first reason is "the extreme necessity we are in of getting into the kingdom of heaven." "We are in a perishing necessity of it," he argued, "Without it we are utterly and eternally lost." In describing this lost-ness outside the kingdom, Edwards utilized the imagery of the people who beat on the door of Noah's ark after it was shut: "All that are without this inclosure will be swallowed up in an overflowing fiery deluge of wrath. They may stand at the door and knock, and cry, Lord, Lord, open to us, in vain; they will be

---

[19] For more information on compatibilism, see J. Matthew Pinson, *40 Questions About Arminianism* (Grand Rapids: Kregel Academic, 2022), 159–66.

thrust back; and God will have no mercy on them; they shall be eternally left of him." A few lines down, he said, "It will be a gone case with them; all offers of mercy and expressions of divine goodness will be finally withdrawn, and all hope will be lost. God will have no kind of regard of their well-being; will take no care of them to save them from any enemy, or any evil; but himself will be their dreadful enemy, and will execute wrath with fury."[20]

What Edwards described here is the case of a reprobate person, someone who, by divine design, is outside the bounds of God's saving grace and, according to Edwards's doctrine of reprobation, without hope—and never had any hope. God had decided from eternity past, according to his own good pleasure, that this person would be reprobate and outside the scope of his eternal elective love, beyond the compass of his final salvific mercy. God had planned it so that this person, of necessity, never could have been the object of his saving mercy. In this way, God arranged it so that this person would be "without this inclosure" of the kingdom and thus would be "swallowed up in an overflowing fiery deluge of wrath." And when the person knocks on the door and cries for mercy, God will have no mercy on him but instead will "execute [his] wrath with fury, and will take vengeance [on him] in an inexpressibly dreadful manner." Notice that this same reprobate person, whom God has purposefully designed to be outside the scope of his saving mercy, Edwards said, is a recipient of an offer of divine mercy. At that last day "all offers of mercy and expressions of divine goodness" that have been shown to that reprobate individual "will be finally withdrawn," and "all hope will be lost."[21]

Edwards here presented a scenario that any other Christian preacher would present: Dear sinner, God has offered you mercy. He has expressed to you his divine goodness. He has given you hope. But if you resist and reject that divine offer of mercy and goodness, you will be deprived of that hope. The trouble is that, while most Christians would not see this sinner as having been designed and predetermined for reprobation—without God's saving mercy and goodness from before the foundation of the world—and thus without hope in God's eternal plan, Edwards believes just that. How can Edwards say that the reprobate

---

[20] Jonathan Edwards, "Pressing into the Kingdom of God," *Sermons and Discourses, 1734–1738, The Works of Jonathan Edwards*, vol. 19, ed. M. X. Lesser (New Haven: Yale University Press, 2001), 280–81.

[21] Edwards, 19:281.

are recipients of an offer of divine mercy? Why would God offer his mercy to people he knows cannot receive it, people to whom he can never be merciful?

The Possibility of Salvation and the Shortness of Opportunity

In the same sermon, Edwards shared some other reasons why people need to press into the kingdom of God. One reason is "the shortness and *uncertainty of the opportunity* to getting into this kingdom." Edwards was warning his hearers that they have only a brief window of opportunity to get into the kingdom: "Our day is limited. God has set our bounds, and we know not where." People outside the kingdom "are in danger every hour of being overtaken with wrath" and so should press into the kingdom before their opportunity comes to an end.[22]

Another reason is the "*possibility* of obtaining. Though it be attended with so much difficulty, yet it is not a thing impossible." Edwards insisted that

> However sinful a person is, and whatever his circumstances are, there is notwithstanding a possibility of his salvation; he himself is capable of it, and God is able to accomplish it, and has mercy sufficient for it; and there is sufficient provision made through Christ, that God may do it consistent with the honor of his majesty, justice, and truth: so that there is no want either of sufficiency in God, or capacity in the sinner, in order to this: the greatest and vilest, most blind, dead, hard-hearted sinner living, is a subject capable of saving light and grace. Seeing therefore there is such necessity of obtaining the kingdom of God, and so short a time, and such difficulty, and yet such a possibility, it may well induce us to press into it (*Jonah 3:8–9*).[23]

Again, these two reasons sound like something that any Christian preacher would say: God has made it possible, through his grace, for you to repent and believe, but you have only a brief opportunity. So do it now! Yet there were

---

[22] Edwards, 19:281. Italics added.
[23] Edwards, 19:281–82.

reprobate people among Edwards's hearers. He was telling them that it was possible for them to be converted and that they needed to repent and believe at that very time, while they have an opportunity, even though they are reprobate. But does his doctrine of reprobation allow him to do this consistently? Is it possible for the reprobate to be converted? Do they have even a short opportunity? Or has God predetermined to give them no opportunity?

Edwards's aim in this sermon was to exhort "all Christless persons to press into the kingdom of God." In doing so, he was sensitive to his hearers' need to know how it is that they are supposed to press into the kingdom:

> Some of you are inquiring what you shall do. You seem to desire to know what is the way wherein salvation is to be sought, and how you may be likely to obtain it: you have now heard the way that the holy Word of God directs to. Some are seeking, but it can't be said of them that they are pressing into the kingdom of heaven. There are many that in time past have sought salvation, but not in this manner, and so they never obtained, but are now gone to hell: some of them sought it year after year, but failed of it, and perished at last: they were overtaken with divine wrath, and are now suffering the fearful misery of damnation, and have no rest day nor night, having no more opportunity to seek, but must suffer and be miserable throughout the never-ending ages of eternity. Be exhorted therefore not to seek salvation as they did, but let the kingdom of heaven suffer violence from you.[24]

Edwards again employed the category of attending to the means of grace, insisting that, though God's gracious influence is necessary for one to press into the kingdom of God, that influence comes through attending to the means of grace. "It is true, persons never will be thoroughly engaged in this business unless it be by God's influence; but God influences persons by means. Persons are not stirred up to a thorough earnestness without some considerations that move them to it."[25]

---

[24] Edwards, 19:282–83.
[25] Edwards, 19:283.

Edwards explained to his hearers that "if ever God bestows mercy upon you, he will use his sovereign pleasure about the *time when*. He will bestow it on some in a little time, and on others not till they have sought it long." He warned his hearers not to grow impatient because others are being converted more quickly than they—"soon enlightened and comforted, while you remain long in darkness." Such an individual needs to "be content to wait, in a way of laborious and earnest striving, till his time comes."[26]

Then Edwards said something that sounds frankly Arminian: "If you refuse, you will but undo yourself; and when you shall hereafter find yourself undone, and see that your case is past remedy, how will you condemn yourself for foregoing a great probability of salvation, only because you had not patience to hold out, and was not willing to be at the trouble of a persevering labor!"[27] Most hearers would hear this as saying, Do not stop attending to the means of grace if God does not choose to bring about your conversion quickly, as he seems to do with others. If you do, you will undo yourself and see that your case cannot be remedied. You will see that you have foregone your conversion, which was very probable. An Arminian preacher could say this. What is notable is that Edwards would give the impression that *it could have been otherwise* for the reprobate whose case cannot be remedied *if the individual had not refused.* Yet Edwards knew that it is necessary, in his concept of the divine arrangement of the world, for reprobates to refuse.

Individuals Who Respond to God's Merciful Assistance Will Probably Overcome

Edwards specified that "there is a great probability, that in a way of hearkening to this counsel, you will live; and that by pressing onward, and persevering, you will at last, as it were by violence, take the kingdom of heaven. Those of you who have not only heard the directions given, but shall, through God's merciful assistance, practice according to them, are those that probably will overcome."[28] What is extraordinary about this is that Edwards was saying that there were some among his hearers who would, through God's merciful assistance, practice the directions Edwards was giving in his sermon. But even these will

---

[26] Edwards, 19:288.
[27] Edwards, 19:288.
[28] Edwards, 19:290.

only "*probably* overcome."[29] Therefore, God is giving his "merciful assistance" to some people whom he has predetermined will not overcome.

God Pours Out His Spirit on the Reprobate, Giving Them an Opportunity to Be Saved

Another remarkable feature of Edwards's preaching here, and his theology of revival in general, is that he believed God was pouring out his Spirit among the elect and reprobate alike. He declared:

> God is pleased at this time, in a very remarkable manner, to pour out his Spirit amongst us; (glory be to his name therefor!). You that have a mind to obtain converting grace and to go to heaven when you die, now is your season![30] Now, if you have any sort of prudence for your own salvation, and have not a mind to go to hell, improve this season! Now is the accepted time! Now is the day of salvation! You that in time past have been called upon, and have turned a deaf ear to God's voice, and long stood out and resisted his commands and counsels, hear God's voice to-day, while it is called to-day! Don't harden your hearts at such a day as this! Now you have a special and remarkable price put into your hands to get wisdom, if you have but a heart to improve it.[31]

The difficulty with this is that Edwards was imploring people to take advantage of this special moment of the pouring out of God's Spirit while they had the opportunity. They had the opportunity that very moment, "if [they] have but a heart to improve it." However, Edwards knew that there were some in his

---

[29] This contradicts John Gerstner's statement, in interpreting Edwards's use of terms such as "possible" and "probable" in "Pressing into the Kingdom," that Edwards believed "any serious seeking would probably issue in salvation." John H. Gerstner, *Steps to Salvation: The Evangelistic Message of Jonathan Edwards* (Philadelphia: Westminster, 1960), 101–2, cited in Cherry, *Theology of Jonathan Edwards*, 228, n. 28. Italics added.

[30] As an aside, note Edwards's use of the traditional language of "go to heaven when you die," in light of the (I think unfortunate) insistence of scholars like N. T. Wright that we need to get away from such language.

[31] Edwards, "Pressing into the Kingdom," 19:291.

hearing whom God has not given a heart to improve it. So, the question presses on us: Why was Edwards implying in this sermon that those who turn a deaf ear to God could have done, should have done, otherwise and will be held accountable for not having done otherwise? And for what purpose—to what end—is God pouring out his Spirit on them, giving them an opportunity to be saved, if he has arranged the universe in such a way as purposefully to prohibit them from "improving it"?

Edwards stressed throughout this sermon the need for sinners to respond at that moment, not to wait, because God was giving them a special opportunity in pouring out the Holy Spirit so extraordinarily. Edwards referred to this as "a day of God's gracious visitation" and "a day of grace." Even though Edwards believed there are special times of outpouring of the Holy Spirit, he mentioned the fact that God's grace is with people throughout life. But "such a time as this is especially, and in a distinguishing manner, a day of grace." And in such special days of grace, he emphasized, "God opens an extraordinary door." Later in the sermon, he said that this was a time "wherein God doth more liberally bestow his grace, and so a time of greater advantage for obtaining it."[32]

Referring to Isaiah 55, Edwards implored his hearers to "seek the Lord while he may be found, and to call upon him while he is near." He declared to his hearers that if they are not "strangely besotted and infatuated," they will "by all means improve such an opportunity as this to get to heaven, when heaven is brought so near, when the fountain is opened in the midst of us in so extraordinary a manner."[33] Edwards stressed to his readers:

> Now is the time to obtain a supply of the necessities of your poor perishing souls! This is the day for sinners that have a mind to be converted before they die, when God is dealing forth so liberally and bountifully amongst us; when conversion and salvation work is going on amongst us from Sabbath to Sabbath, and many are pressing into the kingdom of God! Now do not stay behind, but press amongst the rest! Others have been stirred up to be in good earnest, and have taken heaven by violence; be entreated to follow their example, if you

---

[32] Edwards, 19:291, 295.
[33] Edwards, 19: 292.

would have a part of the inheritance with them, and would not
be left at the great day, when they are taken![34]

Edwards said that his hearers had this divinely provided opportunity in their hands: "How should it move you to consider that you have this opportunity now in your hands! You are in the actual possession of it!" In a remarkable statement, he said that, if the divine opportunity passed by, "it would not be in your power to recover it." However, he stated,

> It is not past; it is now, at this day. Now is the accepted time, even while it is called to-day! Will you sit still at such a time? Will you sleep in such a harvest? Will you deal with a slack hand, and stay behind out of mere sloth, or love to some lust, or lothness to grapple with some small difficulty, or to put yourself a little out of your way, when so many are flowing to the goodness of the Lord? You are behind still; and so you will be in danger of being left behind, when the whole number is completed that are to enter in, if you do not earnestly bestir yourself!"[35]

Later in the sermon, Edwards revisited this theme of opportunities, warning discouraged souls not to worry that they no longer have an opportunity to be saved: "If you lament your folly in neglecting and losing past opportunities," he averred, "then don't be guilty of the folly of neglecting the opportunity which God now gives you. This opportunity you could not have purchased, if you would have given all that you had in the world for it. But God is putting it into your hands himself, of his own free and sovereign mercy, without your purchasing it. Therefore when you have it, don't neglect it."[36]

God is Calling Reprobates

At one point in the sermon, Edwards spoke directly to his listeners and told them, "God is now calling you in an extraordinary manner," and he earnestly

---

[34] Edwards, 19:292.
[35] Edwards, 19:301.
[36] Edwards, 19:301–2.

begged them to press into the kingdom: "Don't stand making objections, but arise, apply yourselves to the work! Do what you have to do with your might. Christ is calling you before, and holding forth his grace, and everlasting benefits, and wrath is pursuing you behind, wherefore fly for your life, and look not behind you!"[37] Here Edwards moved from a more general divine calling to the specific calling of Christ: it is Christ who is calling those under the sound of Edwards's voice. Christ is holding forth his grace. He is holding forth his everlasting benefits to these people, not just to the elect, but to them all. Here Edwards preached straightforwardly just as any Christian preacher would. It reminds me of an old hymn:

> Jesus is tenderly calling thee home—
> Calling today, calling today!
> Why from the sunshine of love wilt thou roam,
> Farther and farther away?

> Jesus is waiting, O come to Him now!
> Waiting today! Waiting today!
> Come with thy sins, at His feet lowly bow;
> Come, and no longer delay.

> Jesus is pleading, O list to His voice!
> Hear Him today! Hear Him today!
> They who believe on His name shall rejoice:
> Quickly arise, come away!

> Calling today! Calling today!
> Jesus is calling, is tenderly calling today![38]

---

[37] Edwards, 19:292.

[38] Fanny J. Crosby, "Jesus is Calling," *Free Will Baptist Hymnal* (Ayden, NC: Free Will Baptist Press, 1958), no. 314. Public domain.

God Knocks at People's Doors Who Will Reject Him

Another image Edwards used in "Pressing into the Kingdom" to describe God's common grace is that of God's knocking on the door of people's hearts.[39] In this sermon Edwards told his auditors that God was specifically knocking on their doors that very day. He was coming "in a very unusual manner amongst us." He was coming to these sinners not just in his word and sacraments, Edwards said, but "by the particular influences of the Spirit of Christ awakening you!" Edwards emphasized to his listeners that Christ was making a special offer to them, and then he reassured them: "You are not passed over. Christ has not forgot you; but has come to your door and there as it were stands waiting for you to open to him." Then Edwards stated, "If you have wisdom and discretion to discern your own advantage, you will know that now is your opportunity." Why is Christ coming this day in an unusual manner, knocking on the door of sinners' hearts, waiting patiently for them to come to him? It is because he has graciously and mercifully designed it or planned it, "upon a gracious and merciful design, a design of saving a number of poor miserable souls out of a lost and perishing condition, and of bringing them into a happy state, in safety from misery, and a title to eternal glory!"[40]

One might object here, "But Edwards was not talking to the reprobate, but to those who will eventually be converted." On the contrary, Edwards made it clear that he was preaching to both elect and reprobate: he stated plainly that there were "probably some here present" who were "concerned about their salvation" who "never will obtain." Not all those who "are now moved and awakened" would be converted. "Doubtless there are many now seeking that will not be able to enter." These are the reprobate, who, even in the midst of the outpouring of the Holy Spirit, when they "inquired with others, what they should do to be saved," failed to do so and grew "hard and secure." All of his hearers that were "now awakened" and had "a mind to obtain salvation . . . probably hope to get a title to heaven, in the time of this present moving of God's Spirit." Yet Edwards had "no reason to think any other, than that some of you will burn

---

[39] It is ironic that Edwards used this language, given the number of discussions I have had with Calvinist friends in which they decried the use in evangelistic literature of Rev 3:20 on the grounds that Jesus does not stand at the sinner's door and knock. Regardless of one's interpretation of that particular passage, which may indeed not be referring to sinners, Edwards eagerly tells the sinners in his hearing that Jesus is knocking on their door.

[40] Edwards, "Pressing into the Kingdom," 19:293.

in hell to all eternity." So, clearly for Edwards, though he did not call them reprobate here, he was preaching to the reprobate, as well as to many who would
eventually be converted.[41]

The Reprobate are Held Accountable for Not Responding to Christ's Gracious Calling

In one of the most striking passages in this sermon, Edwards told his hearers that God the Judge would strictly hold the reprobate accountable for not
improving the special opportunity he was giving them to be saved. They had
every opportunity: God had "set open the fountain of his grace." He had "so
loudly called upon them." He had come to them and had "[striven] with them
in particular, by the awakening influences of his Spirit." Thus they would "have
no good account to give to the Judge, but their mouths will be stopped, and
they will stand speechless before him." The reality of this accountability before
the divine judge should make sinners earnest about their need of salvation:
"You had need therefore to be earnest, and very resolved in this affair, that you
may not be one of those who shall thus fail, that you may so fight, as not uncer-
tainly, and so run, as that you may win the prize."[42]

Edwards went on to say that, after times of "extraordinary effusion of God's
Spirit," God often leaves the unconverted in a harder condition than before
these gracious times. At the beginning of these times of grace, these individuals
are in "a doleful [condition], because in a natural condition." Yet afterwards
they are

> left dreadfully hardened, and with a great increase of guilt,
> and their souls under a more strong dominion and possession
> of Satan. And frequently seasons of extraordinary advantage
> for salvation, when they pass over persons, and they do not
> improve them, nor receive any good in them, seal their dam-
> nation. As such seasons leave them, God forever leaves them,
> and gives them up to judicial hardness.

---

[41] Edwards, 19:294.
[42] Edwards, 19:295.

Therefore, Edwards exhorted his listeners to "improve this opportunity, while God is pouring out his Spirit . . . and while you dwell in that place where the Spirit of God is thus poured out, and you yourself have the awakening influences of it, that you may never wail and gnash your teeth in hell, but may sing in heaven forever, with others that are redeemed from amongst men, and redeemed amongst us."[43]

These are people whom Christ has called and awakened, whom God by his gracious influences on them in particular has placed in an environment where he has poured out his Spirit on them. Yet they are people whom God has determined will ultimately resist and reject Christ. Edwards said that they will have their judgment enlarged because they refused to respond to the gospel, and believers will rise as witnesses against them at the judgment: "Your neighbors, your relations, acquaintances, or companions that are converted, will that day appear against you. . . . They will rise up against you as witnesses, and will declare what a precious opportunity you had, and did not improve." The specific charge that will be made by these witnesses is that the reprobate individual "continued unbelieving, and rejecting the offers of a Savior, when those offers were made in so extraordinary a manner." Yet the individual "was negligent and slack, and did not know the things that belonged to your peace, in that your day. And not only so, but they shall be your judges, your assessors with the great Judge."[44]

"God's Spirit Shall Not Always Strive with Man"

In this sermon as in other places, Edwards used Gen 6:3, "God's Spirit shall not always strive with man," to emphasize the shortness of the opportunity people have to be saved.[45] This verse was commonly used in traditional Arminian preaching, in which the preacher would call on the sinner not to resist the striving of the Holy Spirit. John Wesley's protégé Adam Clarke, for example, stated:

> It is only by the influence of the Spirit of God that the carnal mind can be subdued and destroyed; but those who willfully resist and grieve that Spirit must be ultimately left to the

---

[43] Edwards, 19:295–96.
[44] Edwards, 19: 297–98.
[45] Edwards, 19:302.

hardness and blindness of their own hearts, if they do not repent and turn to God. God delights in mercy, and therefore a gracious warning is given. Even at this time the earth was ripe for destruction; but God promised them one hundred and twenty years' respite: if they repented in that interim, well; if not, they should be destroyed by a flood.[46]

Edwards preached on this theme in his sermon "The Manner in Which the Salvation of the Soul, Is to be Sought."[47] He urged on his hearers: "Men must . . . be diligent in the use of the means of grace" now, while they have an opportunity, for "the Spirit of God will not *always* strive with you."[48] For the people who rejected Noah's message, "it was a day of grace with them, and God's long-suffering all this while waited upon them. . . . All this while they had an opportunity to escape, if they would but hearken and believe God."[49] Just as with those people, who vainly knocked on the door of the ark after the floodwaters began to rise, Edwards preached to his hearers:

> So it will be with you, if you continue to refuse to hearken to the warnings which are given you. Now God is striving with you; now he is warning you of the approaching flood, and calling upon you Sabbath after Sabbath. Now the door of the ark stands open. But God's Spirit will not always strive with you; his long-suffering will not always wait upon you. There is an appointed day of God's patience, which is as certainly limited as it was to the old world. God hath set your bounds, which you cannot pass. Though now warnings are continued in plenty, yet there will be *last* knocks and *last* calls, the last that

[46] Adam Clarke, *The Holy Bible . . . The Text . . . with a Commentary and Critical Notes* (New York: T. Mason and G. Lane, 1837), 1:66.

[47] Jonathan Edwards, "The Manner in Which the Salvation of the Soul, Is to be Sought," *The Works of President Edwards*, 4 vols. (New York: Robert Carter, 1879), 4:368–80; see also Jonathan Edwards, *Sermons, on the following subjects; The manner in which salvation is to be sought. . . .* (Hartford: Hudson and Goodwin, 1780), 7–36.

[48] Edwards, "The Manner in Which the Salvation of the Soul, Is to be Sought," 4:371; Edwards, *Sermons, on the following subjects,* 14.

[49] Edwards, "The Manner in Which the Salvation of the Soul, Is to be Sought," 4:373; Edwards, *Sermons, on the following subjects,* 31.

ever you shall hear. When the appointed time shall be elapsed, God will shut the door, and you shall never see it open again; for God shutteth, and no man openeth.—If you improve not your opportunity before that time, you will cry in vain, "Lord, Lord, open to us." (Matt. xxv. 11, and Luke xiii. 25, &c.) While you shall stand at the door with your piteous cries, the flood of God's wrath will come upon you, overwhelm you, and you shall not escape. The tempest shall carry you away without mercy, and you shall be forever swallowed up and lost.[50]

In this context, Edwards revisited his theme of one's judgment being enlarged for not heeding the warnings of the Spirit. Those individuals who continually "neglect [their] own salvation," when they have been "abundantly warned of the approaching storm of divine vengeance," will receive an ever greater judgment for refusing, in their folly and madness, to "hearken" to the warnings God has so graciously repeated to them. He continued, "You have been once more warned to-day, while the door of the ark yet stands open. . . . Take heed therefore that you do not still stop your ears, treat these warnings with a regardless heart, and still neglect the great work which you have to do, lest the flood of wrath suddenly come upon you, sweep you away, and there be no remedy."[51]

The Spirit's Conviction of Unregenerate People Is Different from Regeneration

In his famous sermon, "A Divine and Supernatural Light, Immediately Imparted to the Soul by the Spirit of God," Edwards distinguished between these convictions and the inward calling that the Spirit gives to the elect: "Those convictions that natural men may have of their sin and misery is not this spiritual and divine light." Such conviction "may be from the Spirit of God" yet only as "assisting natural principles, and not as infusing any new principles." Edwards gave this conviction the name "common grace." Yet, again, he insisted that "common

---

[50] Edwards, "The Manner in Which the Salvation of the Soul, Is to be Sought," 4:379; Edwards, *Sermons, on the following subjects*, 32.
[51] Edwards, "The Manner in Which the Salvation of the Soul, Is to be Sought," 4:380; Edwards, *Sermons, on the following subjects*, 36.

grace differs from special, in that it influences only by assisting of nature; and not by imparting grace, or bestowing any thing above nature." So the light of common grace is "wholly natural," not superior to the light of nature.[52]

Interestingly, however, he argued that the light of common grace is more "than would be obtained if men were left wholly to themselves." The question arises, Why is it that the Holy Spirit brings his grace to bear on people to assist natural principles? Why is this necessary if he does not bestow anything above nature, and if his common grace is more than people would obtain if left altogether to themselves?[53]

Of course, this is the whole problem with Calvinism's understanding of divine calling. There is a general call for everyone and a special call for the elect. However, the real problem comes when the Holy Spirit is exercising grace on people that is more than they would ever obtain if left to themselves. This is said to be a unique opportunity for them that they must improve on, or hell will be hotter for them. Why would God, knowing they will be passed over and not given the ultimate opportunity to be saved, give them a temporal opportunity to be saved through the convicting work of his Spirit? Such an action by God would amount to giving them more grace than they would have by nature alone.

Calvinists often reprint and quote from this sermon, concerning as it does the Calvinist concept of effectual calling or regeneration. Yet the two sermons cited previously, which deal with preparatory stages toward conversion given by God to elect and reprobate alike, seem to be comparatively neglected by contemporary Calvinists.

Edwards went on to state that, in common grace, the Holy Spirit, in convicting unregenerate people, "assists conscience to do this work in a further degree than it would do if they were left to themselves; he helps it against those things that tend to stupify [*sic*] it, and obstruct its exercise." But this grace is to be distinguished from the "sanctifying work of the Holy Ghost," in which "those things are wrought in the soul that are above nature, and of which there is nothing of the like kind in the soul by nature."[54] But why? Why does the

[52] Jonathan Edwards, "A Divine and Supernatural Light, Immediately Imparted to the Soul by the Spirit of God," in *Sermons and Discourses, 1730–1733*, WJE, vol. 17, ed. Mark Valeri (New Haven: Yale University Press, 1999), 410.
[53] Edwards, 17:410.
[54] Edwards, 17:411.

Holy Spirit go to such great lengths to convict people of sin and awaken them with his influences, thus assisting their consciences to help them against those things that stupefy and obstruct the exercise of their conscience, if he has no intention of graciously giving them the ability to repent and believe?

Edwards believed that the Holy Spirit acts in a different manner in the elect than he does in the reprobate. In the case of the reprobate, the Holy Spirit, for Edwards, is only "an extrinsic occasional agent; for in acting upon them he doth not unite himself to them; for notwithstanding all his influences that they may be the subjects of, they are still 'sensual, having not the Spirit' (*Jude 19*)." However, he "unites himself with the mind of" the elect, making the elect "his temple, actuat[ing] and influenc[ing] him as a new supernatural principle of life and action."[55]

Edwards was clear that the Holy Spirit acts on unregenerate people's minds in diverse ways, but he "communicate[s] himself no more than when he acts upon an inanimate creature." The Holy Spirit may "excite thoughts in them, assist their natural reason and understanding, or may assist other natural principles, and this without any union with the soul, but may act, as it were, as upon an external object." However, with the regenerate, the Holy Spirit's actions are "spiritual operations," in which he peculiarly communicates himself to the elect. In speaking of the divine, supernatural light that shines on the elect in regeneration, it is interesting that Edwards earlier referred to common grace as "light." Yet Edwards exhorted everyone "earnestly to seek this spiritual light" of regeneration.[56]

The Holy Spirit Enlightens, Influences, and Illuminates the Reprobate

In his famous *Treatise Concerning Religious Affections*, Edwards noted that, in conviction, the Holy Spirit is enlightening, influencing, and illuminating people, including both elect and non-elect people. "There is a degree of conviction of the truth of the great things of religion," he said, "that arises from the common enlightenings of the Spirit of God." He remarked that those "lively and sensible apprehensions" of religious things that "natural men have who are under awakenings and common illuminations" will give "some degree of conviction of the truth of divine things, beyond what they had before they were

---

[55] Edwards, 17:411.
[56] Edwards, 17:411, 423.

thus enlightened." He also spoke of these people—the "natural man"—as being under "the common influence of the Spirit of God," having "much greater conviction" of God's words and works, as well as "the lively apprehension" of his greatness.[57]

This increased conviction and vital apprehension will tend to make them feel guilty for their sin and afraid of divine wrath, but it will also tend "to cause them more easily and fully to believe the revelation the Scripture makes of another world, and of the extreme misery it threatens, there to be inflicted on sinners." Edwards went on to describe these Spirit-produced convictions and enlightenings and influences as "common illuminations" that cause people to be "more induced to believe the truth of religion." Yet he clearly distinguished these from actual regeneration: "These things persons may have, and yet have no sense of the beauty and amiableness of the moral and holy excellency that is in the things of religion; and therefore no spiritual conviction of their truth. But yet such convictions are sometimes mistaken, for saving convictions, and the affections flowing from 'em, for saving affections."[58]

Ironically, Edwards believed that among the reprobate people who have been under these enlightening influences of the Holy Spirit are the apostates spoken of as having been enlightened in Hebrews 6:

> There the Apostle in the beginning of the chapter, speaks of them that have great common illuminations, that have been enlightened, and have tasted of the heavenly gift, and were made partakers of the Holy Ghost, and have tasted the good Word of God, and the powers of the world to come, that afterwards fall away, and are like barren ground, that is nigh unto cursing, whose end is to be burned: and then immediately adds in the 9th verse (expressing his charity for the Christian Hebrews, as having that saving grace, which is better than all these common illuminations): "But beloved, we are persuaded better things of you, and things that accompany salvation; though we thus speak."[59]

---

[57] Jonathan Edwards, *Religious Affections*, WJE, vol. 2, ed. Paul Ramsey (New Haven: Yale University Press, 1959), 308. As will be seen below, Edwards sees the "enlightening" of Heb 6:4 as the enlightening of the reprobate.
[58] Edwards, 2:308–9.
[59] Edwards, 2:408.

There Is a Difference between Legal and Evangelical Humiliation

Discussing the second stage in the Puritan morphology of conversion—humil-iation—Edwards distinguished between legal humiliation and evangelical humiliation. The subjects of legal humiliation, according to Edwards, are "yet in a state of nature, and have no gracious affections," while evangelical humili-ation is "peculiar to true saints." Legal humiliation is "from the common influ-ence of the Spirit of God, assisting natural principles, and especially natural conscience," while evangelical humiliation arises "from the special influences of the Spirit of God, implanting and exercising supernatural and divine princi-ples."[60] In a "legal humiliation," Edwards explained,

> the conscience is convinced; as the consciences of all will be most perfectly at the Day of Judgment: but because there is no spiritual understanding the will is not bowed, nor the inclina-tion altered: this is done only in evangelical humiliation. In legal humiliation men are brought to despair of helping themselves; in evangelical, they are brought voluntarily to deny and renounce themselves: in the former they are subdued and forced to the ground; in the latter, they are brought sweetly to yield, and freely and with delight to prostrate themselves at the feet of God.
>
> Legal humiliation has in it no spiritual good, nothing of the nature of true virtue; whereas evangelical humiliation is that wherein the excellent beauty of Christian grace does very much consist.[61]

There Is a Back-and-Forth Exchange between the Holy Spirit and Those He Is Humbling

In his "Narrative of Surprising Conversions," Edwards portrayed the Holy Spirit, in this stage of legal humiliation, as being in a back-and-forth relationship with the unregenerate. In this back-and-forth activity, the Spirit is graciously giving them a strong conviction of sin, and they are becoming miserably sorrowful

---

[60] Edwards, 2:311.
[61] Edwards, 2:312.

over their sin and seeking him more diligently. Edwards stated, "Under the sense which the Spirit of God gives them of their sinfulness, they often think that they differ from all others; their hearts are ready to sink with the thought, that they are the worst of all, and that none ever obtained mercy that were so wicked as they." Frequently, "under first awakenings," he said, God leads sinners to reflect on their past sins and leads them to have a "terrifying sense of God's anger." They then often try to live more strictly, confessing their sins and doing their duty, hoping to appease God and make up for their sins. They prayerfully weep and cry out to God, confessing their sins, making much of these confessions, "as though [the confessions and prayers] were some atonement, and had power to move correspondent affections in God too." During these times they have great expectations of a move of God; they feel they are growing and will be converted soon. However, Edwards says, "these affections are but short-lived, they quickly find that they fail."[62]

The Holy Spirit continues influencing them with common grace through all this. They "renew their attempts again and again; and still as their attempts are multiplied, so are their disappointments." They continue praying to God to incline his heart to them, expecting that he will hear their prayer, but he does not. This sometimes makes them tempted to stop seeking God and give up. They continue to struggle with the fear of dying in their sins. Gradually their "former hopes of their religious affections" turn into anger against God because of his lack of pity, his lack of "regard to their distress and piteous cries, and to all the pains they take." Then, when they think of others to whom God has shown mercy, who seemed worse than they are, they sometimes have "dreadful blasphemous thoughts."[63]

Then, as the Holy Spirit continues to convict them, "*not provoked utterly to forsake them*," they begin to feel guilty for these feelings, even fearing they may have committed the unpardonable sin and that God will never show them mercy. This often tempts them to give up in despair. Next, "perhaps, by something they read or hear of the infinite mercy of God, and all-sufficiency of Christ for the chief of sinners," they are encouraged and renewed in their hope that they might be converted. But they feel they are so wicked that Christ will never accept them. This only leads them to try to engage in "fruitless endeavors

---

[62] Jonathan Edwards, "A Faithful Narrative of the Surprising Work of God," in *The Great Awakening*, *WJE*, vol. 4, ed. C. C. Goen (New Haven: Yale University Press, 1972), 164.
[63] Edwards, 4:165.

in their own strength to make themselves better." This leads to greater disappointments, and the cycle continues.[64]

Even though the Holy Spirit is busy influencing them and convicting them of sin and making them feel miserable for it, even though he has created this special opportunity for them and is calling them, they cannot be converted. They "wander about from mountain to hill, seeking rest and finding none: when they are beat out of one refuge they fly to another, till they are, as it were debilitated, broken, and subdued with legal humblings; in which God gives them a conviction of their own utter helplessness and insufficiency, and discovers the true remedy in a clearer knowledge of Christ and his gospel." In this cycle that Edwards refers to as a "labyrinth," he makes it clear that it is not "their own experience only," but the Holy Spirit's convicting influence, that produces these effects.[65]

THE PROBLEM OF FREE OFFER PREACHING
AND THE "TWO WILLS" OF GOD

The concerns of this chapter uncover one of the most difficult issues for Calvinism: its positing of two wills in God. Calvinists posit a secret will that desires the damnation of the reprobate and arranges the world in such a way that the reprobate can never be saved. Yet they also say God has a public will that not only commands people to do what he decrees they can never do but has Jesus "tenderly calling them home" when he knows he has arranged reality so that they can never respond to his call. Edwards explained: "When a distinction is made between God's revealed will and his secret will, or his will of command and decree, 'will' is certainly in that distinction taken in two senses: his will of decree is not his will in the same sense as his will of command is. Therefore 'tis no difficulty at all to suppose that one may be otherwise than the other. His will in both senses is his inclination."[66]

Edwards was quite happy to hold these incongruities in tension without resolution (something that contemporary Calvinists seem to have a harder time doing). He stated:

---

[64] Edwards, 4:165. Italics added.

[65] Edwards, 4:166.

[66] Jonathan Edwards, "Will of God," in *The Miscellanies*, in *WJE*, vol. 13, ed. Harry S. Stout (New Haven: Yale University Press, 1994), 323.

'Tis objected against the absolute decrees of God respecting the future actions of men, and especially the unbelief of sinners and their rejection of the gospel, that this don't consist with the sincerity of God's calls and invitations to such sinners as he has willed in his eternal secret decree never should accept of those invitations. To which I answer: that there is that in God—respecting that acceptance and compliance of sinners, which God knows will never be, and which he has decreed never to cause to be—which though it ben't just the same with our desiring and wishing for that which never will come to pass, yet there is nothing wanting but what would imply imperfection in such a case.... When God, in the manner of existence, came down from his infinite perfection, and accommodated himself to our nature and manner by being made man, as he was in the person of Jesus Christ, he really desires the conversion and salvation of reprobates, and laments their obstinacy and misery; as when he beheld the city Jerusalem and wept over it, saying, "O Jerusalem, Jerusalem, thou that killest the prophets, and stonest them which are sent unto thee, how often would I have gathered thy children together, even as a hen gathereth her chickens under her wings, and ye would not" [*Matthew 23:37*]. So in like manner, when he comes down from his infinite perfection, though not in the manner of being, but in the manner of manifestation, and accommodates himself to our nature and manner, in the manner of expression, 'tis equally natural and proper that he should express himself as though he desired the conversion and salvation of reprobates, and lamented their obstinacy and misery.[67]

Edwards's Free Offer Preaching versus Contemporary Calvinists

All this, of course, revolves around the Calvinist concept of the "free offer of the gospel" or the "well-meant offer of the gospel." Those often known as

---

[67] Jonathan Edwards, "Absolute Decrees. Sincerity of God's Invitation," in *The Miscellanies*, in *WJE*, vol. 18, ed. Ava Chamberlain (New Haven: Yale University Press, 2000), 409–10.

Hyper-Calvinists do not believe in the free offer of the gospel and criticize Calvinists like Edwards for being inconsistent. Most modern-day Calvinists support the notion of the free offer of the gospel. However, it is interesting to note the differences between the tone and terminology of Edwards's free offer and that of many modern-day Calvinists' free offer. Edwards seems content simply to have put the two wills of God out on the table even in his preaching, allowing the loose ends to dangle. He stated very clearly when preaching the gospel that some of those in his hearing are probably reprobate, but he still preached to them just as any non-Calvinist preacher would.

One notable difference between Edwards's preaching and that of contemporary Calvinists is that it is hard to find the latter telling people directly: Jesus is calling you to himself. He is opening a door for you. He is knocking on your heart's door importunately. The Spirit is repeatedly convicting you and awakening you and illuminating you and enlightening you, giving you opportunity after special opportunity. He is pouring himself out on you in a special manner, convicting you of sin and of his saving truth. He is striving with you even now, and if you push him away, this may be your last opportunity to be saved. He may stop striving with you. You may completely fall away, and then you will never have an opportunity to be saved, and you will be held more strictly accountable before a Holy God for your refusal to heed the repeated callings and convictions and awakenings and pleadings of Christ and the Spirit. Hell will be hotter for you because of your repeated refusals to respond to the gracious call of God.

This is the kind of preaching that Edwards engaged in. Yet this is not the kind of preaching that modern-day Calvinists tend to do. This is traditional Arminian preaching. Rather than letting the loose threads hang out there as Edwards does, allowing there to be a little paradox between the secret will of God in reprobating most people and his public call to them to be saved when he knows they cannot, modern-day Calvinists seem more concerned about theological consistency. Thus they do not seem to preach in the same manner Edwards does.

There is also a difference in terminology between Edwards and modern-day Calvinists. Edwards's corpus is shot through with the ideas and terminology presented in this essay. It is central to his Great Awakening context. Talk of Holy Spirit–wrought conviction and awakenings and illuminations and enlightenings and repeated pleadings to the reprobate from Christ and the Spirit are a very important part of his terminology and rhetoric. Yet they are almost absent from much modern Calvinist writing. Either they are downplayed and mentioned only in passing, or in most cases they are not mentioned at all.

A survey of three of the most recent evangelical Calvinist treatments of Edwards bears this out. In *God's Passion for His Glory: Living the Vision of Jonathan Edwards*, John Piper never uses the word *awakening* to refer to the Holy Spirit's working with individual sinners. (This can also be said of the two books later mentioned.) He refers to it only corporately, in the sense of "Great Awakening."[68] What is even more interesting is that Piper turns some of these categories on their heads. He says, in his recent book *A God-Entranced Vision of All Things*, "It is not enough to hear 'the gospel' mentioned in verse 4 or to have 'the knowledge' mentioned in verse 6. There must be a divine work of *illumination or awakening*. God himself, by his Spirit, must do an act of creation as he did at the beginning of the universe when he said, 'Let there be light.' Edwards will call this act of God 'regeneration'—being born again."[69] Yet Edwards used the language of illumination and awakening over and over to speak of what God is doing even for sinners who are reprobate and can never believe the gospel. At the very least, it can be said that this language and these categories that were so important to Edwards are not at all important to Piper.

In Sean Michael Lucas's book *God's Grand Design: The Theological Vision of Jonathan Edwards*, the concept of the Holy Spirit's grace toward the reprobate receives scant attention.[70] Sam Storms's book *Signs of the Spirit: An Interpretation of Jonathan Edwards's "Religious Affections"* comes closer than other contemporary Calvinist treatments to dealing with Edwards's views on the Spirit's activity toward the reprobate. But Storms downplays it; he fails to give it anything like the attention that Edwards gave it. Storms puts most of his emphasis on *counterfeit* convictions, awakenings, and spiritual experiences rather than

---

[68] John Piper, *God's Passion for His Glory: Living the Vision of Jonathan Edwards* (Wheaton: Crossway, 1998).

[69] John Piper, "A Divine and Supernatural Light Immediately Imparted to the Soul by the Spirit of God: An Edwardsean Sermon (2 Corinthians 3:18–4:7)," in John Piper and Justin Taylor, eds., *A God-Entranced Vision of All Things* (Wheaton: Crossway, 2004), 259. Italics added.

[70] Sean Michael Lucas, *God's Grand Design: The Theological Vision of Jonathan Edwards* (Wheaton: Crossway, 2011).

on *Holy Spirit-wrought* convictions, awakenings, and spiritual experiences in the reprobate.[71]

For example, Storms emphasizes Edwards's statement that "there are other spirits who have influence on the minds of men, besides the Holy Ghost." Storms says in passing, "Even if we concede that it is God's Spirit who exerts such influences on the heart, they may not be redemptive or saving in nature but rather may be a manifestation of the 'common grace' of God. The Spirit can convict of sin and influence the mind of a person without him having any saving intent."[72] Edwards would agree. Yet Edwards's and Storms's emphases are radically different. Storms rightly affirms the fact that Edwards thought there are other reasons why people may appear to be regenerate—something with which any Arminian could agree. Yet he fails to stress Edwards's views on preparatory experiences. The reader of Storms's book will come away with an altogether different perception of the importance that Edwards placed on "preparatory" experiences and Spirit-wrought conviction and illumination, even on the reprobate.

Storms mentions it again in a discussion of the "Divine Light" sermon:

> We mustn't forget, however, that there is a degree of conviction concerning the truth of the gospel that arises "from the common enlightenings of the Spirit of God." This is what theologians have traditionally meant when they spoke of the "common grace" of God. The Spirit can awaken in people a measure of conviction concerning the reality of their sin and

---

[71] Sam Storms, *Signs of the Spirit: An Interpretation of Jonathan Edwards's "Religious Affections"* (Wheaton: Crossway, 2007), 64.

[72] Storms, 64. In discussing the morphology of conversion (67–68), Storms downplays conviction and common grace. He mentions "experiences that are preparatory to the reception of saving grace" only in passing, noting that Edwards believed it was possible such experiences could be counterfeited by Satan. This is in contrast to Edwards's constant discussion of preparatory experiences, conviction, awakenings, illuminations, common grace, and other words to describe these gracious experiences. Nevertheless, Storms says, "Even on those occasions when the Spirit is the one responsible for people reacting in fear of hell and judgment, the joy of forgiveness will not necessarily follow. Men and women can quench the Spirit's work and in turn produce for and in themselves a hope and a joy that is grounded in something other than the efficacy of the saving work of Jesus" (68).

the natural perfections of God and the overall truthfulness of Scripture without necessarily regenerating their hearts. . . .[73]

Storms again says that Satan is "capable of misleading people" through counterfeit experiences.[74] It is almost as though Storms is discouraging people from having these experiences of conviction and common grace, whereas Edwards is strongly encouraging them!

In short, readers of these contemporary evangelical Calvinist works on Edwards, as well as other Calvinist works, will come away with a completely different understanding of how God graciously works in the lives of those he intends never to convert. Readers will come away thinking that Edwards's views of common grace are similar to Jenson's comment about the common grace that holds up the world and enables sinners to perform good works. This disparity between Edwards and his modern followers, however, gets to the heart of Calvinism's most profound difficulty: that God publicly calls everyone to salvation and desires everyone's salvation but has secretly determined that most of them can and will never receive the grace necessary for their conversion. Or, as John Piper puts it, "There is a sense in which [God] desires that all be saved and a sense in which he does not."[75]

Edwards's Dilemma

Edwards's account is much more nuanced than that of most modern-day Calvinists. The reason he sounds like an Arminian preacher is that he was not afraid to allow paradox into his preaching and theology. He allowed loose ends to remain untied. So when he engaged in the free offer of the gospel, he did it like the Bible does it, like the Reformed Arminian preacher does it. He said that the Holy Spirit is working graciously and repeatedly with people, striving with them and imploring them to be saved, graciously awakening them and enlightening them, opening a door to them, repeatedly knocking at the door of their hearts, giving them special opportunities to be saved. This is typical

---

[73] Storms, 68.

[74] Storms, 107.

[75] John Piper, *Does God Desire All to be Saved?* (Wheaton: Crossway, 2013), 45–46. For an Arminian response to Piper's arguments, see J. Matthew Pinson, *40 Questions About Arminianism* (Grand Rapids: Kregel Academic, 2022), 109–18.

of non-Calvinist preaching. The difference between the Arminian preacher and Edwards is that the latter is very open with his hearers that God may not indeed, with his secret will, desire their salvation, even though he is perfectly justified in calling them to salvation, pleading with them to come, according to his public will. This is simply not the kind of preaching one hears a great deal of from contemporary Calvinists.

Yet, lest one think that this emphasis of Edwards is something that is peculiar to him or his Great Awakening context, and is more Edwardsean than Calvinist, one should consider a brief quotation from Calvin. In complete agreement with Edwards, Calvin averred that God

> vouchsafes his blessing, for a time, even to reprobates, with whom he is justly angry, in order that he may *gently invite and even allure them* to repentance; and may render them more inexcusable, if they remain obstinate; meanwhile, he curses their felicity. Therefore, while they think they have reached the height of fortune, their prosperity, in which they delighted themselves, is turned into ruin."[76]

Reformed Arminians like the kind of free-offer preaching in which Edwards engaged. Like him, they preach to sinners indiscriminately that Jesus is pleading with them to repent of sin and trust him for salvation. They believe the Holy Spirit is graciously coming to sinners—elect and reprobate alike—and pressing home the call of Christ. They agree that the Holy Spirit is influencing people, convicting them of sin and of the truth of the gospel, that he is awakening and enlightening and illuminating them spiritually, striving with them repeatedly, giving them special opportunities over and over again to respond to God's grace. They believe that even the non-elect are recipients of divine offers of mercy and that there is hope for them. They believe that God is knocking on the door of the hearts of the non-elect, opening a special door for them, and that the Holy Spirit is graciously influencing sinners. They are urging sinners not to spurn these gracious invitations. They believe that, without this grace from the Holy Spirit, no sinners can come to God in their own natural ability. All the precise Edwardsean

---

[76] From Calvin's Commentary on Gen 39:1; John Calvin, *Commentaries on the First Book of Moses Called Genesis* (Edinburgh: Calvin Translation Society, 1850), 2:292. Italics added.

phrases mentioned in this paragraph fit very well into Reformed Arminian theology, preaching, and piety.

Yet Reformed Arminians do not believe that these repeated, individualized strivings of the Spirit can be relegated to the category of "common grace" in terms of the divine grace that keeps the planets spinning and people breathing and gives people the ability to do good deeds. They believe there is a category between common grace of that sort and regeneration. They believe this is the most natural reading of Holy Scripture—the best way to make sense of the dilemma Edwards has between his theology and his preaching. This they call prevenient or enabling grace, whereby the Holy Spirit calls and convicts and woos and awakens and influences sinners to come to him, a grace that God graciously grants them freedom to resist.

Reformed Arminians posit that there is one will in God: that he is "not willing that any should perish but that all should come to repentance" (2 Pet 3:9, NKJV). There is no contradiction between his secret will and his revealed will in the gospel that calls everyone to salvation. He wants all people "to be saved and to come to the knowledge of the truth" (1 Tim 2:4). There is not, as Piper avers, a sense in which God desires everyone's salvation and a sense in which he does not. God is commanding all people everywhere to repent and in his own mysterious time and way will graciously give them the ability to repent, but he also maintains their ability to resist. This is the one will of God. It is the one will of Christ, who, when he looked into the face of the rich young ruler, loved him and had compassion on him. He pleaded with the rich young ruler to come to him, knowing all the while that he would not, yet knowing that he through his grace had made it possible for him to come, if he would. This view comports much better with the kind of free-offer preaching we see in the Bible and the history of the Christian church. And it is the only way to remove the contradiction between Edwards's theology and his biblical gospel preaching.[77]

---

[77] Some of the material in this chapter is adapted from Pinson, *40 Questions About Arminianism*, 129–34.

Chapter 7

Jonathan Edwards against Free Will

Robert E. Picirilli

Jonathan Edwards was both "the theologian of the First Great Awakening" and "the eighteenth century's most powerful exponent of experimental Calvinism."[1] One of the more influential of his prolific writings, originally published in 1754, was entitled *A careful and strict Enquiry into The modern prevailing Notions of that Freedom of Will, Which is supposed to be essential to Moral Agency, Vertue and Vice, Reward and Punishment, Praise and Blame.*[2] In that volume Edwards made his case against free will, and my purpose is to provide both a critical analysis of his treatment and a response.[3]

As I interact with Edwards, I represent a "Reformed-Arminian" perspective.[4] By this I mean the original evangelical soteriology of Arminius himself and of the very first Dutch Remonstrants.

---

[1] Mark A. Noll, *Evangelical Dictionary of Theology*, ed. Walter A. Elwell (Grand Rapids: Baker, 1984), 344.

[2] A more recent edition, which I will cite throughout as "Edwards," is Jonathan Edwards, *Freedom of the Will*, ed. Paul Ramsey (New Haven,: Yale University Press, 1957). I will cite the editor of this edition as "Ramsey."

[3] I have done something similar, in more detail, in *Free Will Revisited: A Respectful Response to Luther, Calvin, and Edwards* (Eugene, OR: Wipf & Stock, 2017).

[4] I sometimes call this "Reformation Arminianism." Some writers in this volume use the term "Reformed Arminianism" with essentially the same meaning. For a more thorough expo-

The "Arminians" whom Edwards opposed were not such. Most of his arguments were directed toward three men: Daniel Whitby, an Anglican clergyman who denied the imputation of Adam's sin to the human race and ultimately expressed Arian and Unitarian tendencies; Thomas Chubb, a Deist; and Isaac Watts, better known as a hymn writer than as a theologian and sometimes called an "uneasy Calvinist."[5] Paul Ramsey, Edwards's editor, observed, "In the eighteenth century there was probably more in common between Edwards' defense of orthodoxy and the restored Arminianism of Arminius, which emerged with new strength and warmth in the Wesleyan revival, than between the latter and some of the 'Arminians' whom Edwards opposed."[6] Douglas Sweeney claims that none of those to whom Edwards responded were technically "Arminian."[7] Edwards never cited Arminius himself.[8]

THE METHOD OF EDWARDS

Significantly, Edwards's argument against the freedom of the will is neither biblically nor theologically based. Instead, he depended almost entirely on philosophical reasoning.[9] His objections to freedom of the will are grounded in logic and so lack the power of biblical exegesis. In this he was entirely unlike two great theologians who, before him, had written treatises against free will: Luther and Calvin.[10] Perhaps he considered their biblical and theological arguments sufficient and hoped to add another weapon to the arsenal of arguments against the doctrine of free will.

---

sition of soteriology from this perspective, see my *Grace, Faith, Free Will: Contrasting Views of Salvation: Calvinism and Arminianism* (Nashville: Randall House, 2002).

[5]   For more on these three, see Ramsey, "Editor's Introduction," 65–118.

[6]   Ramsey, 3.

[7]   Douglas A. Sweeney, *Jonathan Edwards and the Ministry of the Word* (Downers Grove : IVP Academic, 2009), 149, n. 9.

[8]   Whether he had access to Arminius's original Latin works I do not know; the English translation came later.

[9]   The significant exception is his chapter demonstrating from Scripture that God possesses exhaustive foreknowledge of the moral choices of human beings, discussed later in this chapter.

[10]   For Luther's volume, see *Martin Luther on the Bondage of the Will: A New Translation of De Servo Arbitrio (1525), Martin Luther's Reply to Erasmus of Rotterdam*, trans. J. I. Packer and O. R. Johnston (Westwood, NJ: Revell, 1957). For Calvin's, see John Calvin, *The Bondage and Liberation of the Will: A Defence of the Orthodox Doctrine of Human Choice against Pighius*, ed. A. N. S. Lane, trans. G. I. Davies (Grand Rapids: Baker, 1996).

There is, of course, more than one way to argue for truth. Among the possible grounds are at least three: reason, experience, and divine revelation. At risk of oversimplification, we may characterize the methods that capitalize on these three as rationalism, empiricism, and biblical exegesis, respectively. The last of the three grounds truth claims in biblical-theological exposition, and this was the way of Luther and Calvin. Empiricism depends on human experience and is the method of the sciences (and of some philosophers[11]), insisting that only that which can be confirmed in experience—ultimately, sense experience—can be known. Rationalism attempts to gain knowledge from reason alone, seeking for self-evident truths and then using logic to flesh out the implications of those truths.

The last of these has been the method of a number of well-known philosophers in the history of Western thought.[12] It is the method Edwards chose to use in his argument against free will. Ramsey observed that much of Edwards's book consists "wholly of philosophical clarification and reasoning" and that he "returns again and again to philosophical analysis."[13] Another interpreter of Edwards called this book "a debater's triumph."[14]

I cite the following as an example of Edwards's use of the method:

> What is self-existent must be from eternity, and must be unchangeable: but as to all things that *begin to be*, they are not self-existent, and therefore must have some foundation of their existence without themselves. That whatsoever begins to be, which before was not, must have a cause why it then begins to exist, seems to be the first dictate of the common and natural sense which God hath implanted in the minds of all mankind, and the main foundation of all our reasonings about the existence of things, past, present, or to come.[15]

---

[11] Locke, Berkeley, and Hume come to mind.

[12] Descartes, Spinoza, and Leibniz are often mentioned.

[13] Ramsey, "Editor's Introduction," 9.

[14] Perry Miller, *Jonathan Edwards* (Lincoln, NE: University of Nebraska Press, 2005), 251. Subsequently, Miller noted that Edwards "seemed satisfied with dialectics. . . . Edwards seems through most of this book to be altogether happy with Dr. [Oliver Wendell] Holmes's characterization of it: that logic is logic is all he says" (259).

[15] Edwards, *Freedom of the Will*, 181.

The words indicate Edwards's reliance on rationalistic method: self-evident truths, first causes, and cause-effect relationships as logically compelling. First and foremost, this is an argument for the existence of God, the First, Uncaused Cause.[16] In Edwards's hands it also became an argument that all events, including human choices, are necessary and traceable to a First Cause.

Rationalistic method tends to rely on *analysis* of opponents' propositions, breaking them down to be able to show that they are logically self-defeating. Edwards was a master of this approach. Even so, one must be careful to evaluate his "self-evident" assumptions and the logic that follows. As I will attempt to show, some of his key arguments do not hold up under close scrutiny.

EDWARDS AGAINST FREE WILL: AN OVERVIEW

Given the limitations of a single chapter, I can provide only an overview of Edwards's treatise so that the reader can understand his approach and the nature of his reasoning. There is a short preface, four main parts, and a conclusion. Part One treats the terms and definitions involved in the discussion of free will. In Part Two, the lengthiest part, Edwards applied logic to consider whether there can be any such thing as what Arminians mean by free will. Part Three asks—and answers in the negative—whether the kind of free will Arminians insist on is essential to moral agency, virtue and vice, praise and blame. Part Four counters the main arguments of Arminians. All of these Edwards discussed rationalistically. Only in the Conclusion did he indicate that what he had said about free will is thoroughly coherent with the teachings of Calvinism. But he used none of those doctrines as a basis for his argument against free will.

Edwards defined important terms in Part One. The *will* is a "faculty or power or principle of mind by which it is capable of choosing."[17] To *determine* the will is, in consequence of some action or influence, to *cause* the choice it makes.[18] *Necessity* means that there is an infallible connection between an event, including human volition, and anything antecedent to it that is the ground or reason for its being what it is. There are two kinds of necessity.

---

[16] This reminds one of the cosmological argument for the existence of God as employed by contemporary advocates of evidentialist apologetics like Norman Geisler in *Christian Apologetics* (Grand Rapids: Baker, 1976).

[17] Edwards, *Freedom of the Will*, 137.

[18] Edwards, 141.

Natural necessity involves the force of natural law and prevails without regard to the will. *Moral* necessity, which Edwards predicated of all human volition, is in effect when a person's biases, inclinations, or motives are so strong that the choice made cannot be otherwise.

Opposite to necessity is *contingency*, something that comes to pass without any connection to a cause or antecedent and thus "has absolutely no previous ground or reason."[19] By definition, then, there can be no such thing. There is *liberty*, however, which means simply the ability to choose *as one pleases*—even though moral necessity means that what the person pleases and chooses cannot be other than what it is. So long as the person is not forced against his will, he is at liberty and so is a moral agent and is responsible.

Among the logical arguments that Edwards marshaled against free will in Part Two, the first is of central importance and undergirds all the rest. Arminians, he said, define free will to mean the power of *self-determination*, which he defined to mean that the self "determines its own acts by choosing its own acts." He proceeded to object that this requires an act of the will that determines the act of the will, so that every free act of choice is preceded by another free act of choice. This, he argued, must lead us either to infinite regress or to an initial act of choice that was *not* "free," and this means that none of the acts that follow in the chain were free. Either way, the idea that acts of the will are self-determined, Edwards maintained, is absurd.[20]

Equally important is Edwards's argument from cause and effect. He insisted that all events, including human volitions, are the effects of causes. A *cause* he defined broadly as any antecedent that is connected to an event in such a way that it is "the ground or reason" of the event, even *if it exerts no positive influence* and is "perhaps rather an occasion than a cause, most properly speaking."[21] In fine, rationalistic form, he affirmed that anything not self-existent (and so eternal) must begin to be, and anything that begins to be must have a cause; otherwise we have no way of knowing anything, including the existence of God. Volitions are among the things that "begin to be." Edwards therefore ridiculed the idea of Watts that spirits can originate ideas without causes.

Similarly, Edwards ridiculed the Arminians' claim that for the will to be free, it must act in *indifference*, which illogically implies that one exercises

---

[19] Edwards, 155.
[20] Edwards, 172.
[21] Edwards, 180–81. Italics added.

preference without having a preference![22] He insisted that (1) this would require *absolute* freedom from all prior inclinations, which is not possible, and that (2) when a will is already inclined, it is bound and cannot act except as it is inclined.[23]

Edwards proceeded, then, to argue his case from foreknowledge, again using logical demonstration—to which I will respond later in this chapter. Most important, he insisted that Arminians must either acknowledge necessity in acts of the will or be left with nothing but randomness and chance, since the opposite of necessity is contingency and contingency means not being caused.

In Part Three of the work, Edwards argued that free will is not essential to moral responsibility or to considerations of virtue and vice or praise and blame. For one thing, God himself is *necessarily* good and yet is certainly praiseworthy. There is therefore no logical contradiction between necessary behavior and the kind of responsibility required of a moral agent or of that agent's deserving praise or blame. Indeed, the Arminians' "liberty of indifference" is not only unnecessary to true virtue but inconsistent with it since being morally indifferent is certainly not virtuous but wicked. Indeed, any habitual tendency toward good or evil, which everyone acknowledges as praise- or blameworthy, would violate that indifference.

Edwards devoted Part Four to countering the main arguments of Arminians. Among other things, he attacks the Arminians' "metaphysical" notions of action and agency: they require that the action of an agent be uncaused, and yet they hold that one's action is the effect of its own determination. He proceeded then to answer Arminian objections that if humans act entirely by necessity, all means and efforts toward good are in vain and men are mere machines. He observed that such means are part of the chain of connected events, and Watts was incorrect in denying that God himself acts by necessity.

At length, Edwards responded to the argument that Calvinism makes God the author of sin. God is not a sinner, nor the agent, actor, or doer of sin, but he is the permitter—or not the hinderer—of sin. He "disposes" all events in such a way that sin "will most certainly and infallibly follow," but he does so for his own "wise, holy and most excellent ends and purposes," and only in that sense is he the "author" of sin—although Edwards does not prefer that

---

22 Edwards, 196.
23 Edwards, 205.

wording.[24] God may "in his providence so dispose and permit things" that will certainly and infallibly be connected to evil without himself being guilty of any evil.[25] In this connection Edwards discussed the entrance of the first sin into the world: God, when he created man, so ordered "his circumstances, that from these circumstances, together with his [God's] withholding further assistance and divine influence, his [man's] sin would infallibly follow."[26] This is not inconsistent with God's moral character but manifests his *disposing* will ("what he chooses as a part of his own infinite scheme of things") and not his *perceptive* will (what God loves, as expressed in his counsels and invitations).[27] Indeed, the Arminians' insistence that choices arise without any connection to or dependence on anything foregoing—and so to being uncaused and without any ground or reason—is what really leads to atheism.[28]

THE CONCEPT OF FREE WILL EDWARDS OPPOSED

Unlike Luther and Calvin, who were resisting the free will of Roman Catholicism in their day, Edwards wrote against the free will of Anglicans and Dissenters in England in the eighteenth century. In summary, Edwards's "Arminians" held three main concepts, to which he returned often, as follows. First, they held that real "liberty" is grounded in *self-determination*, meaning that volitions, or acts of the will, cannot be dependent on any cause outside the self or on anything before those acts. Second, they held that a will, to be free, must act from indifference, which Edwards took to mean that the mind is in a state of equilibrium before volition, not already inclined one way or the other. Third, they held that whatever is done freely must be contingent, as opposed to necessary or to having a "fixed and certain connection with some previous ground or reason of its existence."[29]

Responding to the Arminians of his day, Edwards said they required that "the determination of volition is without a cause" and that "the free acts of the will are contingent events," not done by necessity.[30] This means, to Edwards,

---

[24] Edwards, 399.
[25] Edwards, 406.
[26] Edwards, 413.
[27] Edwards, 415.
[28] Edwards, 420.
[29] Edwards, 164–65.
[30] Edwards, 179, 192.

that Arminians regard contingency as the opposite of constraint or of a consequence where one thing infallibly follows from another.[31] It also means that for
Arminians, if an act is made necessary—that is, caused—by something outside
the self, the act has no moral value; only if caused from within the self is the
person blame- or praiseworthy.[32] Likewise, any "action" that is necessitated by
the action of another is not an action, and the doer is not an agent. Arminians
consider that "necessary agent" is a contradiction.[33]

EDWARDS'S CONCEPT OF THE WILL

Edwards insisted that the human will is at liberty—"free"—to choose as it
pleases: in other words, in accord with its own desires. To exercise the will is
the same as to choose,[34] and a person never "wills anything contrary to his
desires, or desires anything contrary to his will."[35]

If this explains how fallen humans are free only to choose evil, it does not
explain how the original parents became sinners. As already noted, Edwards
affirmed that God placed them in circumstances where their choice of sin was
necessary, although he did so for a holy purpose.[36]

Equally important to Edwards's concept of the will is that all its volitions are caused. A volition is an "existent" (that which exists), and yet it is
not self-existent. Anything that begins to exist (and so did not always exist)
must have a cause outside itself to account for its existence. Cause-effect relations apply to everything except God himself; the volitions of persons are not
exceptions. True, a "cause" is not necessarily a mechanical force like that which
exists between a strike of lightning and the peal of thunder that follows. Yet
the mental understandings antecedent to volitions are the causes of those volitions. Such understandings are formed by various kinds of influences, including appeals, motivations, warnings, and the like. The connection between these
and the choice made by the person is an infallible one and therefore qualifies as
a cause-effect relationship. People always choose whatever makes the strongest
appeal to their minds. Choices infallibly follow from prevailing motivations

---

[31] Edwards, 213.
[32] Edwards, 338.
[33] Edwards, 343.
[34] Edwards, 137.
[35] Edwards, 139.
[36] Edwards, 413–14.

and inclinations, from what "appears most agreeable and pleasing, all things considered."[37]

According to Edwards, then, all volitions, like all events, occur by moral necessity. This means that every act of will follows when a person's understanding or biases or inclinations or motivations are strong enough that they inevitably lead to the choice made, when there is a "perfect connection between moral causes and effects."[38] Conversely, moral inability consists in the absence of an inclination, or of one strong enough, or "of sufficient motives, to induce and excite the act of the will to the contrary."[39]

Consequently, Edwards's concept of the human will and its "freedom" is in accord with a view called *compatibilism* (although he does not use the term itself, which was apparently not coined until the twentieth century). Compatibilists believe that one can hold to determinism and freedom at the same time without being logically incoherent. They say that freedom of will does not require being able to make either of two (or more) contrary choices, only that one is free to act in accord with the sum total of all the circumstances, including mental and emotional states, bearing on him or her at the time of choice.

EDWARDS'S REASONS FOR REJECTING FREE WILL

The preceding discussion has already made clear the arguments Edwards lodged against the Arminian concept of free will. My purpose here, then, is to summarize his major contentions in preparation for responding to them in the final section of this chapter.

1. The law of cause and effect. Edwards relied heavily on cause-effect relationships in his resistance to free will, arguing that human choices, like all events, must have causes. Our volitions have not always existed and are therefore not *self-existent*. Anything that is not self-existent has to have a cause for its existence other than itself, and that applies to human volitions as well as to the existence of humans themselves.

Human choices, then, cannot arise—willy-nilly, as it were—out of thin air. Lying behind them are various circumstances deriving from information, understanding, motivations, inclinations, influences, passions, desires, and the

---

[37] Edwards, 147.
[38] Edwards, 156–57.
[39] Edwards, 159.

like. These are the causes of the volitions. In fact, they make the specific choices infallible or necessary; they cannot be otherwise.

2. All-inclusive necessity. Closely related to this is Edwards's concept of necessity as prevailing in all actions in the world. For Edwards this can be seen from either of two different perspectives, but both lead to the same unerring conclusion that everything that takes place does so by necessity.

One perspective is found in what has just been said about cause and effect. Every effect, including human volition, has a cause that renders the effect infallible and necessary. The other perspective is found in divine foreknowledge. Whatever God knows, and he knows the future exhaustively, cannot but come to pass. That, too, indicates necessity.

As already noted, Edwards distinguished between physical necessity, involving natural law, and moral necessity, involving the volitions of moral agents. But the latter are just as necessary, although of a somewhat different nature, as things that must be what they are because of natural law. I will discuss Edwards's concept of necessity further in the section on foreknowledge. He tends to confuse the issue by equating *necessity* with (mere) *certainty*.

3. The logical absurdity of self-determination. Closely related to the preceding two reasons, Edwards seized on the term *self-determination* and never tired of attacking it as logically self-contradictory or absurd.

In summary, here is Edwards's argument. The Arminians insist that acts of the will are "self-determined." This requires a self behind every choice, determining the choice, which means that the act of determining precedes the choice! However, for that act of determining to be self-determined, there would then have to be yet another volition before it, determining it. And this leads to infinite regress, which all logicians know is a dead end.

If that infinite regress is to be avoided, one must go back to a *first* choice, one that initiated the whole chain of choices. Then one faces a dilemma. If that first choice is uncaused, then it arises out of nothing, without any explanation or reason for its existence. If, however, it is caused, then one is left with the self-contradictory notion of a *first* cause that was itself caused by a prior cause, and that of course cannot be.

A CRITICAL RESPONSE TO EDWARDS'S
ARGUMENT FROM CAUSE AND EFFECT

My purpose now is to respond to the rationalism of Jonathan Edwards in opposition to free will. First, I refer to the logical arguments he set forth that are dependent on his commitment to cause-effect relationships.

To begin with, I feel constrained to say that I do not think rationalism is the way to do theology. Even so, I am aware that many people find Edwards's approach impressive, and so I do not ignore this line of argument. There are two main logical arguments to address, then: (1) Edwards everywhere assumed the universal applicability of cause-effect relationships to everything that transpires in the universe, and (2) on this grounds he ridiculed the concept of self-determinism as self-defeating and absurd. I will deal with these two major aspects of his approach in reverse order.

Edwards against Self-Determinism

Apparently growing out of his commitment to universal cause-effect relationships, Edwards felt compelled to hold up for ridicule the idea of self-determinism, insisting that this "Arminian" notion requires that human volition be both an effect and its cause and thus two logically distinguishable "events." This analysis undergirds his most basic argument against the Arminian view of free will as he understood it.

The following lengthy quotation from Edwards captures his argument. It comes after his assertion that the Arminian notion of liberty means that there is a "sovereignty in the will, whereby it has power to determine its own volitions."

> If the will determines itself, then either the will is active in determining its volitions, or it is not. If it be active in it, then the determination is an *act* of the will; and so there is one act of the will determining another. But if the will is not active in the determination, then how does it exercise any liberty in it? These gentlemen [advocates for free will] suppose that the thing wherein the will exercises liberty, is in its determining its own acts. But how can this be, if it ben't active in determining? Certainly the will, or the soul, can't exercise any liberty in that wherein it don't act, or wherein it don't exercise itself. So that

if either part of this dilemma be taken, this scheme of liberty, consisting in self-determining power, is overthrown. If there be an act of the will in determining all its own free acts, then one free act of the will is determined by another; and so we have the absurdity of every free act, even the very first, determined by a foregoing free act. But if there be no act or exercise of the will in determining its own acts, then no liberty is exercised in determining them. From whence it follows, that no liberty consists in the will's power to determine its own acts: or, which is the same thing, that there is no such thing as liberty consisting in a self-determining power of the will.[40]

At least a few comments are in order. First, it is an excellent example of what is often elaborate, not to say torturous, reasoning, nearly impossible to follow! Oliver Wendell Holmes is reported to have said, of *Freedom of the Will*, that it is like "the unleavened bread of the Israelite: holy it may be, but heavy it certainly is."[41]

Another observation is that the paragraph illustrates well Edwards's rationalistic method, first by analysis framing the argument in two mutually exclusive possibilities: if the will determines itself, it is either active in doing so or not. From that comes the argument that if it *is* active, there must be one act of the will preceding and determining the other, and if it is *not* active, it is not exercising liberty at all. Then follows the conclusion that, either way, the idea that human beings are at liberty to exercise self-determining power is self-defeating.

Edwards's argument depends on his analysis of the proposition that the Arminian conception of freedom of the will entails a power to determine one's own volitions. That analysis reveals, for Edwards, that in the Arminian notion of liberty, there are two events, as indicated by two words: namely, the *determining* (as the cause) and then the *volition* that follows from it (as the effect). It is this analysis that sets up his logical argument.

Edwards was defining *self-determination* to mean that the will must choose its own actions in order to determine them. This means that there is an act of

---

[40] Edwards, 176.

[41] Oliver Wendell Holmes, "Jonathan Edwards," *The International Review* 9 (1880): 3.

the will that determines any given act of the will, a choice preceding a choice, as it were. But if all human choices are self-determined, then the choice preceding the choice must likewise have a choice or volition that precedes it. And this will lead us to infinite regress, with every choice requiring a preceding choice and no place to stop, going back into the infinite past.

Edwards offered two solutions to this problem of infinite regress. (1) Stop with some past choice that was *not* "caused" by a prior choice and so was uncaused. This is not possible since anything uncaused must either exist eternally or cannot exist at all. (2) Stop with a past choice that was caused by some agent outside the self. But that would make the first choice *not* self-determined or "free," which would then mean that the resulting volitions in the whole chain of cause-effect events would also not be self-determined. (For Edwards this uncaused first cause is, of course, God.)

There are at least two things wrong with these solutions. First and most important is finding in the power of self-determination two events instead of one. One simply does not first will to make a choice or volition and then exercise his will in choosing. Persons do not choose to choose; they simply choose—regardless of what influences are involved and exist before the choice. In other words, no one who holds to self-determinism means by it what Edwards (deliberately, I assume) took it to mean!

For that matter, Edwards himself appears to have realized that this is not what those who defend free will mean. In one discussion he acknowledged that the Arminian really means that "the person in the exercise of a power of willing and choosing, or the soul acting voluntarily, determines [a course of action]"[42]—thus undermining his analysis as so much quibbling over words. This is, I suspect, what Allen Guelzo means when he observes that the arguments of *Freedom of the Will* are "predicated on a risky series of analytic propositions about the terms and processes of human volition."[43]

Even so, it would be impossible to overstate the importance of this argument for Edward's entire volume. Again and again he returned to the very same analysis and wove it into his argument.[44] He was apparently convinced that the

---

[42] Edwards, *Freedom of the Will*, 172.

[43] Allen C. Guelzo, "The Return of the Will: Jonathan Edwards and the Possibilities of Free Will," in *Edwards in Our Time: Jonathan Edwards and the Shaping of American Religion*, eds. Sang Hyun Lee and Allen C. Guelzo (Grand Rapids: Eerdmans, 1999), 90.

[44] Edwards, *Freedom of the Will*, 192, 219–20, 228–29, 234–35, 359, etc.

Arminian logically *had* to mean what he took self-determinism to mean rather than what the Arminian *really* meant.

The second flaw in Edwards's analysis is this: even if it were true that there were two free acts in a given volition, Edwards was wrong to indicate (partly by implication here, but by direct statement in other places) that this must lead to the impossible infinite regress. My reason for saying this is, I think, fairly obvious. Any Christian, including the one who believes in self-determination, traces the beginning of persons back, not to infinite regress, but to a self-existent Creator-God. This God created *persons*, and persons are the selves that make choices or—as Edwards himself put it, cited above—voluntarily determine a course of action. Edwards obfuscated this by insisting that the Arminians said that the *will* has power to determine its volitions. Defenders of free will either do not say that or, if they do, say it carelessly. They say, instead, that *persons* determine their volitions. *Self*-determination means that the *self* or *person* wills and in that volition chooses or determines or decides on a course of action. And Arminians do not affirm that when God created the first person, he also made necessary all his choices.

I cite the editors of a recent edition of some of Edwards's writings, commenting on his insistence that freedom is "the 'liberty' or opportunity to do as one pleases in the absence of any hindrance":

> Edwards is, of course, assuming that this is the meaning of liberty in "common speech," and he takes advantage at this point of the ambiguity previously noted about whether the issue is the freedom of the *person* or the freedom of the *will* to insist on the former, declaring that liberty belongs to the person and not to the will. Accordingly, he can claim that the notion of a self-determining *will* is incoherent because it is supposed to be independent of any prior conditions, and this leads to an infinite regress: before any free act, there must be another free act and so on, and in order to stop the regress, there must be a first act that is not free. But if this is so, no subsequent act can be free. Here we have the basic contention of the entire

treatise, and for Edwards it was enough to overcome the Arminian position.[45]

I cannot imagine that *anyone*—Arminian or otherwise—would ever have thought that freedom of the will means anything other than freedom of the *person* to exercise his or her will.

As a final observation on this point, I note that Calvin himself approvingly used the term *self-determination* to refer to human exercise of the will. In his discussion of the difference between coercion and necessity, he noted, "We describe [as coerced] the will which does not incline this way or that of its own accord or by an internal movement of decision, but is forcibly driven by an external impulse. We say that it is self-determined when of itself it directs itself in the direction in which it is led, when it is not taken by force or dragged unwillingly." He continued, "According to these definitions we allow that man has choice and that it is self-determined, so that if he does anything evil, it should be imputed to him and to his own voluntary choosing."[46]

To be clear, Calvin did not believe in free will as the power of alternative choice. He immediately added a note about humanity's innate wickedness that necessarily drives them to evil: "We locate the necessity to sin precisely in corruption of the will, from which it follows that it is self-determined."[47] Later he said, "I do not want to fight over words if it is once and for all established that freedom should be applied not to a power or ability to choose good and evil alike, but to a movement and an agreement which is self-determined."[48] Again: "We hold that the will can be called free only because it moves by a self-determined volition."[49] He also cited Augustine to agree with the concept of self-determination.[50] For Calvin, then, the problem with free will lies not in some logical absurdity in the notion of self-determination but in the very real effects of depravity, which is an entirely different matter.

I note, in passing, that Edwards's disdain for the notion of self-determination has proved unpopular with many, from his day until the present. One recent

---

[45] John E. Smith, Harry S. Stout, Kenneth P. Minkema, eds., *A Jonathan Edwards Reader* (New Haven: Yale Nota Bene, 1995), xvi.

[46] Calvin, *Bondage and Liberation of the Will*, 69–70.

[47] Calvin, 70.

[48] Calvin, 103.

[49] Calvin, 122.

[50] Calvin, 140–41.

analysis mentions three examples: (1) In 1770 Calvinist James Dana "pro-
tested . . . that a man can simply look into his own breast and know that he
has inward freedom of the sort Edwards denied." (2) Henry Philip Tappan, in
1839, published the longest attack on Edwards's view, insisting that "only a self-
determining will stands the test of an 'appeal to consciousness.'" (3) "Even in the
twenty-first century, some philosophers still dismiss Edwards's theory on the
ground that it does not agree with the prevailing view of self-determination."[51]

Edwards and the Logic of Cause and Effect

For Edwards free will fails because it leaves human choices without causes.
Fundamental to all of Edwards's arguments is the basic assumption that the law
of cause and effect applies to everything that occurs in the universe, including
specifically the choices that persons make.

I think Edwards himself would acknowledge that if this foundational
assumption of universal cause and effect were undermined, his argument
against free will as a whole would crumble. He made no bones about its importance for his position. He regarded this as "the first dictate of the common and
natural sense which God hath implanted in the minds of all mankind." Then he
said, "If this grand principle of common sense be taken away, all arguing from
effects to causes ceaseth, and so all knowledge of any existence, besides what
we have by the most direct and immediate intuition. Particularly all our proof
of the being of God ceases."[52]

What did Edwards mean by *cause*? He observed that the word is often
used narrowly to refer only to "that which has a positive efficiency or influence to produce a thing, or bring it to pass." He would use the term, however,
"in a sense which is more extensive," he said, "to signify any antecedent . . . on
which an event, either a thing, or the manner and circumstance of a thing, so
depends, that it is the ground and reason, either in whole, or in part, why it is,
rather than not; or why it is as it is, rather than otherwise." "In other words," he
said, a *cause* is "any antecedent with which a consequent event is so connected,

---

[51] Michael J. McClymond and Gerald R. McDermott, *The Theology of Jonathan Edwards*
(New York: Oxford University Press, 2012), 346.
[52] Edwards, *Freedom of the Will*, 181.

that it truly belongs to the reason why the proposition which affirms that event, is true; *whether it has any positive influence, or not.*"[53]

I have two relatively brief comments. First is the fact that Edwards was indeed giving *cause* a meaning that is broader than the one it usually has. Later in the same section, he made it broad enough to include the "occasion" for an event. As becomes clear in his subsequent discussion of the fact that God is not the author of sin, this allowed him to include God's permissive decree about sin as *cause*. Thus any antecedent event that has a necessary connection to an event is its cause. Apparently Edwards, were he watching a modern football game, would say that a defender's failure to intercept a pass was a cause—*the* cause?—of the opposing team's touchdown! This is not the way the word is typically used in theological discussion—or if it is, then we can fearlessly say that God is the cause of sin. (And anyone who says this on that basis is not affirming what I am denying when I say that God is *not* the cause of sin.)

More important is the fact that Edwards was applying the same cause-effect law that governs actions in the physical world to actions in the psyche, and that is questionable indeed. Even on his broad definition of *cause*, he ought not to have used the language of cause and effect to define human volition. In the material world, this language indicates mechanical connections that cannot be other than they are and are as regular as clockwork. Edwards said that "if every act of the will is excited by a motive, then that motive is the cause of the act of the will"; for him motives do what they do "by their influence; and so much as is done by their influence, is the effect of them."[54] No. An influence is not properly named a cause; an influence can be resisted.

It is true, of course, that promptings arising in the psyche can themselves be responsible for motions (actions) in the physical world. A murderer pulls the trigger of a gun and kills someone, all actions growing out of inner promptings. All the physical actions are purely mechanical, manifesting inviolable cause-effect laws. The question, however, is whether the decision to kill is likewise mechanical, manifesting inviolable cause-effect laws.

---

[53] Edwards,180–81. Italics added.

[54] Edwards, 225. Guelzo reads Edwards to say, furthermore, that "the presentation of these motives in all future moments has already been fixed." I do not doubt that Edwards thought so, but his argument in *Freedom of the Will* does not make this point: *certain*, yes, but not *fixed*—which I take to be the same as *necessary* as I have defined the word. See the discussion on Edwards and foreknowledge to follow. Guelzo, "Return of the Will," 92.

I think not. Instead, decisions of the will are not the inevitable effects of prior causes. Furthermore, if they are, then like all the manifestations of natural law, they go back either into infinite regress or to an uncaused Cause of everything who becomes responsible for them all. But the mental and spiritual world does not function like the physical world. Decisions of the will do not "spring up" without antecedents, of course; they follow from ideas, persuasions, influences, and the like. They do not, however, "spring up" infallibly or necessarily. The concept of influence and response provides a much better framework for the discussion of the mind and its functions, including the will, than cause and effect—as has been persuasively affirmed by Leroy Forlines.[55]

To go back to Edwards's analysis of his opponents' view of free will into two acts, I would simply observe that the only *causal* reality antecedent to a volition is the *self*. Edwards himself is much better on this point when he defines *will* as a "faculty or power or principle of mind by which it is capable of choosing: an act of the will is the same as an act of choosing or choice."[56] Indeed, and it is the *person* who makes the choice. That is what self-determination or (libertarian) free will means.

I acknowledge that there are questions that result from the kind of "dualism" I am affirming. If our minds and wills are not part of the material world and do not function like the material world, there is a genuine difficulty in understanding how a mental prompting can in fact *cause* a physical motion. This is the classic problem of philosophy called "the mind-body problem." If the psyche is a sort of "stuff" that is radically different from the "stuff" of my physical body, how can they interact?

René Descartes speculated that that there is some sort of connection or nexus between the mind and the body in the pineal gland. That "solution" is no solution at all, as also are a number of solutions proposed by various philosophers. Some claim that the physical world is, after all, part of the mind.[57] Some take the opposite approach and say that the so-called mind is nothing more than a physical brain with electric currents. That "solution" leads, of course, to

---

[55] Leroy Forlines, *The Quest for Truth: Theology for Postmodern Times* (Nashville: Randall House, 2001), 144–45 (and in other places throughout his work as indicated in the index under "influence and response," 530).

[56] Edwards, *Freedom of the Will*, 137.

[57] This is philosophical idealism. I tend to think that a biblical worldview can be expressed either as dualism or as idealism. However, discussing that goes well beyond the purposes of this chapter.

philosophical materialism, which affirms that everything that exists is matter. In a materialistic world, it works very well to affirm that all events are effects of prior causes. I find it infinitely harder to believe that this works in a biblical view of God, people, and things.

In other words, one of the powers of the human psyche is to "originate" ideas and to translate those ideas into actions that extend into the physical world. Our volitions are included among these. This does not mean, of course, that the self operates in a vacuum. We live in and are influenced by the world about us and by others. From the moment we are born, we have experiences, and those experiences contribute to who we are and how we think. We are affected by all the things that have influenced us at any time.

This means that at times our free choices will be very predictable. Yet it does not mean that *all* our choices are necessary or fixed. To think they are is to hold to hard determinism or to soft determinism (also called compatibilism). To hold to self-determinism, instead, means that regardless of the strength of our influences, when we have the information and influence that enables us, we are free to choose between alternatives. That is, in fact, a given in human experience which both hard and soft determinism fail to explain.

Edwards was indeed a compatibilist, one who claims that determinism and free will are compatible. But the "free will" that is compatible with determinism is not really free. Instead, it is bound in a world where just one choice is possible, a choice that is the infallible effect of a complex of causes that make it necessary.

A CRITICAL RESPONSE TO EDWARDS'S ARGUMENT FROM FOREKNOWLEDGE

My purpose now is to focus specifically on Edwards's argument, also in *Freedom of the Will*, that God's foreknowledge of the future rules out the possibility of free will as conceived by Arminians. As in the rest of his work on free will, this argument is—with one exception to be noted—entirely rationalistic. Edwards held that God's foreknowledge of the future means that the future is *necessary*— and therefore that there is no such thing as free will. As Guelzo notes, "For

Edwards, the ontology of an eternal God who holds an infallible foreknowledge of all events *ipso facto* eliminated any notion of human self-determination."[58]

In Part II of *Freedom of the Will*, Edwards treated the topic of foreknowledge, assigning himself two tasks: (1) to show that God has certain foreknowledge of the voluntary acts of moral agents, and (2) to show how it follows from this that such volitions are not contingent but necessary and therefore not free in the Arminian sense of the word.

Edwards's Argument from the Foreknowledge of God

In Section 11 Edwards attempted the first of these two tasks and succeeded admirably,[59] compiling what Sam Storms calls "an impressive body of exegetical evidence that he believes proves that God infallibly foreknows human volitions."[60] I could wish that all the advocates of open theism, for example, would carefully read this chapter. It is by far Edwards's best chapter, the only chapter in which he draws his argument from the Scriptures rather than from philosophical reason. I am in full agreement with him: God most certainly knows all the future, including human volitions and the moral acts—right or wrong—that express them.

Consequently, I need not give much space to reproducing his treatment. Even so, it may be helpful to share Edwards's outline, as follows (in my words).

Argument 1: God predicts the future volitions of moral agents, events that are dependent on those volitions, and his consequent judicial proceedings—none of which could be foretold if not foreknown.

Argument 2: God foreknew the fall of man, and of angels, else he could not have foreknown the great things consequent on those events such as all things pertaining to the great work of redemption, including the incarnation, life, death, and resurrection of Jesus Christ, plainly said to have been settled before the foundation of the world (Eph 1:3; 3:11; 1 Pet 1:2, 20; 2 Tim 1:9; Titus 1:2, etc.).

---

[58] Guelzo, "Return of the Will," 99.

[59] Edwards, *Freedom of the Will*, 239–56.

[60] Sam Storms, "Open Theism in the Hands of an Angry Puritan: Jonathan Edwards on Divine Foreknowledge," *The Legacy of Jonathan Edwards: American Religion and the Evangelical Tradition*, eds. D. G. Hart, Sean Michael Lucas, and Stephen J. Nichols (Grand Rapids: Baker, 2003), 117.

Argument 3: If God were ignorant in advance of human volitions, it would follow that he must often repent and wish he had done otherwise.

Argument 4: Then God must also be frequently liable to changing his mind and intentions about his future conduct.

Argument 5: Then furthermore, God, after creating the world, must also have been liable to be wholly frustrated in his purpose for the world.

These points, especially the first two, are liberally supported by extensive biblical evidence and persuasively presented in that light. My summary is woefully inadequate in comparison with Edwards's careful and impassioned presentation.

I found myself, while reading this, estimating how the neo-Arminian open theists would answer each of Edwards's points and the biblical passages he discusses. Open theists generally explain divine predictions of the future, in the Bible, in one of three ways: (1) as inferences that God draws from his understanding of the nature of the persons and circumstances involved, or (2) as promises of actions he has determined to take regardless of further circumstances; or (3) as promises of actions he will take that are conditioned on human response, even when the conditions are not stated as such. It follows that, at least in the first of these, God may sometimes be mistaken.

I am satisfied that open theism's denial of God's exhaustive foreknowledge of the future, including the free, moral acts of human beings, does not work. Though not the only problem with that viewpoint, its Achilles' heel is found in the fact that God had to know the sinfulness of Adam and the rest of the race "before the foundation of the world" in order to plan for the redemptive work of Jesus before the existence of the created order. This alone destroys both the assumptions and the arguments of open theism.[61] In short, I have no doubt that Edwards's affirmations in Section 11 stand on sound biblical footing: God has perfect, intuitive knowledge, in advance, of all the volitions, good and evil, of human beings.

It is important to note here that in *Freedom of the Will*, Edwards does not give "foreknowledge" the active meaning it often has in the works of traditional

---

[61] For a more thorough treatment and critique of open theism, see my "An Arminian Response to John Sanders's *The God Who Risks: A Theology of Providence*," *Journal of the Evangelical Theological Society* 44:3 (September 2001), 467–91. See that essay for reference to the works of open theists. See also my *God in Eternity and Time: A New Case for Human Freedom* (Nashville: B&H Academic, 2022), especially the chapter "Why Open Theism Doesn't Work."

Calvinism. He uses "prescience" as a synonym of foreknowledge more than once, including in his introduction to the subject in the opening paragraphs of Section 11.[62] Never does he suggest that it is the equivalent of foreordination. I think Guelzo is reading too much from Edwards's other writings when he says, in commenting on *Freedom of the Will*, that "he allowed . . . no distinction to open up between God's foreknowledge and divine foreordination of all events, since for Edwards the eternality of God guarantees that what is foreknown by God can only be thus foreknown because it has already been foreordained."[63] Indeed, Edwards does not say, anywhere in this work that I noticed, that foreknowledge is the effect of foreordination (or predestination), as Calvinists usually do.[64]

Even so, I do not doubt that Edwards *believed* that foreknowledge requires foreordination. In his conclusion to the volume, he observes, "I might also shew, how God's certain foreknowledge must suppose an absolute decree, and how such a decree can be proved to a demonstration from it: but that this discourse mayn't be lengthened out too much, that must be omitted for the present."[65] That, then, is not his argument in *this* volume, being rationalistic as it is; here he assumes only that foreknowledge is knowledge before the fact. That being the case, the Arminian can respond on Edwards's own grounds.

Edwards's Argument that Foreknowledge Disproves Free Will

This brings us to Section 12, where Edwards undertakes his second task: to show that certain foreknowledge means that all future volitions are *necessary*, and that therefore there is no freedom of the will as Arminians define that freedom. His argument, in summary, is that since God knows perfectly what volitions every person will have in the future, those volitions must *necessarily* come to pass—which means that there is neither any contingent event nor free will in the universe.

---

[62] Edwards, *Freedom of the Will*, 239; see also 265, for example.

[63] Guelzo, "Return of the Will," 93.

[64] See, for example, Louis Berkhof, *Systematic Theology* (Grand Rapids: Eerdmans, 1949), 102, where he observes that "the decree of God is . . . the foundation of His free knowledge" (which includes foreknowledge) and insists that "this must be maintained over against all those who believe in a conditional predestination."

[65] Edwards, *Freedom of the Will*, 435.

To flesh out this argument in more detail, God foreknows all things by necessity, and that knowledge is therefore a necessary "existent" (something that exists). Then the things foreknown, being indissolubly connected with the foreknowledge, must likewise be necessary existents. They cannot therefore be contingent existents since anything contingent may or may not exist and therefore could not be certainly foreknown. To suppose that God certainly foreknows something uncertain is a contradiction and impossibility. Consequently, Edwards argued, even an Arminian, if agreeing that God certainly foreknows all events, must agree that all events are necessary and not contingent, which eliminates the possibility of free will.[66]

This sort of argument was not new with Edwards. The underlying claim— that since God knows the future perfectly, all events *must* happen as he knows they will—is common, both in and out of theological discussion. Ordinary people, without thinking this through, may believe that it is so (a word about this later). But many theologians have likewise accepted this as obvious, going all the way back to the first Protestant himself, Martin Luther, who chided Erasmus:

> Do you suppose that He [God] does not will what He foreknows, or that He does not foreknow what He wills? If He wills what He foreknows, His will is eternal and changeless, because His nature is so. From which it follows by resistless logic, that all we do, however it may appear to us to be done mutably and contingently, is in reality done necessarily and immutably in respect of God's will.[67]

Some contemporary theologians express the same notion, among them Francis Beckwith, who poses the problem thus: "If God has perfect knowledge of future events including human actions, and if God cannot be wrong about what he knows, then all human actions will turn out only one way."[68]

---

[66] Edwards, 257–69.

[67] Luther, *Bondage of the Will*, 80.

[68] Francis J. Beckwith, "Limited Omniscience and the Test for a Prophet: A Brief Philosophical Analysis," *Journal of the Evangelical Theological Society* 36 (1993), 357. One notes that his use of "*will* turn out" (rather than "*must* turn out") actually affirms only certainty, not necessity, as will be explained below.

The open theists have also accepted this logic. Richard Rice, for example, writes, "In spite of assertions that absolute foreknowledge does not eliminate freedom, intuition tells us otherwise. If God's foreknowledge is infallible, then what he sees cannot fail to happen. . . . And if the future is inevitable, then the apparent experience of free choice is an illusion."[69]

As a result, open theists make a crucial mistake: they deny God's foreknowledge. Storms summarizes their syllogism: "The Bible portrays human choice as morally significant. . . . Therefore, human choice cannot be necessary. A foreknown choice is a necessary choice. Therefore, God does not foreknow human choice."[70] As I hope to make clear, this is mistaken and unnecessary, both logically and biblically.

Even so, this is the position of Edwards. He said, for example, that "if there be any infallible knowledge of future volitions, the event is necessary; or, in other words, that it is impossible but the event should come to pass."[71] Also: "On the whole, I need not fear to say, that there is no geometrical theorem or proposition whatsoever, more capable of strict demonstration, than that God's certain prescience of the volitions of moral agents is inconsistent with such a contingence of these events, as is without all necessity; and so is inconsistent with the Arminian notion of liberty."[72]

Edwards's Use of Terms

Essential to a discussion of Edwards's position is an understanding of the key words involved: *necessity, certainty,* and *contingency.* Everything in the discussion depends on the way one uses those words. Careful definition of the terms is absolutely essential to clarity and understanding. I will first define them as Edwards uses them, then show an inadequacy that requires more careful definition.

Contingency, according to Edwards, originally meant what comes to pass by chance or accident. In other words, people use the word when they cannot

---

[69] Richard Rice, "Divine Foreknowledge and Free-Will Theism," *The Grace of God, the Will of Man,* ed. Clark H. Pinnock (Grand Rapids: Zondervan, 1989), 127.

[70] Storms, "Open Theism in the Hands of an Angry Puritan," 116.

[71] Edwards, *Freedom of the Will,* 258.

[72] Edwards, 268–69. One notes again, by his comparison with geometrical theorems and his use of "strict demonstration" (meaning logical demonstration), his reliance on rationalistic method in this work.

discern the causes or antecedents of a thing, and so it comes to pass without their being able to predict it or incorporate it into their plans. Yet the word has another meaning, which Edwards adopted: something that comes to pass which *has no connection* with a cause or antecedent and therefore "has absolutely no previous ground or reason."[73] Since Edwards was confident that all events have a cause, then for him contingent events do not exist.[74]

Necessity, for Edwards, is therefore the opposite of contingency. Again, Edwards made a distinction between the "original" sense of a term and the way terms may be used in philosophical reasoning ("terms of art" he calls the latter). Commonly, necessity means something that comes to pass in spite of our opposition to it, something we cannot help. But "philosophical necessity" is "nothing else than the full and fixed connection between the things signified by the subject and predicate of a proposition, which affirms something to be true."[75] Here one sees again the rationalistic method of Edwards, in the analysis of propositions and drawing logical deductions from them. He meant, of course, that for any sentence (subject and predicate) that states a truth, there must be a "necessary" connection between its subject and predicate; there must be some antecedent in the subject that makes the predicate necessary.

For Edwards, then, any event—including a human volition—that has an antecedent that is the ground or reason for its being what it is, is a *necessary* event. Once again we see his reliance on the law of cause and effect—even if *cause* is more broadly defined than usual, as explained earlier.

There is an important caveat here. We must take note that in Edwards's argument *necessity* is nothing more than *certainty*, as he acknowledged: "Metaphysical or philosophical necessity is nothing different from certainty. I speak not now of the certainty of knowledge, but the certainty that is in things themselves, which is the foundation of the certainty of the knowledge of them; or that wherein lies the ground of the infallibility of the proposition which affirms them."[76] Again, he observed: "The only way that anything that is to come to pass hereafter, is or can be necessary is by a connection with something that is necessary in its own nature, or something that already is, or has been; so that

---

[73] Edwards, 155.
[74] Edwards, 214, 216.
[75] Edwards, 153; the entire discussion (150–55) must be carefully read; Edwards's verbiage sometimes gets in the way.
[76] Edwards, 151–52.

the one being supposed, the other *certainly* follows. . . . This is the necessity which especially belongs to controversies about the acts of the will."[77]

Indeed, in a letter that followed publication of *Freedom of the Will*, Edwards observed, "I have largely declared, that the connection between antecedent things and consequent ones . . . which is called moral necessity, is called by the name 'necessity' improperly. . . . Such a necessity as attends the acts of men's will, is more properly called 'certainty.'"[78] Concerning this, Edwards's editor commented: "Thus Edwards tended sometimes to remove the very word 'necessity,' after spending so much time giving it new meaning, in favor of another [certainty] whose 'original and proper meaning' was more suitable."[79]

Two things need to be said about this equation of necessity and certainty. First, the usage is confusing, and it would be better if the two words were distinguished; I will return to this. Second, it may very well mean that *Edwards was not arguing what his interpreters usually think he was arguing.* If indeed, as seems likely, Edwards really meant nothing more than that the future is *certain* to be what God knows it to be, then he was in fact not arguing against classic Arminianism on that score. I readily acknowledge that God's absolute foreknowledge of the future, including the volitions of human beings, entails the fact that everything in the future is *certain* to be what it will be.

An example of Edwards's reasoning along these lines may help clarify what I am saying. At one point in his discussion, to illustrate his claim that God's knowledge of the future means that the future is necessary, he offered a supposition:

> Let us suppose future existences some way or other to have
> influence back, to produce effects beforehand, and cause
> exact and perfect images of themselves in a glass [mirror],
> a thousand years before they exist, . . . that these images are
> real effects of these future existences, perfectly dependent on,
> and connected with their cause; . . . this proves . . . that the

---

[77] Edwards, 153–54. Italics added.

[78] Edwards, 456. The source is "Remarks on the *Essays on the Principles of Morality and Natural Religion*, in a letter to a Minister of the Church of Scotland." Even Luther (81) admitted as much: "I could wish, indeed, that a better term was available for our discussion than the accepted one, *necessity*, which cannot accurately be used of either man's will or God's." *Certainty* is the term he needed!

[79] Ramsey, "Editor's Introduction," 46.

existence of the things which are their causes, is also equally sure, firm and necessary.[80]

Then he observed that, in the same way, God's knowledge of the future is the effect of that future and likewise proves the *necessity* of that future. I am not entirely comfortable with applying the language of cause and effect to facts and knowledge, but Edwards was on to something here. Once one substitutes the words *certain/certainty* for *necessary/necessity*, any of us can agree with him. *And it is clear that his discussion does not really prove anything more than that— even though he treats it as though it does!*

A Better Definition of the Terms

This leads me to a better way of using the three key terms, as follows, and as best used in discussing the freedom of the will.[81] A *contingency* is anything that a person really can decide in more than one way: any event or volition that is not the inevitable consequence of natural law or an act of God. (It does *not* imply that something happens by mere chance or is random or uncertain.) A *certainty* is whatever event or volition is or was or will be. A *necessity* is an event or volition that *must* be because of some force other than itself, whether natural law or an act of God; it is actively caused, in other words, in such a way that no other effect is possible.

It is confusing to equate certainty with necessity, both because people mean different things by the words and because the words originate from different perspectives. The *certainty* of any event relates entirely to its "factness," *that* it is. The *necessity* of any event relates, instead, to its nature, to the kind of thing it is, to *how* or *why* it is. We can say, for example, that a given event came to pass "by necessity"; we would not say that something happened "by certainty."

To say that a future event or volition is *certain* is simply to say that it *will* be, without saying that it *must* be. Our Spanish-speaking friends say *Que será, será,* "What will be, will be." Yes, and to say "will *certainly* be" adds nothing. As it stands, the sentence is mere tautology, exactly like saying "A brown cow is a brown cow" or "what will be = what will be." But to say "must be" or "will

---

[80] Edwards, *Freedom of the Will*, 266.

[81] For a more thorough discussion of these terms and how they relate to the freedom of the future, see my "Foreknowledge, Freedom, and the Future," *Journal of the Evangelical Theological Society* 43:2 (2000), 259–71.

necessarily be" (as the words are often used and understood) is to say something more.[82]

In other words, everything that occurs—past, present, or future—does so *certainly*, which expresses nothing more than its factuality. Of all certain things, some occur *necessarily*, as the inevitable result of a cause like an act of God or natural law. Some other certain things occur *contingently*, as a result of a free choice when a different choice is possible. Events can be both certain and contingent, or certain and necessary, but not contingent and necessary.[83]

As a criticism of Edwards, then, I would suggest that he did not use the terms well. It would have been better had he used them as I have just defined them. Even then, he (like many Calvinists) might have denied, against me, that there are any such things as true contingencies in the history of the world. So be it. But at least I would have known for sure whether he meant to affirm that all future events, given God's foreknowledge, are both certain and necessary in the sense I have used the words. As it is, I can be sure only that he was in agreement with me that all future events are certain. Storms, agreeing with Edwards against open theists, words Edwards's claim more precisely: "*God foreknows the voluntary, free choices made by the people* and knows them in such a way that they remain *both voluntary and free*, on the one hand, and *absolutely certain to occur*, on the other."[84] If that is an accurate representation of Edwards, then we really have no argument, and I can only assume, of Edwards, that he had not read Arminius or any Arminian theologian who, like me, readily acknowledges the certainty of future volitions.[85] At the same time, I am fairly confident that Edwards himself must have thought that he was proving necessity and not mere certainty.

---

[82] Words can be tricky; I will consistently use the verb *will* to express certainty and the verb *must* to express necessity.

[83] That these terms *can* be used differently hardly matters; this is the way I am using them, and I am confident that it is the way most people will understand best when freedom and foreknowledge are discussed. I would suggest, then, that accepting these definitions and using the words thus is the way forward in the discussion. If these very words, defined in this very way, are not used, then *some* set of words with these meanings differentiated will be required for meaningful discussion.

[84] Storms, "Open Theism in the Hands of an Angry Puritan," 124.

[85] I am not immediately aware of any, later than Arminius himself, whom Edwards could have read on this point. For a good example later than Edwards, see the Wesleyan theologian Richard Watson (1781–1833), *Theological Institutes* (New York: Nelson & Phillips, 1850), 1:378–81.

Certainty Does Not Close the Future and is Not Opposed to Freedom of the Will

Some, upon hearing me say that the future is *certain* but not *necessary*, will say that I am playing with words, that this distinction matters not. Either way, they assume, if the future is foreknown, and is certain to occur, then it can be no other way; it *has* to be ("must be") as it will certainly be. I will readily acknowledge that this *seems* to be the case to many people on first thought about it, but I am confident in denying that this is so. To say that something *will* be a certain way in the future is no stronger than saying that some course of action *was* a certain way in the past. If we can believe that what happened in the past was not necessary but was a free choice that someone made when he or she could have made a different choice (a contingency, in other words), then the same thing applies to the future. My knowledge of the past did not cause it to be necessary, nor does God's knowledge of the future cause the future to be necessary.

I do not want the reader to think that I invented this notion or am alone in holding it. Evangelical Arminians have consistently affirmed both the exhaustive foreknowledge of God and the libertarian freedom of persons. Arminius himself said, for example, "If [God] resolve to use a force that . . . can be resisted by the creature, then that thing is said to be done, *not necessarily* but *contingently*, although its actual occurrence was certainly foreknown by God."[86] He proceeded in the passage to use as an illustration the prophecy that Jesus's bones would not be broken, denying that they *could* not have been broken but affirming the certainty that they *would* not.

Richard Watson, perhaps the leading early Wesleyan theologian, gave an extended treatment to the terms and their relationships, from which I quote but a few lines:

> The position, that *certain* prescience destroys *contingency*, is a mere sophism. . . . The great fallacy in the argument . . . lies in supposing that *contingency* and *certainty* are the opposites of each other. . . . Contingency in moral actions is, therefore, their *freedom*, and is opposed, not to *certainty*, but to *necessity*. . . .

---

[86] Jacobus Arminius, *The Writings of James Arminius*, trans. James Nichols and W. R. Bagnall (Grand Rapids: Baker, 1956), 1:291. The entire discussion makes a strong case that the same event cannot be both a necessity and a contingency but is a certainty.

> The question is not ... about the *certainty* of moral actions,
> that is whether they *will* happen or not; but about the nature
> of them, whether free or constrained, whether they *must* hap-
> pen or not. ... The foreknowledge of God has then no influ-
> ence upon either the freedom or the certainty of actions, for
> this plain reason, that it is *knowledge* and not *influence*; and
> actions may be certainly foreknown, without their being ren-
> dered necessary by that foreknowledge. ... But [some will say]
> if a contingency *will* have a given result, to that result it *must*
> be determined. Not in the least.[87]

To illustrate, let us suppose that tomorrow I will go for a walk in the woods
on a path I am not familiar with and that I will come to a fork in the path,
knowing only (from the signs, perhaps) that either one will finally lead me to
the same destination. I can choose either fork. I will not make the choice until
I come upon the fork. God knows which one I will choose, but it would be
backward to say that his knowledge means I *must* make the choice I am going
to make. Instead, the opposite is true. The choice I will make is the grounds
of his knowledge, not the other way around. (As already noted, even Edwards
acknowledged that the certainty that is in things themselves is the foundation
of the certainty of the knowledge of them.[88]) That he knows which choice I will
make does not close the future. It will not be reality until I make the choice, and
until the choice is made, I can make either one.

God also knows, by the way, all that will follow if I am going to make the
other choice.[89] Furthermore, he knows what sort of influences or circumstances
might incline me to one choice or the other, and if he should have any interest
in my choosing the right or the left, he *could* bring to pass those influences or

---

[87] Watson, *Theological Institutes*, 1:378–81.

[88] Edwards, *Freedom of the Will*, 151–52; cf. 265: "Knowledge of futurity, supposes futurity;
and a *certain knowledge* of futurity, supposes *certain futurity*, antecedent to that certain knowledge."

[89] As the philosophers like to express this, he knows "all possible worlds."

circumstances accordingly—thus using what some philosophers call "middle knowledge."[90] And I would still choose freely![91]

I hasten to insert that the Arminian position on this matter has no need for what is called Molinism, the view that the ordinary way God maintains his control or government of the world is by using his "middle knowledge" to provide all the circumstances in human situations in which we will do what he needs us to do for the achievement of his plans. For the Arminian, true libertarian freedom rests on the ability of the person to choose in either of two or more ways *in the same set of circumstances*, and God's government will be successful no matter which choice a person makes. That God knows which choices we will make, when we really can make either, and knows what will follow from either, goes hand in hand with his ordinary method of government in testing us (as he did Adam) by giving us true freedom of choice between options we really can choose. That way he needs no knowledge except foreknowledge; he does not need to tilt us in one direction or the other in order to achieve his objectives.[92]

God knows contingencies as well as necessities, and he knows the difference between them. Although the future is certain, then, it is not closed or fixed until it actually occurs. The choice of the person in time is what makes the event certain, but God knows it in advance as certain. Were the person to make a different choice when the time came, God would never have known anything different from that choice.

For that matter, *even if the future were not known, it would still be certain*, given that *certain* means only that it will be whatever it is when the time comes. Even Edwards acknowledged that an absolute decree of God regarding an event

---

[90] For "middle knowledge," see William L. Craig, "Middle Knowledge: A Calvinist-Arminian Rapprochement?", in *The Grace of God, the Will of Man*, ed. Clark H. Pinnock (Grand Rapids: Zondervan, 1989), 141–64; William L. Craig, *The Only Wise God* (Grand Rapids: Baker, 1987), 135, where he says, "Since [God] knows what any free creature would do in any situation, he can, by creating the appropriate situations, bring it about that creatures will achieve his ends and purposes and that they will do so *freely*." While this may help us understand how God succeeds in his wise government of the world *at times*, it does not speak to the problem of whether foreknowledge closes the future.

[91] God can, in fact, by sending rain, keep me from going to work in my garden, as I had planned, without interfering with my free will. But this takes us somewhat far afield, and I am not convinced that this is God's *ordinary* way of ensuring the success of his government.

[92] I might add that, for me, this means that God knows what will follow from either choice we make. It strikes me that if we really can choose option A or option B, so that either is actually possible, God must fully know both options and their consequences, and that libertarian freedom entails this.

adds nothing at all to its certainty.[93] If I am going to choose the right fork, God knows I am going to choose it. If I am going to choose the left fork, he knows that. Indeed, if I am going to choose, he knows I am going to choose—and that I am free to make either choice! He only knows what I am going to do if I am going to do it, so that *his interaction with me is the very same as if he learned it only when I chose it.*[94] God deals with us in time.

For that matter, it is also true that if my best friend knows which fork I am going to choose, I will choose that fork. He could not *know* it unless I was going to choose it. The same is true of God's knowledge of the future. To say that if God knows I will choose the right fork, for example, then I will choose the right fork, is no different from saying that if I will choose the right fork, I will choose the right fork. Back to *Que será, será!* The reason this discussion troubles some people is the fact that in some way they take the fact that God knows something in the future to mean that it is already a reality. In the realm of free human decision-making, it is the making of the decision that makes something reality.

To use the illustration that Erasmus and Luther argued about, God knew that Judas would betray Jesus. But in no way does that simple fact of knowledge settle that Judas *had* to betray him—and the fact that Luther brought foreordination into the discussion may show that he realized this. I do not know whether Judas could have chosen differently, although I assume he could have. But whether he could have or not is not settled by God's foreknowledge of the event. That much is clear.

There is an interesting and significant illustration of God's foreknowledge of contingencies in 1 Sam 23:1–13. David, doing his best to stay beyond Saul's hostile reach, continues to skirmish with the Philistines, who have attacked the village of Keilah. Obtaining the Lord's direction, he and his fighting men go to help and succeed in delivering Keilah from the invaders. Saul learns where David is and makes preparation to go and capture him there. David learns of this and, seeking God's direction once again, consults Abiathar the priest who—apparently by means of Urim and Thummim—answers David's questions. The first question is, "Will Saul come down?" The answer: he will. The

---

[93] Edwards, *Freedom of the Will*, 261.
[94] Except, of course, that by knowing all possibilities, he can act in a providential way for me even before I am aware of his work.

second question is based on that: "Will the men of Keilah deliver me into Saul's hands?" The answer: they will.

Now, in fact, neither of these two things came to pass! David and his men left the vicinity in order to avoid the foreknown contingencies that God revealed. Saul learned that they had gone and did not go to Keilah. And the inhabitants of that village did not betray David to Saul. All these were contingencies, conditional events foreknown as such. God knew they would occur only *if* David remained in Keilah, and he answered accordingly. Did God also know that David, once informed, would leave? Of course he did. But that he knew which of two possible sets of events would transpire does not change the fact that there were two possible sets of events and he knew what would transpire either way. It was not *necessary* that David go or stay. The choice was a *contingency* and was not settled until David decided. It was *certain* that those of Keilah would deliver David to Saul *if* he stayed, and it was *certain* that Saul would not capture him there if he left; it was *certain* that David would leave. Thus Edwards is right to say that God cannot know uncertainties, but he is wrong to say that contingencies are uncertainties.

I am the first to acknowledge that some people, including some who agree with me about human volition, find it difficult to grapple with the fact that God knows our choices—as the certainties they are—and yet we can choose differently. Reasoning like that which I have given in the preceding paragraphs often does not help them see this. In one sense, one simply has to "see" that the certainty of the future does not make it a necessary future. God knows the choices we will make, but we do not have to make them. Not *all* decisions are that way, of course, but there are decisions to be made when we are free not only to make the ones we make but also to make different ones. Foreknowledge does not close the door to the future.

One who has difficulty with this may find it helpful to focus on and accept a few interwoven truths: (1) that the certainty of the future means nothing more fatalistic than the certainty of the past; (2) that God's knowledge of the future no more makes it necessary than our knowledge of the past; (3) that what "will be" means nothing more than what "will be," whatever it is; and (4) that (for contingencies) what "will be" will be *only* if it is what is actually chosen in time.

What remains, then, is for the evangelical Arminian to insist that the future is just as open, and human volition just as free, as it would be if God did not know the future. In my earlier response to John Sanders, I commented on his objection that God could not really *test* Abraham, as to the offering of Isaac, if he already knew the story of his life in advance. The answer is that Abraham was not tested until he was tested *in time*. Until then, he really could pass or fail the test. God knew in advance that he would pass, of course, but *only because he did in fact pass the test in time*. God created space and time, understands this realm perfectly, and operates interactively with us in this realm—or else neither creation nor the incarnation would be possible.[95]

Perhaps saying all this yet another way will help. Logically, there are only two possibilities for the future: either the future that will be, or no future at all. If there is any future, it is the future that will be, and that future is certain—which adds nothing at all to the mere fact that it will be; to say it is the future that will be is what makes it logically certain. This affirmation, however, says absolutely nothing about *how* it will come about, whether necessarily or contingently. It will be only if and when it comes to pass, and for all contingent events that depend on free, human choices, those choices will bring it to pass, and only then will it be fixed. Until then, all such events remain to be determined when the free choices are made—even though God knows now what those choices will be.

In spite of this, someone who resists may say (as is often said) that since God knows the way we will choose, we must choose that way or else he would be wrong in his knowledge. That is standing foreknowledge on its head, and the answer is that he knows what we will choose *only* if indeed we are going to choose it. To return to the testing of Abraham, it would be foolish to say that he could not have failed because God knew he would pass. It would be just as wrongheaded for me to say that Joe Biden *had* to be elected president, or that Donald Trump could not have been reelected, *because* I know that Biden won. God's foreknowledge will always be right, of course, but only because he knows what will be.

I may add another important observation about Edwards's argument for the necessity of every human volition, based on foreknowledge and relying on cause-effect relationships. As a rational argument not based on biblical exegesis,

---

[95] My volume *God in Eternity and Time: A New Case for Human Freedom* (mentioned in an earlier note) develops this line of thinking about creation as an argument for freedom; a large section of that work is devoted to the issue of foreknowledge, including a response to Paul Helm's argument against freedom based on foreknowledge. Though couched in somewhat different terms, Helm's argument is logically the same as that of Edwards.

it does not affirm that the will is not free because of depravity, for example. Given the nature of his argument, then, *it must likewise apply to the first sin of Adam and Eve before the fall.* That means, therefore, that the choice to eat the forbidden fruit was, in Edwards's terms, likewise the necessary effect of all the causal influences in their circumstances. I am fairly confident that Edwards would have affirmed this, but he could do so only if "necessary" means nothing more than "certain." Indeed, as I have already noted, he regarded God's decree to *permit* Adam's sin as included in the meaning of "cause" as he broadly defined it. Again, then, one could easily argue the same for every sin of the human race after Adam, once more showing only that such volitions are certain but not necessary in the usual sense of the word. Any evangelical Arminian can agree with this.

CONCLUSION

I have responded to Edwards's two great arguments against free will. To the first I have countered that the minds of persons are not part of the cause-effect system that prevails in the natural realm. If I am right, Edwards's argument from cause and effect loses its power, his *necessity* is abrogated, and the *person* is free to will. His second argument, from foreknowledge, I have shown to be empty of force. It confuses necessity and certainty and finally reduces to the unjustified claim that what God knows will happen *must* happen—a claim that requires more than foreknowledge to sustain. Both of these arguments should be dropped.

Then we can go back to the primary considerations that have always governed the issue of free will. On biblical grounds, does God's sovereign, all-inclusive providential government of the world require that human beings cannot be allowed to determine for themselves whether to accept God's free and gracious gift of salvation or to reject it? And does human depravity mean that God must first regenerate persons before they can believe the gospel? These, and related questions, express the biblical and theological issues that have always dominated the debate about free will. That is the context in which the issue should be decided.

As for Edwards himself, I am not quite saying that, after all, he defined "cause" so broadly (as including an antecedent that does not exercise positive influence) and "necessity" so loosely (as mere "certainty") that one cannot be sure that he really denied free will. Regardless of his failure in terminology and argument, he was no doubt a true Calvinist. It remains, therefore, to offer a summary.

Edwards most certainly meant to affirm that free will means only that a person is free to make the choice he or she makes, to do as one pleases, not free to choose between live alternatives. In other words, Edwards did not believe in *libertarian freedom*—to use a phrase that has come to represent the power of alternative choice. In the end, he agreed with Luther and Calvin that human beings are free only to do evil. This is compatibilism (also called *soft determinism*), the view that people always (and "freely") choose what the sum total of their inclinations at the time dictates.

"Soft" or not, compatibilism is still determinism. It is not freedom, and those who hold compatibilism retreat into an unfalsifiable position: no matter how energetically I insist that I am often in situations where I can make either of two or more choices (including moral ones), they confidently affirm that I am fooling myself, that—after all—I always make the choice I make! Furthermore, the compatibilist is finally forced to say that every sin we commit has been the only possibility since (and including) Adam's sin. In the end, the compatibilist has it only a little better than a materialistic hard determinist. This is the reason secular science ultimately destroys freedom of the will, as Guelzo notes in citing Steven Pinker to the effect that "the scientific mode of explanation cannot accommodate the mysterious notion of uncaused causation that underlies the will."[96] That is the issue, then—and for Edwards as well.

The sum of Edwards's argument against freedom of the will is not, after all, strong against a *truly* Arminian perspective of freedom. Douglas Sweeney explains that Edwards maintained a distinction "between a fallen sinner's 'natural ability' (constitutional capacity) to repent and live a life that honors God and her 'moral inability' (ineradicable unwillingness) to do the very same (without the help of saving grace)."[97] If this means that human depravity renders a person unwilling and unable to respond to the gospel without a gracious work of the Holy Spirit that enables a positive response,[98] then I can enthusiastically say that no evangelical Arminian I know would affirm otherwise. This in no way curtails the moral freedom of a person to choose for or against God.

---

[96] Guelzo, "Return of the Will," 96.
[97] Sweeney, *Jonathan Edwards and the Ministry of the Word*, 151.
[98] Arminius called this "prevenient grace."

But Edwards, I think, meant more than this. In Calvinism, and no doubt in Edwards, the "saving grace" Sweeney refers to *begins* with regeneration, without which there is no enabling of the non-elect to exercise faith.

Chapter 8

Jonathan Edwards on Perseverance

Matthew McAffee

INTRODUCTION

Jonathan Edwards is likely the most prominent figure in the Calvinistic tradition this side of the Atlantic. In recent decades, John Piper's efforts in exploring the theology of Edwards and its relevance for spirituality and pastoral ministry have produced a wave of interest in Edwards among American evangelicals.[1] The academy has long held in high regard the prolific output of Edwards the pastor/scholar as well, considering it a worthy object of theological inquiry. In fact, Edwardsean scholarship has firmly established itself as a scholarly discipline.[2] One is justified in dubbing Edwards the American Calvinist *par excellence*.

The works of Edwards are not only of interest to those from within the Calvinistic tradition, however. They also hold value for those who stand outside

---

[1] See, e.g., John Piper, *A God Entranced Vision of All Things: The Legacy of Jonathan Edwards* (Wheaton: Crossway, 2004); *God's Passion for His Glory: Living the Vision of Jonathan Edwards* (Wheaton: Crossway, 2006).

[2] Note, e.g., the resources amassed by *The Jonathan Edwards Center* at Yale University for the purpose of scholarly research, http://edwards.yale.edu.

his theological framework. Reformed Arminianism finds in Edwards a useful conversation partner in Calvinist-Arminian discussions on soteriology.[3] One of the goals of this chapter is to validate this observation through an Arminian reading of Edwards on the perseverance of the saints. Though Edwards disagreed with Arminianism on a number of theological points, at times he was candid about how his Calvinistic sensibilities influenced the interpretation of key biblical texts on perseverance. In typical exchanges of theological discourse, advocates for one theological position or another commonly talk past their interlocutors in defense of a given interpretation. The writings of Edwards furnish a third party in such conversations, one somewhat removed from our own context yet fully invested in many of the same questions. One particularly fruitful area ripe for theological engagement between Arminianism and Calvinism is Edwards's views on the nature of perseverance.[4]

In this chapter I will explore the writings of Edwards that expound the nature of perseverance, examining them specifically from a Reformed Arminian theological framework. I will analyze Edwards from three vantage points: (1) perseverance and its relationship to election, (2) perseverance and its relationship to justification, and (3) perseverance and the significance of scriptural warnings. It is my hope that the following interaction with Edwards—from a non-Edwardsean specialist—will contribute meaningfully to the Calvinism/Arminianism conversation on the nature of perseverance.

---

[3] Throughout this essay I have adopted the term "Reformed Arminian," which is an adaptation of Robert E. Picirilli's "Reformation Arminian" as articulated in *Grace, Faith, Free Will: Contrasting Views of Salvation: Calvinism and Arminianism* (Nashville: Randall House, 2002), 35–64. For a full defense of this terminology, see J. Matthew Pinson, *40 Questions about Arminianism* (Grand Rapids: Kregel Academic, 2022), 55–80. F. Leroy Forlines utilized the term "Classical Arminianism" as a way of signaling alignment with the thought of Arminius in his own historical context as distinct from Wesleyan Arminians. See F. Leroy Forlines, *The Quest for Truth: Theology for Postmodern Times* (Nashville: Randall House, 2001), xvii–xviii. As Pinson explains, Arminius's theology was "distinctively Reformed" and was "a *variety* of Reformed theology rather than a *departure* from it" (*40 Questions about Arminianism*, 65). This understanding will also be assumed in this chapter for the term "Arminian" or "Arminianism" unless otherwise indicated.

[4] Earlier theologians of Arminian persuasion also realized the influence of Edwards's writings and attempted to respond to him in some fashion. One such example is the book-length treatment of perseverance and apostasy produced by Albert Nash, *Perseverance and Apostasy: Being an Argument in Proof of the Arminian Doctrine on that Subject* (New York: N. Tibbal, 1871).

PERSEVERANCE AND ELECTION

In reading Edwards's remarks on perseverance, it becomes clear that his understanding of the subject stems from his doctrine of the effectual calling of God's elect, which falls in line with the Calvinistic tradition. Perseverance is, therefore, the byproduct or outflow of God's sovereign work of grace in calling the sinner to conversion. In the words of Edwards, it would be "impossible, in the strictness of speech, that God should prosecute a design or aim at a thing, which he at the same time most perfectly knows will not be accomplished, as that he should use endeavors for that which is beside his decree."[5] In other words, it is unconscionable to suggest that God would proceed in his initial workings of grace, enabling conversion with the knowledge of that individual's failure to persevere in the faith. For Edwards such an outcome calls into question the efficacy and integrity of God's sovereign design. He continued to argue this point, asserting that "if the beginning of true faith and holiness, and a man's becoming a true saint at first, don't depend on the self-determining power of the will, but on the determining efficacious grace of God; it may well be argued, that it is so also with respect to men's being continued saints, or persevering in faith and holiness."[6] In the same way that God sovereignly elects certain persons to salvation without respect to the will of man, so God determines to complete this redemptive work in the individual to the end. Edwards elaborated:

> The conversion of a sinner being not owing to man's self-determination, but to God's determination . . . and it being very evident from the Scriptures, that the eternal election which there is of saints to faith and holiness, is also an election of them to eternal salvation; hence their appointment to salvation must also be absolute, and not depending on their contingent, self-determined will. From all which it follows, that it is absolutely fixed in God's decree, that all true saints shall persevere to actual eternal salvation.[7]

---

[5] Jonathan Edwards, *Freedom of the Will* in *The Works of Jonathan Edwards*, vol. 1, ed. Paul Ramsey (New Haven: Yale University Press, 1957), 435.

[6] Edwards, 1:436.

[7] Edwards, 1:436.

As already noted, Edwards's position on the certainty of the future condition of believers falls within the confines of classic Calvinistic thinking.
Edwards followed Calvin himself on this point, who, on the basis of God's sovereign election, concludes "that there is no danger of falling away, since the Son
of God, who asks that their piety may prove constant, never meets with refusal.
What then did our Saviour intend to teach us by this prayer [Lk. 22:32], but just
to confide, that whenever we are his our eternal salvation is secure?"[8]

Arminius differed from Calvinistic teaching on election and as a result
held to a slightly more nuanced view of perseverance than the predestinari-
ans of his day, and by extension differed significantly from its later proponents
like Edwards. For Arminius, predestination is rooted in God's foreknowledge,
in that he "has known from all eternity those individuals who through the
established means of his prevenient grace would come to faith and believe, and
through his subsequent sustaining grace would persevere in the faith. Likewise,
in divine foreknowledge, God knew those who would not believe and persevere."[9] God in eternity past decreed that salvation would be obtained through
the obedience of the Son in his destruction of sin by his own death, that he
would receive those who repent and believe in Christ and damn those who
would not, and that he would administer the necessary means for repentance
and faith "in a sufficient and efficacious manner."[10] Election is therefore conditioned on one's response to God's predestined means of grace (which are sufficient and efficacious, according to Arminius) and is initiated by the convicting,
drawing work of the Spirit.[11] The sinner's conversion is entirely dependent on
God's grace, while at the same time contingent on the individual's not resisting
that grace.

As election is contingent on not resisting divine grace, so perseverance
is conditioned on believers' not resisting that grace.[12] In the same way that

---

[8] John Calvin, *Institutes of the Christian Religion*, 2 vols., trans. Henry Beveridge (Grand
Rapids: Eerdmans, 1994), 3.24.6, 2:246.

[9] W. Stephen Gunter, *Arminius and His* Declaration of Sentiments: *An Annotated Translation
with Introduction and Theological Commentary* (Waco, TX: Baylor University Press, 2012), 135.

[10] Gunter, 135.

[11] Cf. Calvin's description of the Spirit's work in regeneration with the use of the term "enlighten":
"For those whom Christ enlightens with the knowledge of his name." See *Institutes*, 3.24.6, 2:245.

[12] Note also the explanation of Nash in his critique of Edwards: "The prayer of faith is
answered in the bestowment of the grace necessary for the accomplishment of the contem-
plated end. But men may either co-operate with, or resist the grace given. These conclusions are
necessarily involved in man's responsibility to God." Nash, *Perseverance and Apostasy*, 45.

Edwards's and his Calvinistic predecessors' view of unconditional election determines that their understanding of perseverance be unconditional, so the Arminian view of conditional election necessitates that perseverance be conditional.

PERSEVERANCE AND JUSTIFICATION

Edwards in many places defined perseverance in relation to justification, arguing that perseverance is one of a number of conditions for justification.[13] By condition, Edwards meant that "the promise of acceptance is made only to a persevering sort of faith, and the proper evidence of its being of that sort is actual perseverance."[14] It is important for Edwards to distinguish between the cause and condition, or as Jason Achmoody puts it, "causal conditionality and noncausal conditionality."[15] Samuel Logan, whose discussion informs Achmoody on this point, notes that in *Freedom of the Will*, Edwards scrupulously maintained that only God's action provides the cause of justification. At the same time, he allowed for several conditions that serve to confirm the reality of justification in the individual.[16] Faith is one of the more prominent and unique of these conditions, but among them Edwards also offers the condition of perseverance.[17]

---

[13] It should be noted that Edwards viewed faith as unique from all other conditions. See especially Samuel T. Logan, "The Doctrine of Justification in the Theology of Jonathan Edwards," *Westminster Theological Journal* 46 (1984), 34–42. Edwards explained the unique role of faith as the instrument of receiving justification: "Whereas it was not intended that faith was the instrument wherewith God justifies, but the instrument wherewith we receive justification; not the instrument wherewith the justifier acts in justifying, but wherewith the receiver of justification acts in accepting justification." Jonathan Edwards, "Justification by Faith Alone," *Works of Jonathan Edwards, Volume 19. Sermons and Discourses, 1734–1738*, ed. M. X. Lesser (New Haven: Yale University Press, 2001), 153. Edwards proceeded to specify in the same section of this sermon that "Christ, the mediator by whom, and his righteousness by which, we are justified, is more directly the object of this acceptance and justification, which is the benefit arising therefrom more indirectly; and therefore, if faith be an instrument, it is more properly the instrument by which we receive Christ, than the instrument by which we receive justification" (153).

[14] Jonathan Edwards, "Perseverance in Faith," in *The Miscellanies*, WJE, vol. 13, ed. Harry S. Stout (New Haven: Yale University Press, 1994), 480.

[15] Jason Achmoody, "Jonathan Edwards' Doctrine of Perseverance As It Relates to the Nature of Saving Faith and Christian Assurance," (Th.M. thesis, Dallas Theological Seminary, 2002), 22, following Logan, "The Doctrine of Justification," 33.

[16] Logan, 33.

[17] On faith's uniqueness as a condition of justification, see Achmoody, "Jonathan Edwards' Doctrine of Perseverance," 23–24.

Traditionally, scholars of Edwards have attempted to plant his views on perseverance firmly within the broader Reformed tradition. From what we find in seminal works like *Freedom of the Will*, for example, Edwards appears to have stood in this tradition by emphasizing that the regenerate will most certainly persevere. Not all scholars have agreed on this assessment, however. Some have interpreted Edwards as somewhat innovative regarding perseverance. Achmoody picks up on this difficulty, conceding that there are those who have argued that Edwards's view concerning the relationship between perseverance and faith "virtually destroys the doctrine of justification by faith alone."[18]

Thomas Schafer's work on Edwards and justification is to date the most comprehensive attempt at showing Edwards veering slightly away from Reformed orthodoxy on matters of justification and its relationship to obedience, claiming that one "cannot help feeling that the conception of 'faith alone' has been considerably enlarged—and hence practically eliminated."[19]

Jeffrey Waddington comes to Edwards's defense by arguing, among other things, that Schafer has misread Edwards without proper sensitivity to the Reformed context within which he operated.[20] Waddington then concludes that the great New England preacher and theologian "on all points . . . falls within the confines of Reformed Protestant orthodoxy" with regard to the doctrine of justification by faith.[21] We might agree with Waddington's corrective here, at least from the vantage point of Edwards's own self-perception and sense of belonging to the Reformed tradition that emerges from his writings. More recently, however, Gary Steward stresses that Reformed defenders of Edwards on justification have failed to recognize how he blends faith and obedience in a way that makes continued justification dependent on them.[22] As Steward explains, "Future acts of faith, for Edwards, have the same function in

[18] Achmoody, 34–35.

[19] Thomas A. Schafer, "Jonathan Edwards and Justification by Faith," *Church History* 20 (1951): 60. Achmoody, "Jonathan Edwards' Doctrine of Perseverance," 35, cites Schafer as referring specifically to the relationship between perseverance and faith, though Schafer himself does not use the term "perseverance."

[20] Jeffrey C. Waddington, "Jonathan Edwards's 'Ambiguous and Somewhat Precarious' Doctrine of Justification?" *Westminster Theological Journal* 66 (2004): 359.

[21] Waddington, 372.

[22] Gary Steward, "What Is Saving Faith Really? Jonathan Edwards' Departure from Reformed Theology, Part 2," *Credo* (May 17, 2022), 4, https://credomag.com/2022/05/what-is-saving-faith-really-jonathan-edwards-departure-from-reformed-theology-part-2/.

justification as the first act of faith," meaning that believers "persevere in faith and obedience *in order to be justified*."[23]

All parties must concede, however, that Edwards felt that, at least to some degree, more needed to be said regarding the necessity of perseverance for salvation than the Calvinistic tradition had thus far offered. In his *Miscellanies* 729, he offered a defense of his own interest in matters relating to the "manner" of perseverance, lamenting that "though perseverance is acknowledged by Calvinian divines to be necessary to salvation, yet it seems to me that the manner in which it is necessary has not been sufficiently set forth."[24]

Ava Chamberlain notes a development in Edwards's thinking on perseverance as reflected in his extant writings on the topic. She points out that in earlier entries from his collection of notes entitled *Miscellanies*, Edwards maintained that union with Christ accepted by faith "was the sole condition of justification," while in subsequent entries he "modifies this viewpoint."[25] Chamberlain goes on to explain that although Edwards continued to affirm that a person is justified at the first act of faith, he gave perseverance "a status almost equivalent to faith by arguing that perseverance is contained 'virtually in that first act.'"[26] The motivation for such a development in Edwards's thinking appears to be largely pragmatic (perhaps even pastoral) in nature. This feature becomes all the more clear when understood against the backdrop of the historical circumstances surrounding his ministry and his ever-growing attack against antinomianism and the popular Arminianism of his day.[27] This acknowledgment should temper Chamberlain's claim that Edwards is simply making theological adjustments, which seems to me to be an oversimplification.

As Edwards took up the task of explaining the "manner" of perseverance, his discussion became rather complex, at times exhibiting a surprisingly Arminian tone. For example, consider the following remarks concerning the necessity of perseverance for the attainment of eternal life:

---

[23] Steward, 6–7.

[24] Jonathan Edwards, "Perseverance," in *The Miscellanies*, in *WJE*, vol. 18, ed. Ava Chamberlain (New Haven: Yale University Press, 2000), 353.

[25] See Edwards, 18:22, where Chamberlain notes Nos. 795 and 808.

[26] See Edwards, 18:13.

[27] See the helpful summary of this background in Logan, "The Doctrine of Justification," 26–30. One should note that in Edwards's attacks on Arminian doctrine, it becomes increasingly clear that his theological opponents were not what we are calling Reformed Arminian. To some degree the Arminianism he was arguing against was much more akin to Pelagianism than to the teachings of Arminius himself.

'Tis owned to be necessary as a *sine qua non*; and also is expressed by that, that though it is not that by which we first come to have a title to eternal life, yet is it necessary in order to the actual possession of it, as the way to it; that it is impossible that we should come to it without perseverance, as 'tis impossible for a man to go to city or town without traveling throughout the road that leads to it. But we are really saved by perseverance, so that salvation has a dependence on perseverance, as that which influences in the affair, so as to render it congruous that we should be saved. Faith is the great condition of salvation; 'tis that *by* which we are justified and saved.[28]

These are strong words, words that certainly provide fodder for Chamberlain's argument that Edwards had adjusted his views on faith and justification.[29] Yet Edwards did maintain justification through the primary condition of faith, describing perseverance as a property of faith: "Though a sinner is justified on his first act of faith, yet even then, in that act of justification, God has respect to perseverance, as being virtually in that first act; and 'tis looked upon as if it were a property of faith, by which the sinner is then justified."[30] The term "virtual" continues to feature prominently, as he explains that perseverance is a promise, or guarantee, once the first act of faith has occurred. This promise is not conditioned ultimately on believers' continued obedience in and of themselves but finds certainty in the fact that it is divinely accomplished, as believers rely on the certainty that "we shall have salvation."[31]

---

[28] See Edwards, "Perseverance", and Edwards, "Perseverance, in What Sense Necessary for Salvation," *WJE* 18:353–4. Note that Edwards utilizes the imagery of traveling to a town in illustrating perseverance elsewhere, as in his sermon on this topic in *WJE*, 19:602.

[29] See Edwards, *The Miscellanies* 18:22, where Chamberlain argues that in earlier entries Edwards indicated that faith was the "sole condition" of justification, while in later entries he expanded his thinking on the matter, elevating perseverance to a level "almost equivalent to faith." Yet Achmoody prefers to emphasize the uniqueness of faith among Edwards's noncausal conditions, pointing out that its unique role in justification is related to the believer's union with Christ (Achmoody, "Jonathan Edwards' Doctrine of Perseverance," 24 n. 39).

[30] Edwards, "Perseverance, in What Sense Necessary for Salvation," 18:354. Cf. Calvin's remarks on justification being a "symbol" of election: "In regard to the elect, we regard calling as the evidence of election, and justification as another symbol of its manifestation, until it is fully accomplished by the attainment of glory" (*Institutes*, 3.21.7, 2:211).

[31] Edwards, "Perseverance, in What Sense Necessary for Salvation," 18:356.

It is when Edwards entertains the potential problem that would ensue if perseverance were not to accompany justification that an Arminian reader might be surprised. For example, all the while maintaining that "by divine establishment it shall follow," he posited that without perseverance, "the act of justification should be suspended, till the sinner had persevered in faith."[32] The entertainment of such a possibility reminds us of the challenges that inevitably arise on a practical level. Edwards himself acknowledged these challenges as he attempted to maintain the certainty of perseverance and the need for perseverance, both at the same time.

Commenting on several biblical passages where perseverance might appear to be in question, Edwards conceded that these texts imply "that if true believers should fail of a persevering in faith they would therein fail of a title to salvation, or a state of salvation, and would be in a lost state."[33] In one place Edwards reflected on the Lord's prayer in John 17 and Jesus's discussion of the vine in John 15, and in connection with the "plucked out" language from John 10:28. Edwards concluded, "So believers being overthrown in their faith, or their [not] knowing Christ's voice and following him, is called being plucked out of Christ's hand; and it is implied that the consequences would be their perishing. And it also seems to be implied [that] their possession to eternal life by Christ's gift depends on their perseverance."[34]

When the theology of divinely determined perseverance collides with practical exhortations in Scripture to persevere, there is little difference between the approach of Edwards in handling these texts and what one would find in the Reformed Arminian tradition. For both, the warnings of Scripture are undeniably strong and warrant the scrutiny of their interpreters. The problem for Edwards and others within the Calvinist tradition, however, is that it is difficult for these biblical texts to maintain their motivational teeth, so to speak, when they are prefaced by the certainty of perseverance. Even Calvin apparently sensed this practical dilemma when he stated:

> But anxiety arises as to our future state. For as Paul teaches,
> that those are called who were previously elected, so our

---

[32] Edwards, 18:354.
[33] Edwards, "Justification by Faith Alone, Perseverance of Faith," 18:510–11.
[34] Edwards, 18:511.

Saviour shows that many are called, but few chosen (Matt. 22:14). Nay, even Paul himself dissuades us from security, when he says, "Let him that thinketh he standeth take heed lest he fall" (1 Cor. 10:12). . . . In fine, we are sufficiently taught by experience itself, that calling and faith are of little value without perseverance, which, however, is not the gift of all.[35]

This difficulty will become more evident as we turn our attention to Edwards's treatment of the more prominent warning passages from the book of Hebrews.

PERSEVERANCE AND SCRIPTURAL WARNINGS

The Scriptures contain many warnings for the believer regarding the perils of falling away or straying from the faith. Time and space do not permit us to discuss Edwards's interpretation of every warning passage found in the Bible. Thus we will limit the major portion of our discussion to his remarks regarding the warnings from the New Testament letter to the Hebrews (6:4–6; 10:25–29).[36] Our treatment will also require brief comment on the sin against the Holy Spirit from the Gospels (Matt 12:31–32; Mark 3:28–30; Luke 12:10). Before turning our attention to these texts, however, we will explore Edwards's view regarding the purpose of scriptural warnings in the economy of perseverance.

In the application section of one of his major sermons on perseverance, Edwards outlined two divine purposes in giving exhortations for saints to persevere and not fall away. The first, he argued, is to stimulate self-examination in the individual as a means of determining whether one's faith is of the

---

[35] Calvin, *Institutes*, 3.24.6, 2:245–46. Elsewhere Calvin remarked, "For although he loves the gifts which he daily bestows upon us, inasmuch as they proceed from that fountain, still our duty is to hold fast by that gratuitous acceptance, which alone can support our souls; and so to connect the gifts of the Spirit which he afterwards bestows, with their primary cause, as in no degree to detract from it" (Calvin, *Institutes*, 3.14.21, 2:89).

[36] See the following commentaries for an Arminian perspective on these passages: Paul Ellingworth, *The Epistle to the Hebrews: A Commentary on the Greek Text*, NIGTC (Grand Rapids: Eerdmans, 1993), 317–25, 531–44; Stanley Outlaw, *The Book of Hebrews*, The Randall House New Testament Commentary, gen. ed. Robert E. Picirilli (Nashville: Randall House, 2005), 118–31, 251–59; Gareth Lee Cockerill, *The Epistle to the Hebrews*, NICNT (Grand Rapids: Eerdmans, 2012), 267–79, 481–95. Other significant warnings from Hebrews include 2:1–3a; 3:6; 3:7–19; 4:1–13; and 10:32–39.

persevering type.[37] The second use is a means of divine influence in the life of the true believer. Note the words of Edwards on this aspect of scriptural warnings:

> Though it be promised that true saints shall be so influenced and assisted, as that they shall persevere; yet this is one means by which God influences them, viz. counsels and warnings against falling away; in many places that have already been mentioned. And those that don't earnestly endeavor to persevere, it looks dark and doubtful whether or no they are such as God has promised to influence [and assist].[38]

It is remarkable that Edwards described one of the uses of these warnings in terms of influence. Theologically, the Calvinistic tradition has typically explained the divine relationship with humanity in the work of redemption as causal. Reformed Arminian theologian F. Leroy Forlines adopted an "influence and response" framework for his understanding of God's relationship to humanity in the work of redemption, contending that interpersonal relationships do not operate under the rubric of cause and effect.[39] From an Arminian standpoint, the nature of God's preemptive drawing activity is one of influence and response wherein the Holy Spirit convicts individuals of sin, calling and enabling them to respond to the offer of grace in Christ's provisional atonement.[40]

---

[37] Edwards, "Persevering Faith," 19:603.

[38] Edwards, 19:608.

[39] Forlines, *The Quest for Truth*, 312–14. Forlines explained, "A person is one who thinks with his mind, feels with his heart, and acts with his will. In the simple sense of the terms *cause* and *effect*, one person cannot *cause* another person to do anything. This does not depend upon the lack of ability that one person has to influence another. Rather, the inability of one person to cause another person to do something grows out of the nature of what it means to be a *person*. When an appeal is made to a person, it is inherent with the nature of a person to consider the appeal and then make a decision. There is no such thing as a person doing or not doing something *without having made a decision*. This is true regardless of how strong the influence may be upon him or her" (313).

[40] On the reception of the Holy Spirit "by faith," note especially Gal 3:2, 5, 14; John 7:39; Eph 1:13; Acts 11:17; 15:7–9, as well as the discussion of these passages in Picirilli, *Grace, Faith, Free Will*, 170–72.

In our examination of the warning passages throughout the Scriptures, it is reasonable and consistent to conclude that God continues to exert his influence in the life of believers, urging them to persevere to the end.[41] This kind of language, however, is not consistent with the divinely determined perseverance Edwards espoused, leading him to wonder if those who do not persevere were ever truly converted in the first place. Yet this suggestion would seem to question the effectiveness of God in influencing perseverance, if one of the purposes of these texts is to do just that.[42] This point becomes even clearer when we consider God's desire for perseverance, as even Edwards pointed out from Deut 5:29, "Oh that they had such a heart as this, to fear Me and to keep all My commandments all day long, so that it would be good for them and for their sons forever."[43] However, we all know that this divine desire was not fully realized among the Israelites. Many, if not most, did not persevere.

Warnings from Hebrews

Edwards discussed at length the aforementioned warning passages from the book of Hebrews in several places. The first place we find a major discussion of Heb 6:4–6 is in a collection of sermons and essays entitled *Ethical Writings*.[44] The second major discussion of this passage is found in his *Notes on Scripture*.[45] In both places, Edwards also discussed the parallel warning passages from Heb 10:25–29.

Interpreters have long noted the difficulties that these warnings present for any theologian, and even Calvin himself exposed misuses of Hebrews 6 in particular.[46] His initial remarks on verse 4 would almost lead one to believe that

---

[41] Nash, *Perseverance and Apostasy*, 45, utilizes this same terminology to describe God's work in "influencing" perseverance: "While, therefore, real perseverance involves the active co-operation of free beings with divine *influence*, neither the prayers of Christ, nor the prayers of good men for the preservation of saints, is any proof of their infallible perseverance." Italics added.

[42] Edwards's way around this theological conundrum would be to say that they are intended to influence true believers, not false professors. Arminians charge that such an argument, however, amounts to theological finagling and cannot be supported from these texts. On the contrary, the Arminian view argues that the addressees are assumed to be believers in the truest sense.

[43] This translation is my own.

[44] Jonathan Edwards, "Love More Excellent Than Extraordinary Gifts of the Spirit," in *Ethical Writings*, vol. 8, ed. Paul Ramsey (New Haven: Yale University Press, 1957), 162–66.

[45] Jonathan Edwards, *Notes on Scripture*, in *WJE*, vol. 15, ed. Stephen J. Stein (New Haven: Yale University Press, 1998), 176–77, 272, 598–99.

[46] See John Calvin, *Commentaries on the Epistle of Paul the Apostle to the Hebrews*, trans. John Owen (Edinburgh: Calvin Translation Society; reprint, Grand Rapids: Baker Books,

he understood the expressions "having been enlightened," "having tasted the heavenly gift," "having become sharers of the Holy Spirit," and "having tasted the goodness of the word of God and the powers of the age to come" to be descriptions of true believers, especially when he remarked, "Let us know that the Gospel cannot be otherwise rightly known than by the illumination of the Spirit, and that being thus drawn away from the world, we are raised up to heaven, and that knowing the goodness of God we rely on his word."[47] Yet for Calvin, and perhaps for all serious interpreters of this passage, the crux of the matter has to do with the nature of falling away. In an attempt to maintain his view on effectual calling, Calvin suggested that it is not unreasonable to assume that God has also granted the reprobate "some taste of his grace," that he has illuminated their minds "with some sparks of his light," that he has granted "some perception of his goodness," or that he would "in some sort engrave his word on their hearts."[48] In the tradition of Calvin and his followers, this is what it means to fall away: illumined reprobates fall away from the limited workings of the Holy Spirit in their hearts, workings that are short of true conversion.

Edwards's view of falling away does line up with this traditional Calvinistic interpretation. At the same time, however, we might argue that in his attempt to offer further elucidation for this theological difficulty, he created additional problems for Calvinism. In the taxonomy of Edwards, there is a distinction between the "extraordinary" and "ordinary" gifts of the Spirit.[49] His distribution of this terminology is not always consistent and at times seems contradictory. At one point Edwards stated that the extraordinary gifts of the Spirit result in the conversion of sinners and the edification of the saints in holiness, "which is the fruit of the ordinary influences of the Spirit."[50] Elsewhere he called these same extraordinary gifts "miraculous influences" that accompanied the apostolic ministry of the early church and held remarkable sway over observers.[51] It would seem, then, that the "ordinary" gifts are those works that bring about regeneration. This distinction provides the means of explaining the descriptions from Heb 6:4–5 outlined above: they refer to the Holy Spirit's miraculous

---

1999), 135.

[47] Calvin, 137.

[48] Calvin, 138.

[49] Edwards, "Love More Excellent," 8:162.

[50] Edwards, 8:162.

[51] Edwards, 8:165.

(thus the term "extraordinary") work in and among those whom he did not actually regenerate. The language Edwards employed to articulate the status of these individuals is rather unique for the Calvinistic perspective, especially in his willingness to allow for their "having" the Holy Spirit in a limited sense: "'Tis not probable that they should *have* the Holy Ghost with respect to his miraculous influences, and not feel anything of the power of it in their souls."[52]

At this juncture Calvinism encounters serious difficulty in its effort to exegete a divinely determined perseverance from texts like Hebrews 6. The Arminian perspective often raises objections to Calvin's denial of true regeneration here with one simple question: if they were not regenerate, from what are they falling away? Edwards would then answer, they are falling away from the extraordinary influence of the Spirit. Once they "had received the Holy Ghost in his extraordinary gifts," to turn away from such divine illumination would be to sin against the Holy Spirit[53] and thus commit apostasy.[54]

Once the illumined reprobate individual has rejected the Spirit's miraculous workings within him or her, it is impossible to restore that person to repentance. Yet one thing remains rather perplexing: in what sense would those who have never truly repented be incapable of a second repentance? The language of repentance (*metanoeō*, "to repent"/*metanoia*, "repentance," often with *pisteuō*, "to believe") in the New Testament becomes a technical term denoting one of the key elements of conversion, regardless of whether we believe the Spirit, by regeneration, has enabled the sinner to repent (Calvin) or the sinner has not resisted the prevenient grace of the Spirit (Arminius).[55] Therefore, in the clear

---

[52] Edwards, 8:165. Italics added.

[53] For Edwards, the sin against the Holy Spirit (Matt 12:31–32; Mark 3:28–30; Luke 12:10) equals the sin of falling away mentioned in the book of Hebrews. In the words of Edwards, "Reproaching the Holy Ghost in his extraordinary and miraculous gifts and operations was this blasphemy against the Holy Ghost. So did they to a degree who themselves had those extraordinary gifts, that yet totally apostatized from Christianity and turned persecutors, spoken of, Hebrews 6:4–6, 'For 'tis impossible for those who were once enlightened, and have tasted of the heavenly gift, and were made partakers of *the Holy Ghost*, and have tasted the good word of God, and the powers of the world to come, if they shall fall away, to renew them again to repentance; *seeing they crucify to themselves the Son of God afresh, and put him to open shame*'" (Edwards, "Sin against the Holy Ghost," 18:310). This was also true for Arminius, who included the warning passages from Hebrews in his treatment of the sin against the Holy Spirit. See Jacobus Arminius, *The Works of James Arminius*, trans. James Nichols and William Nichols, 3 vols. (Nashville: Randall House, 2007), 2:731–54, "A Letter on the Sin against the Holy Spirit."

[54] Edwards, "Love More Excellent," 8:164.

[55] On *metanoeō*, "to repent," see Matt 3:2; 4:17; Mark 1:15; 6:12; Acts 17:30; 26:20. On *metanoia*, "repentance" see Matt 3:8 (cf. Luke 3:8); Luke 15:7; 24:47; Acts 5:31; 11:18; 20:21; 2 Tim

language of the writer of Hebrews here in 6:4–6, once a person has repented (i.e., experienced regeneration), were he or she to fall away from that regenerate state, he or she could not repent a second time. Not only does this text close the door on the possibility for repeated regeneration, but it also poses serious problems for Edwards and his insistence on the fact that the passage addresses false professors.

One of the unintended (but nonetheless necessary) consequences of Edwards's proposal regarding the Spirit's extraordinary gifts in his interpretation of Heb 6:4–5 is that it brings into question the Calvinistic way of understanding the sovereign work of the Spirit. In some instances, the work of the Spirit within the sinner produces regeneration, but in other cases the Spirit's activity in the sinner does not. On this point, Edwards was moving rather close to the Arminian view that the Spirit of God extends the offer of grace that the sinner must then receive through faith. We can only say that Edwards came close, however, since the Spirit is conducting two distinct works: one that leads to salvation and one that does not. This perspective seems only to obfuscate the matter of Heb 6:4–6 by sidestepping the straightforward reading of the text and is difficult to maintain from Scripture elsewhere.[56]

An Arminian Exegetical Response

Arminians believe it is extremely hard to argue from Heb 6:4–6 that the writer of Hebrews had anything in mind other than describing genuine believers who renounce their faith and thus fall away. The list of descriptions in verses 4–5 is rather impressive and tends to heighten the severity of this warning. Particularly significant is the author's use of *metochos*, "partakers", in the expression *metochous genēthentas pneumatos hagiou*, "having become partakers of the Holy Spirit" (6:4). From the internal evidence of the book of Hebrews, we

---

2:25; 2 Pet 3:9.

[56] It also seems strange for Edwards to make this appeal to the Spirit's work being that of the miraculous apostolic kind considering his cessationist views. Note especially his remarks in a sermon he preached attempting to curtail certain abuses he perceived in believers making claims about the miraculous workings of the Spirit. He stated, "Those influences of the Spirit giving immediate revelations were designed to be continued only while the church was in a state of childhood, in the sense explained, and never were intended for any stated continuance in the church of God. 'Tis plainly implied in the text that faith, hope, and charity shall abide when the church in some sense shall have become adult, at a time when prophecies and [visions] shall have ceased and vanished away." Jonathan Edwards, "Extraordinary Gifts of the Spirit are Inferior to Graces of the Spirit," *WJE*, vol. 25, ed. Wilson H. Kimnach (New Haven: Yale University Press, 2006), 285. I would like to thank Barry Raper for pointing this out to me.

find that the author uses this word in 3:1 to refer rather explicitly to genuine believers: *adelphoi hagioi klēseōs epouraniou metochoi*, "holy brethren, partakers of the heavenly calling." Here, *metochos* means "partake" in the sense of full and complete participation, as indicated by the fact that it is in apposition to *adelphoi hagioi*, "holy brethren."

Arminians observe another important feature of this description arising from the use of *geuomai*, "to taste, experience": *geusamenous te tēs dōreas tēs epouraniou*, "and after tasting of the heavenly gift" (6:4). Interpreters often argue that the meaning of this term is akin to our English sense of the word "taste," which can indicate a partial sampling just short of the full experience. It is true that throughout the New Testament (and Greek literature in general), the word *geuomai* sometimes means "to taste partially," but it is always limited to physical objects, such as food, for example.[57] Yet, whenever this verb is used metaphorically (i.e., accompanied by an object that is anything other than food or drink), it indicates the full experience of the verbal object. One of the more notable examples of this usage is when it takes the object *thanatos*, "death" (lit. "to taste death"), meaning "to die."[58] The immediate context of Hebrews strengthens the case for this meaning here since in 2:9 the author utilizes this verb in reference to Jesus experiencing death on behalf of everyone: *hopōs chariti theou huper pantos geusētai thanatou*, "thus by the grace of God he might taste death for everyone." Another metaphorical use of *geuomai* occurs in 1 Pet 2:3, which unquestionably refers to a full experience: *ei egeusasthē hoti chērstos ho kyrios*, "if you have tasted that the Lord is good." Peter goes on to address those who have tasted the goodness of God, declaring that they are being built up as a "spiritual house" (*oikos pneumatikos*) to become a "holy priesthood" (*hierateuma hagion*) (1 Pet 2:5).

Coming back to Heb 6:5, this same verb occurs again, only this time with yet another object: *kalon geusamenous theou hrēma*, "having tasted the good word of God." What would it mean to experience fully "the good word

---

[57] E.g., a meal (Luke 14:24; Acts 10:10; 23:14), water (John 2:9), poisonous plants (Matt 27:34).

[58] E.g., Matt 16:28; Mark 9:1; Luke 9:27; John 8:52. Note that this discrepancy also holds true for the broader corpus of Greek literature, where the metaphorical use of *geuomai* is "to fully experience something." H. G. Liddell and R. Scott state that the metaphorical sense often indicates making a proof of something through full experience, not to mention an instance where it denotes the experience of a married woman, which is by no means a partial taste. Liddell and Scott, *Greek-English Lexicon with a Revised Supplement* (Oxford: Clarendon, 1996), 346.

of God"? It is significant to note the Septuagint's use of *panta ta hrēmata ta kala*, "all the good words," to translate the Hebrew expression *hakkol haddābār haṭṭôb*, "all the good words," in Josh 23:15. In this context, "all the good words" is contrasted with "all the bad words" (Septuagint: *panta ta hrēmata ta ponēra*; Hebrew: *kol haddābār hārā ʾ*), the former referring to the blessings/promises of the covenant and the latter to the curses of the covenant.

In other words, the good words of God for his people are those blessings he promises to those who enter into his covenant and who exercise obedience to his covenant stipulations. Consequently, the Old Testament background for this rather specific designation makes it highly unlikely that the writer of Hebrews would use it here to speak of a partial experience. On the contrary, the good word would be experienced only by those who have become true members of God's covenant and have responded in obedience to his commands.[59] The ultimate end of these promises is viewed in light of the final age to come, as the author emphasizes that these individuals have not experienced the blessings of the promises only in this life but also in the powers of the age to come: *dynameis te mellontos aiōnos*, "and the powers of the age to come."

Finally, consider the author's use of *phōtizō*, "to shine, enlighten," at the beginning of Heb 6:4: *tous hapax phōtisthentas*, "those once having been enlightened." The writer uses the same terminology elsewhere with reference

---

[59] This terminology also appears in Josh 21:45 (*ou diepesen apo pantōn tōn hrēmatōn tōn kalōn*, "There did not fall from all the good words," i.e., not one of the promises of God failed) and Zech 1:13 (*apekrithē kyrios pantokratōr tō angelō tō lalounti en emoi hrēmata kala*, "the Lord Almighty answered the angel speaking with me with good words," i.e., good words that were spoken in response to what appeared to be a failure on God's part to fulfill his promises to Israel), both of which refer to the promises of God to his covenant people. Another instructive example, though it is from outside a covenant context, is that of 1 Kgs 18:24 and the showdown between Elijah and the prophets of Baal at Mount Carmel. Unlike the above examples, where the adjective *kalos* is in the attributive position, here it is in the predicate position: *kalon to hrēma ho elalēsas*, "the word is good which you speak" (translating the Hebrew *ṭôb haddābār*, "the word is good"). The sense of the predicate construction here indicates certainty. In other words, the people indicate that they believe Elijah's proposition to construct altars and sacrifices without fire, waiting for the superior deity to light the sacrifice, is a reliable means of determining which god is the true God. This meaning is essentially the same as those above, in that we are dealing with one's reliable word. For more on this expression in the Old Testament, see Matthew McAffee, "The Good Word: Its Non-Covenant and Covenant Significance in the Old Testament," *Journal for the Study of the Old Testament* 39 (2015): 377–404. On the significance of this expression for the warnings of Hebrews, see Matthew McAffee, "Covenant and the Warnings of Hebrews: The Blessing and the Curse," *Journal of the Evangelical Theological Society* 57 (2014): 537–53.

to the sufferings that the addressees had endured after they had been enlightened: *phōtisthentes pollēn athlēsin hypemeinate*, "after being enlightened you endured much contest" (Heb 10:32). Hebrews 10 yields another warning for believers against falling away, wherein those who would fall away from the faith are warned that there remains no further sacrifice for their sins and that such an act profanes the blood of the covenant by which they were sanctified (10:26, 29).[60] Toward the end of this section, the writer cites Deut 32:36, "The Lord will judge his people," emphasizing that even those who are legitimately God's people are not beyond the reaches of his judgment, even to the point of apostasy, if they put him to the test. False professors are not in view. These same people, whom the writer addresses as "his people" via Deut 32:36, are then described as at one time "being enlightened," no doubt by the gospel itself (Heb 10:32). Paul similarly uses this same terminology in Eph 1:18 and 3:9.

At the end of the day, Arminians believe that the burden of exegetical proof remains squarely on the shoulders of those who would deny that the individuals described in Heb 6:4–6 (and 10:26–29) are anything less than true believers. If we had to rely on only one of these descriptions from Heb 6:4–6 at the exclusion of the others, the case for their being genuine believers might be more challenging to make, though not impossible. However, at great lengths our author removes all doubt concerning the identity of these individuals lest we should be tempted to think it could not apply to true believers. This point only strengthens the potency of the warnings themselves.

CONCLUSION

Jonathan Edwards's writings on perseverance demonstrate a strong resemblance to the Calvinistic tradition of which he clearly viewed himself to be a part. This conclusion finds support in his insistence that God's sovereign electing and effectual calling of the individual demand that the true believer will ultimately persevere. Anything less than this, according to the Calvinistic view, would bring God's sovereignty into question. It is in the more familiar works of Edwards such as *Freedom of the Will* and *Religious Affections* that his affinity to traditional Calvinism is its strongest.

---

[60] Again, there is no biblical support for the notion that this kind of expression would describe anyone other than a genuine believer.

There is a sense, however, in which Edwards broke new ground in several places, perhaps in three most notable areas: (1) his discussion of perseverance as a condition (though noncausal) of justification, (2) his robust appeal to the need for perseverance in the life of the believer practically, and (3) his serious attempt to exegete the warning passages of the New Testament without undermining their potency.

As noted previously, Edwards believed that more needed to be said regarding the relationship between perseverance and justification. This is specifically true as it relates to the manner in which perseverance is a condition of justification. In describing perseverance as a property of faith, he places himself firmly in the tradition of Hebrews 11, where the writer showcases the perseverance of the ancient saints in all that they accomplished "by faith." For Edwards, this would be the faith that is of the persevering kind. Nonetheless, Edwards's view of faith as a condition of justification does not resemble the mainstream Calvinistic view. Edwards calls faith a condition by which the sinner accepts God's grace,[61] which he later qualifies by adding that one of the manifest properties of true faith is perseverance.[62]

Yet here Edwards came much closer to Arminianism than is often recognized, at least on a pragmatic level. As Edwards emphasized the need for perseverance in the life of the believer, at the same time he found himself needing to maintain that the true believer will ultimately persevere in the end. Nevertheless, his willingness to entertain the possibility of having justification "suspended" if a true believer did not persevere and his insistence that the final salvation of the believer is held only "virtually" seem inconsistent in defense of a divinely determined perseverance.

Edwards attempted to handle the warning passages from the New Testament in an exegetically rigorous way, at least in his treatment of the warnings in the book of Hebrews. As far as I have been able to determine, Edwards did not appeal to the hypothetical nature of these warnings as a means of avoiding their application to true believers. Instead, he argued that the warnings address true

---

[61] Again, it is worth noting how closely this explanation resembles the Arminian view of faith as the means of accepting God's offer of grace. For Edwards and Arminians alike, faith is not a work.

[62] On Edwards's treatment of justification from an Arminian perspective, see Kevin Hester's discussion on this topic in chapter 4.

believers as a divine means of influencing their perseverance.[63] Those false professors who have indeed become partakers of the extraordinary or miraculous
works of the Holy Spirit without having become truly regenerate would be the
only ones who could truly fall away. But of course, this poses a predicament.
The warnings cannot be a means of influencing believers to persevere and a
warning to false professors against falling away at the same time, since the text
offers no indication of such a distinction.

Furthermore, as we have already seen, the end result of Edwards's distinction between the extraordinary and ordinary workings of the Spirit
poses serious problems for Calvinism's view of divine sovereignty. One of the
major tenets of Calvinism is to maintain that the Spirit causes some sinners
to accept the gospel call and withholds grace from others. Here, Edwards
allowed for a middle ground wherein the Spirit works his miraculous signs
with one of two results: some take on the appearance of a regenerate person,
while others truly become regenerate. Although the warning passages from
the Scriptures provide a means of influence, in the end they fail to convince
false professors to the point of regeneration and thus cannot effectively keep
them from falling away from their false profession. Arminianism, on the
other hand, maintains that the Holy Spirit comes to sinners with prevenient
grace, to which they must respond in faith, the condition of justification.
Consequently, as the Scriptures clearly indicate, the regenerate must also
exhibit a continuance in faith, or in the words of Edwards, the property of
faith called perseverance.

In reading Edwards, it becomes increasingly clear that he did not always
maintain his Calvinistic framework consistently. His serious reading of the
Scriptures often led him into conflict with his theological system, and the practical application of divinely determined perseverance is difficult to maintain.
As a result, the writings of Edwards on perseverance offer important insights
for the ongoing conversation between advocates of Calvinism and Arminianism, two significant theological strands of the Christian tradition. These observations from Edwards call all parties to approach the text with a renewed sense

---

[63] Note the similarity of this approach with Thomas R. Schreiner's "means of salvation" view.
See Thomas R. Schreiner, "Perseverance and Assurance: A Survey and a Proposal," *Southern
Baptist Journal of Theology* 2 (1998): 52–58. See also Thomas R. Schreiner and Ardel B. Cane-
day, *The Race Set Before Us: A Biblical Theology of Perseverance and Assurance* (Downers Grove:
IVP, 2001), 142–215.

of humility in an attempt to articulate an understanding of perseverance in our theology of redemption.

About the Editor

J. Matthew Pinson has served as president of Welch College, where he also serves as professor of theology, for twenty-two years. After attending Welch, he earned a B.A. and M.A. from the University of West Florida and an M.A. in religion from Yale University, where he met his wife, Melinda, also a graduate student at Yale. He later received a doctorate from Vanderbilt University. Before going to serve at Welch, he was a pastor for twelve years. Pinson has authored, coauthored, or edited more than ten books including *40 Questions About Arminianism* (Kregel Academic), *Four Views on Eternal Security* (Zondervan), and *Perspectives on Christian Worship* (B&H Academic). He and his wife Melinda have been married for thirty years and have two adult children, Anna and Matthew. Pinson speaks widely at churches and conferences across denominational lines and serves on several boards.

About the Contributors

Paul V. Harrison is senior pastor of Madison Free Will Baptist Church in Madison, Alabama. A longtime adjunct professor of church history and Greek at Welch College, he has served as both the associate editor and editor for *Integrity: A Journal of Christian Thought*. He is creator of *Classic Sermon Index*, a subscription-based online index of nearly 60,000 sermons. He is author of a number of articles in journals such as the *Journal of the Evangelical Theological Society* as well as a commentary on James and Jude in the Randall House New Testament Commentary series. Harrison earned his B.A. from Welch College and his M.Div. and Ph.D. from Mid-America Baptist Theological Seminary. He and his wife Diane have two grown sons.

Kevin L. Hester serves as Vice President and Dean of the School of Theology at Welch College, where he has served for twenty years. With expertise in both Patristics and the Reformation era, he is author of a number of scholarly and popular articles as well as two books, including *Eschatology and Pain in the Theology of Gregory the Great* (Paternoster). He holds a B.A. from Welch College, an M.Div. from Covenant Theological Seminary, and a Ph.D. from Saint Louis University. He serves as the associate editor of *Integrity: A Journal of Christian Thought* and as an editor of the *Biblical Higher Education Journal*. He has also served as chair of the Commission on Accreditation of the Association for Biblical Higher Education. He and his wife Leslie have four adult sons.

Matthew McAffee is Provost and Professor of Biblical Studies at Welch College and Dean of Welch Divinity School. He holds a B.A. from Welch College, an

M.Div. from Southern Baptist Theological Seminary, and an M.A. and Ph.D. from the University of Chicago. McAffee is author of a number of articles on the biblical theology of salvation and has published in journals such as the *Journal of the Evangelical Theological Society*, the *Journal of Biblical Literature*, the *Journal of the American Oriental Society*, and the *Bulletin of Biblical Research*. He is coauthor with H. H. "Chip" Hardy of *Going Deeper with Biblical Hebrew* (B&H Academic) and has also authored *Life and Mortality in Ugaritic: A Lexical and Literary Study* (Penn State University Press). He and his wife Anna have five children.

Robert E. Picirilli is author or editor of more than twenty-five books, including *God in Eternity and Time: A New Case for Human Freedom* (B&H Academic), a finalist for *Christianity Today*'s 2023 Book Awards in the academic theology category. His book *Paul the Apostle* (Moody) has been widely used as a college and seminary text, while his recent *Free Will Revisited* (Wipf and Stock) responds to the thoughts of Luther, Calvin, and Edwards on freedom of the will. General Editor of the twelve-volume Randall House New Testament Commentary, he has written articles that have appeared in journals such as *Journal for the Study of the New Testament*, *Journal of the Evangelical Theological Society*, and *Evangelical Quarterly*. Picirilli earned his B.A. at Welch College and his M.A. and Ph.D. at Bob Jones University. His service to Welch College extended over fifty years, both as professor and Academic Dean. He is now Professor Emeritus of New Testament and Greek at Welch. He was married to his late wife Clara for fifty-eight years. He has five grown daughters, nine grandchildren, and ten great-grandchildren.

Barry Raper is Associate Dean of Welch Divinity School and Associate Professor of Christian Ministry. He has taught at Welch for the past sixteen years. He has more than twenty years of ministry experience, the past fourteen as senior pastor of Bethel Free Will Baptist Church in Chapmansboro, Tennessee. He received his B.A. from Welch College and his M.Div. and D.Min. from Southern Baptist Theological Seminary. Raper's academic emphasis has been spiritual formation in ministry. He is author of numerous articles, has contributed a chapter to *The Promise of Arminian Theology: Essays in Honor of F. Leroy Forlines* (Randall House Academic), and is a columnist for *ONE* Magazine. He and his wife Amanda have five children.

Name and Subject Index

Scripture Index